Mastering Project Uncertainty

Uncertainty permeates every thinkable aspect of project work and mastering information awareness and availability is the key to controlling benefits, budgets, and timelines. This book offers a theoretical framework and practical guidelines to systematically minimize uncertainty, thereby increasing the chances of project success.

To paraphrase Henry Ford, transitioning from traditional risk management to mastering project uncertainty implies abandoning the quest for faster horses in favor of driving cars toward your project's destination. This book presents the road map to this transition, with Part I providing a theoretical foundation for uncertainty management using systems thinking. Part II introduces strategies supported by practical techniques to master uncertainty through:

1 Raising information awareness
2 Increasing information availability
3 Improving the effective use of information
4 Maximizing information efficiency.

This book's combined theoretical and highly practical approach, is essential reading for scholars, academics, business leaders, project managers, strategists, and policymakers to bring the organization's vision for a sustainable future to life.

Paul Cuypers is an experienced and certified program-, project-, change-, and test manager, agile coach, and independent researcher working in Norway. Over the years, he has engaged in defense, industrial, banking, shipping, and IT-related projects. He is an international speaker and course instructor on project methodology, Power Kanban, agile rolling wave planning, capability thinking, and uncertainty management. He enjoys developing next-generation project management techniques and is passionate about creating the supporting theoretical models.

Mastering Project Uncertainty

A Systems Thinking Approach

Paul W.M. Cuypers

Routledge
Taylor & Francis Group
NEW YORK AND LONDON

First published 2024
by Routledge
605 Third Avenue, New York, NY 10158

and by Routledge
4 Park Square, Milton Park, Abingdon, Oxon, OX14 4RN

Routledge is an imprint of the Taylor & Francis Group, an informa business

© 2024 Paul W.M. Cuypers

The right of Paul W.M. Cuypers to be identified as the author of this work has been asserted in accordance with sections 77 and 78 of the Copyright, Designs, and Patents Act 1988.

All rights reserved. No part of this book may be reprinted or reproduced, or utilised in any form or by any electronic, mechanical, or other means, now known or hereafter invented, including photocopying and recording, or in any information storage or retrieval system, without permission in writing from the publishers.

Trademark notice: Product or corporate names may be trademarks or registered trademarks and are used only for identification and explanation without intent to infringe.

Library of Congress Cataloguing-in-Publication Data
Names: Cuypers, Paul W. M., author.
Title: Mastering project uncertainty : a systems thinking approach / Paul W.M. Cuypers.
Description: New York, NY : Routledge, 2024. | Includes bibliographical references and index.
Identifiers: LCCN 2023034407 (print) | LCCN 2023034408 (ebook) | ISBN 9781032557335 (hardback) | ISBN 9781032557274 (paperback) | ISBN 9781003431961 (ebook)
Subjects: LCSH: Project management. | Leadership. | Management--Technological innovations.
Classification: LCC HD69.P75 C89 2024 (print) | LCC HD69.P75 (ebook) | DDC 658.4/04--dc23/eng/20231020
LC record available at https://lccn.loc.gov/2023034407
LC ebook record available at https://lccn.loc.gov/2023034408

ISBN: 978-1-032-55733-5 (hbk)
ISBN: 978-1-032-55727-4 (pbk)
ISBN: 978-1-003-43196-1 (ebk)

DOI: 10.4324/9781003431961

Typeset in Sabon
by MPS Limited, Dehradun

Contents

Introduction

Why care about projects

In the epic movie *The Matrix* (1999), machines have taken over the Earth, hunting down the remaining free humans. When interrogating the resistance leader, a robot named Agent Smith (Hugo Weaving) shares a revelation. It dawned on him that humans do not classify as mammals but remind him of a virus: Moving to an area and multiplying until every natural resource is consumed. The only way to survive is to spread to another location, eventually killing their host. The need to change our way of life has become apparent in the face of climate change, rising pollution, drought, and hunger; insights from killing robots are no longer required.

The problem for humans is that there is no other host. The famous phrase is: There is no Planet B! The Martian colony envisioned by Elon Musk could only survive with regular supplies from the Earth. Our technological challenge is not interplanetary travel but accommodating an ever-increasing population on a progressively polluted planet with steadily scarcer resources. Saving the world means changing our way of life. Through innovation projects, we must develop sustainable technologies to supply food, water, and energy; clean up the environment; and stop species extinction. Projects are the vehicles of change: If innovation is an engine, knowledge is the fuel, and project capability is the oil that makes the parts work frictionless together. Project capability enables the makeover of our eroding consumer-based lifestyle to secure the world for future generations.

The importance of projects has grown beyond the ability to create a competitive advantage and economic growth; project capability catalyzes the technological development that is imperative to our existence and survival.

Project uncertainty

Uncertainty affects all theoretical and practical aspects of projects, including project management as a science. Starting with science, after 40 years of research into a definition of project success, the result is inconclusive. A consensus exists that project success is a subjective, multidimensional, time, context, and stakeholder-dependent construct (Ika 2009; Frefer et al. 2018). Which is an elaborate saying: We know that we do not know. Our inability to define project success represents a significant obstacle. The justification for any project management method is a measurable increase in the likelihood of project success. How do you determine if one method is more effective compared to another without knowing what success looks like?

DOI: 10.4324/9781003431961-1

In addition to the definition of success, the project methodology concept is obtuse and needs clarification. In project management circles and scientific publications, methods like Agile, PMBOK, and PRINCE2 are systematically referred to as methodologies. In research, the *methodology* is the systematic study of methods concerning their effectiveness, efficiency, limitations, and application. The methodology is the cornerstone in the scientific quest for finding the truth; it is the meta-method to study methods. The critical question in any research is: Provided we used another method, could we potentially have arrived at a different conclusion? The analog methodology question regarding a project is: Had we used another project method, could we have achieved more success? Alternatively, could project failure have been avoided?

Projects are unique undertakings; they cannot be repeated using another method nor allow for establishing a control group. How do you objectively prove that a particular project management method was the decisive factor in achieving project success? Might there be a placebo effect? Does mere belief in a method create a sense of control and accomplishment? There must be sound economic reasons for selecting one project management method over the other, as any hour spent on controlling goes at the expense of the hours available for creating deliverables. The failure to establish a logical concept of project methodology as the meta-method to evaluate method effectiveness markedly inhibits knowledge development in theory and practise.

But the troubles for the scientific community do not stop here. The very definition of uncertainty is, you guessed it, uncertain. Authors, scholars, and scientists struggle to systematically define the theoretical relationships between risk, threat, opportunity, and uncertainty. Uncertainty can have positive or negative effects (Perminova, Gustafsson, and Wikström 2008). Some use risk management to denote negative effects; others consider risk management an umbrella process for managing threats and opportunities (Hillson 2003). This academic approach collides with the everyday language use of the words risk and opportunity.

Chapman and Ward (2003) introduced uncertainty management as the preferred designation for managing risk and opportunity. However, project uncertainty encompasses more than suppressing unwanted events that negatively affect the plan; projects also require decision-making, problem-solving, and sometimes crisis management. Defining uncertainty management as a combination of risk and opportunity only partially covers the true challenges.

Although project management is a firmly established praxis with numerous institutions, bodies of knowledge, and certifications, the theoretical foundation is implicit, narrow to nonexistent (Koskela and Howell 2002; Pollack 2007). Project management methods are mainly prescriptive; the typical project guide contains instructions on what to do, like a recipe for baking a cake. The downside of applying procedures unsupported by theoretical understanding is that it is hard to pinpoint the cause of the failure, make improvements, or prevent failures from reoccurring.

Compared with ancient sciences like medicine, project management is still in the alchemistic stage: A set of practices based on a mixture of experience, tradition, and beliefs, with an added hint of science. The breakthrough in medication came when we learned to isolate the active ingredients in medicinal herbs and produce them synthetically. Using singular drug components rather than mixed potions, the effects of a substance on the human body could be tested. Today, our understanding of medical drugs is based on chemical and biological theory backed by clinical tests using control groups and placebos. Likewise, we need to identify the working elements of our experience-based practices, and create sound theories to support their application confirmed by field testing.

Moving over to the practitioner side, there has been a growing realization that risk management alone is insufficient to ensure project success. Traditional risk management has severe shortcomings. First, semi-scientific scoring methods like risk matrices and heat maps are rampant, while only some organizations use qualitative data simulations to assess risk (Hubbard and Evans 2010). The second reason is that project problems are not caused exclusively by risk, where *risk* is defined as a possible event with negative effects. Unidentified prerequisites, dependencies, constraints, assumptions, stakeholders, or requirements will negatively impact the plan and implicitly, the chances of project success.

Third, traditional risk management strands on its presumptions:

1 That you are capable of knowing all the risks the project is subject to
2 The risks haven't happened yet.

There are two types of risks: Those you are aware of and those you are not. One can establish better control over the identified risks, for example, by using Monte Carlo simulations. But what about risks you do not see? These risks might be considerably scarier than the ones you are currently addressing. How do you discover them? Support in finding unknown risks is limited to checklists and brainstorming sessions, another practice lacking conclusive evidence of its effectiveness (Mullen, Johnson, and Salas, 1991).

Similar logic applies to problems: There are problems you know and those you do not. Imagine a car with a leaky oil pan unbeknownst to the owner. At some point, the oil level gets too low, leaving the driver stranded by the side of the road. Projects can suffer from issues that have transgressed beyond the risk stage at inception. Also, having a problem and knowing that you have one are different things. Problem symptoms may take time before they emerge and sometimes even longer before they are recognized. The classic risk strategies of avoidance, mitigation, or transfer do not apply when problems are already a fact.

In summary, merely improving risk management is a quest for faster horses; we need a vehicle called *uncertainty management* to get our projects successfully over the finish line. Here is the paradox; in the absence of a sound theoretical foundation, a practical definition of project success, and objective proof regarding the effectiveness of our methods, we invest more and more in project work. HBR estimates that by 2027, some 88 million people worldwide are expected to be working on projects, and the value of project-oriented economic activity will have reached $20 trillion. However, research shows that only 35% of the projects undertaken worldwide are successful—implying an extravagant waste of time and money (Nieto-Rodriguez 2023).

Note the catch; without a generic definition of project success, how was the 35% rate determined?

The structure of this book

Considering the above-mentioned issues, it may be clear that work is to be done. In this book, we will focus on the theory behind and practical solutions to the following list:

- How to select the correct work form
- How to determine project success
- How to define project methodology
- How to visualize the concept of project uncertainty
- How to systematically reduce uncertainty in projects.

This book is divided into two parts. As you cannot manage what is not defined, Part I provides a theoretical foundation for uncertainty management based on systems thinking:

- Chapter 1, Organizing for success, discusses the relationship between the standing and temporary organization including a short review of programs, portfolios, projects, task forces, crisis, and incident teams
- Chapter 2 addresses the methodology question and provides the rationale for selecting systems thinking approach to model project uncertainty over process analysis, functional analysis, capability thinking, and empirical methods
- Chapter 3 presents the uncertainty matrix as a generic model to define uncertainty and a systems thinking model of project uncertainty consisting of the main elements:
    - Assignment
    - Context
    - Decisions
    - Method
    - Scenarios.
- Chapter 4 details the components of the project assignment, discussing uncertainty related to stakeholders, benefits, deliverables, activities, and resources
- Chapter 5 describes the components of the project context in terms of prerequisites, constraints, threats, opportunities, and interdependencies
- Chapter 6 details the components of decision-making under uncertainty, qualifiers, alternatives, logic, effects, and confirmation
- Chapter 7 breaks down the method into the approach, communication, tools, techniques, and coordination
- Chapter 8 describes the components of scenario uncertainty, the plan, risk, problem, crisis, and posture based on pre-emptive-, counter-, and contingency measures.

Now that we know what we are up against, the next step is to define actions. Part II contains practical models, tools, and techniques to reduce uncertainty in your project:

1 Raising information awareness (Chapter 9)
2 Increasing information availability (Chapter 10)
3 Improving the effective use of information (Chapter 11)
4 Maximizing information efficiency (Chapter 12).

For clarity and self-study purposes, each chapter is structured as follows:

- Introduction
- Definitions
- Elements
- Principles
- Techniques
- Artifacts
- Concepts
- Questions.

The intended audience

Mastering project uncertainty is relevant for anyone who has a vested interest in project success, ranging from program managers; portfolio owners; project management office representatives; project sponsors; steering committee members; architects, project, test, and quality teams. Although the central theme is project uncertainty, the comprehensive theoretical and practical coverage of projects makes this book suitable as a primer for anyone aspiring to a career as a project manager. Seasoned project managers and agile practitioners will appreciate the next-generation techniques such as Power Kanban and agile rolling wave planning. The book requires no previous project knowledge, the questions and exercises make it suitable as a study book for students or self-study. This guide provides actionable insights and techniques for practitioners and a fundamental theory for academics and scholars. Although specifically aimed at projects, the system thinking modeling approach can be extended to other fields and industries, such as business strategy, insurance, economics, law enforcement, and defense.

Paul Cuypers
HYVES Project Research
Næroset, Norway
2023

References

Chapman, C.B., and S.C. Ward. 2003. *Project Risk Management: Processes, Techniques, and Insights*, 2nd ed., Chichester: Wiley.

Frefer, A. A., M. Mahmoud, H. Haleema, and R. Almamlook. 2018. *Industrial Engineering & Management*, (7)1.

Hillson, D. 2003. *Effective Opportunity Management for Projects: Exploiting Positive Risk*, 1st ed., Boca Raton: CRC Press.

Hubbard, D., and D. Evans. 2010. "Problems with Scoring Methods and Ordinal Scales in Risk Assessment." IBM Research and Development, 54, no. 3.

Ika, L. A. 2009. "Project Success as a Topic in Project Management Journals: A Brief History." *Project Management Journal* 40, no. 4: 6–19.

Koskela, L., and G. A. Howell. 2002. The underlying theory of project management is obsolete. *Paper presented at PMI® Research Conference 2002: Frontiers of Project Management Research and Applications*, Seattle, Washington. Newtown Square, PA: Project Management Institute.

Mullen D., C. Johnson, and E. Salas. 1991. "Productivity Loss in Brainstorming Groups: A Meta-Analytic Integration." *Basic and Applied Social Psychology* 12, no. 1: 3–23.

Nieto-Rodriguez, A. 2023. The project economy has arrived. *Harvard Business Review*. Available at: https://hbr.org/2021/11/the-project-economy-has-arrived (Accessed: April 15, 2023).

Perminova, O., M. Gustafsson, and K. Wikström. 2008. "Defining Uncertainty in Projects—A New Perspective." *International Journal of Project Management* 26: 73–79.

Pollack, J. 2007. The Changing Paradigms of Project Management. *International Journal of Project Management* 25: 266–274.

The Matrix 1999. *Directed by L. Wachowski and L. Wachowski, [Feature Film]*. Burbank: Warner Bros.

Part I: Theoretical foundation

Introduction

In part I, a conceptual model of project uncertainty is created by projecting the uncertainty matrix over a system model of a project.

DOI: 10.4324/9781003431961-2

Chapter 1

Organizing for success

Introduction

The first uncertainty to address is to find the best work form given the nature of the assignment. When asked how humans differ from animals, people will commonly mention our ability to use technology. Indeed, technology has developed extremely fast, and so has our welfare. From the time of the first motorized flight by the Wright brothers in 1903 to the day Neil Armstrong was able to say the famous words, 'That's one small step (a) for man, one giant leap for mankind,' took only 66 years. Armstrong was not alone; Buzz Aldrin accompanied him in the lunar module, while Mike Collins flew the command module circling the moon. Back on Earth, the mission control center was operated by 30 people around the clock. Estimates vary, but making that step involved approximately 400,000 people working on the Apollo program (Thimmesh 2015).

Traveling to the moon and back was an extraordinary undertaking for multiple reasons; one being that the program had to invent the technology to get there. But what about an everyday technology like a steel knife in your kitchen drawer? Could you make one? Even a low-tech knife requires a worldwide federation of organizations work together in a coordinated fashion. The making of a knife requires miners to bring up the iron ore, steel factory workers, designers, production plant operators, logistics, marketing, and salespeople. Technology may define *Homo sapiens*, but it is our ability to organize work that allows us to invent, innovate, and operate technology at an unprecedented scale.

The Apollo program illustrates the importance of organizations; they enable us to achieve objectives we cannot realize as individuals. Going to the moon requires many tasks, from engineers building rockets to janitors cleaning the control center. Even if we theoretically can do the work ourselves, organizations relieve us from mundane jobs, freeing up our time to pursue other goals in life. We bring our children to kindergarten, allowing us time to work, study, or do sports. Rather than getting up at four o'clock in the morning and baking bread ourselves, we buy bread instead at the bakery and sleep a couple of hours extra. From birth to school, sports, work, politics, and healthcare, organizations shape our lives.

The choice of a fitting organizational work form, given the characteristics of the assignment, is a fundamental step to maximizing the chances of success. Suppose you have a unique work assignment the standing organization is ill-equipped to handle. What temporary work form do you choose: A program, a portfolio, a task force, a project, an incident team, or a crisis team, and why? This question leads to several others: What role do projects play in the organization? Why were projects invented in the first place? How do

DOI: 10.4324/9781003431961-3

projects differ from other temporary work forms? Selecting the proper organization type is the first crucial step to reducing uncertainty.

Definitions

Mission

The organization's *mission* is the raison d'être of an organization, the ability to deliver value to society, in the form of products, services, capabilities, or opinions. IKEA and Volvo provide products; airline companies offer transportation services; Uber and Airbnb provide capabilities to connect and sell; while environmental and political organizations shape opinions. Organizations also provide *secondary value*, such as salary, career, learning opportunities, status, and a social arena.

Vision

A *vision statement* is a short, concise, and inspiring sentence that describes a future state; for example, Microsoft formulated their vision during the eighties: 'A computer on every desk and in every home.' During the 1970s, computers were the domain of companies that could afford them in terms of money and the space they took. Some initially perceived the Microsoft vision as over-ambitious, even borderline science fiction. Looking back, given the smartphones in our pockets, essentially a computer combined with a radio transmitter, this vision became more than true.

Strategy

A *strategy* is a winning approach to achieve victory or realize a vision based on unique insight into a situation, competitor, or enemy. A strategy serves as a protective layer around the organization, capitalizing on opportunities, exploiting internal strengths, concealing weaknesses while shielding it from threats. Any strategy must consider and address relevant internal and external trends and forces affecting the outcome of the endeavor. Tesla's vision is to make a decent profit based on mass-produced, affordable electric cars. Being outsiders to the automobile industry and a start-up, they needed substantial resources and capabilities to achieve economies of scale.

Rather than going the usual start-up road of creating a minimally viable product, like a cheap, stripped-down version of an electric vehicle, Tesla started at the other end of the spectrum and built a luxury car: The Tesla Roadster. Going from 0 to 100 kilometers per hour in just above 2 seconds and associated with the winning image of Elon Musk, Tesla made their mark in the industry. Driving small electric cars like the Buddy was associated with ideology-driven environmentalists who could not afford a 'real' car; driving a Tesla became hip and a sign of success. Tesla cars are an example of reconfiguration innovation: All components are existing technology, batteries, electric motors, computers, IoT, reshaped to create a new product.

The challenge to building the Roadster was not technological but supply chain related: Tesla could not rely on outsourcing or depend on suppliers to achieve mass-production benefits. The critical component was batteries, and to prevent bottlenecks, Tesla took control of the supply chain and invested in battery manufacturers. This diversification created synergy; the same batteries can also be used in Tesla's parallel business ventures, such as Powerwall, an integrated battery system for storing solar energy in the event the electricity grid goes down, enabling the power to stay on. Apart from dealing with threats, strategies implicitly focus on optimizing strengths. The investment capital needed for the bold supply chain moves was amassed due to Musk's reputation for success, which is a solid recipe for getting the attention of investors. Tesla analyzed the car industry's business environment and, given its strengths, built a winning strategy rather than following conventional wisdom (Mangram 2012).

Goals

Goals. A *goal* is a high-level statement of an intention, direction, or end result that must be achieved.

Objectives

Objectives. A goal can be divided into one or more objectives. Where a goal can be high level and somewhat fuzzy, an objective must be formulated so that you can know whether the objective has been achieved or not. The acronym SMART is useful to state objectives: Specific, Measurable, Achievable, Realistic, and Time-related. For example, reduce the companie's turnover from 9% to 3% within one year.

Elements

Standing and temporary organization

The *standing organization* conducts routine activities in support of the organization's mission. The adjective 'standing' is used in favor of 'permanent' as organizations evolve as visions and conditions change. Over time, the standing organization becomes highly specialized to do the organization's core business effectively and efficiently. As a result of the

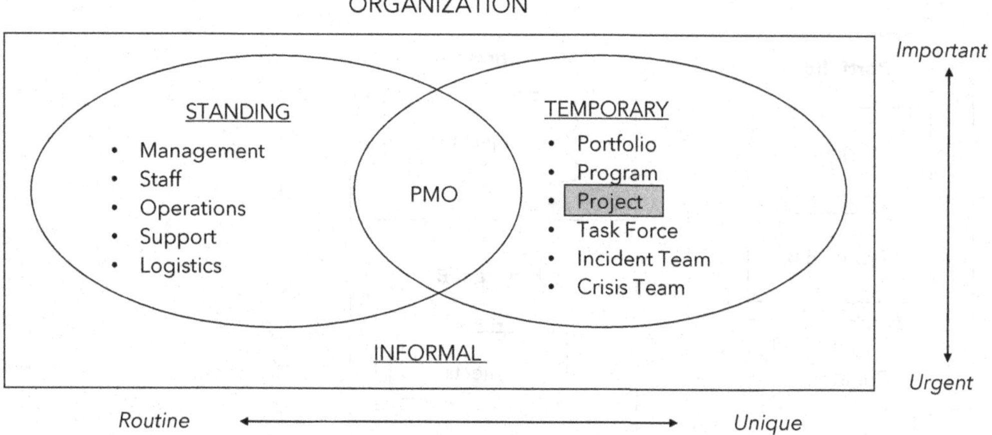

Figure 1.1 The role of projects in the organization.

focus on routine work, they are less suitable for out-of-the-ordinary tasks. On the other hand, *temporary organizations* like projects are time-bound work constellations created to accomplish unique assignments and they are disbanded once their objectives are met (Figure 1.1).

Informal organization

The *informal organization* is the unofficial social structure determining how people work together in practice whereas the formal organization leaves a vacuum. The informal organization consists of an ever-changing network of relationships and communities driven by common interests, beliefs, or emotions. The informal organization complements the formal organizational structures, workflows, and routines. The upside is that informal organizations potentially accelerate the response to unanticipated events and problem-solving efforts that require people to collaborate across administrative boundaries. The downside of the informal organization is that it is often invisible and, therefore, uncontrolled. If the formal and informal goals do not coincide, progress can stagnate.

Portfolio

The noun portfolio comes from the Italian *portafoglio* with the literal meaning of 'a case for carrying loose papers.' It originates from the Latin words – *portare*, 'to carry,' and *folium*, which means 'sheet' or 'leaf.' Imagine Michelangelo walking through Florence with a set of sketches for a project under his arm. In management, a *portfolio* refers to a collection of programs or projects combined by a particular aspect, such as a customer or technology, or competing for similar resources. A portfolio can contain both programs and individual projects. Where a program is an aggregation of projects, a portfolio is an aggregation of assets. Portfolio management involves decisions to invest or to divest. The goal of the portfolio is to create long-term value for the stakeholders by achieving the best possible financial and business outcomes (Figure 1.2).

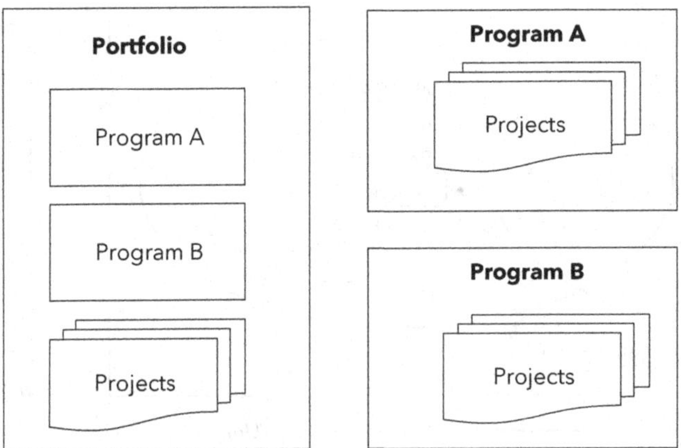

Figure 1.2 The elements of portfolios and programs.

Program

A *program* is a group of related projects managed in a coordinated way to obtain benefits of scale and control not available from managing them individually. A program could contain similar projects to capitalize on the economies of scale, like building several ships of the same class. Alternatively, it can include projects of different natures supporting a common goal. The Apollo program from NASA ran from 1968 to 1972, and its purpose was to land people safely on the moon and bring them back to Earth. The program contained multiple projects ranging from how to drink, sleep, and eat under zero gravity conditions to rocket engine development and space navigation.

Projects

A *project* is a temporary organization tasked with an assignment for which the standing organization is ill-equipped to succeed. A project leader is mandated to manage a hand picked team working under his direct control across departmental and organizational boundaries. As such, projects are exempt from standard operating procedures and free to adopt an approach that best fits the assignment while minimizing administrative overhead. The project organization is dismantled once the work is completed, and the team returns to their day-to-day activities or consultant houses.

Specialization and optimization of the standing organization have a cost; dealing with out-of-ordinary assignments is where highly functional organizations struggle. For a car company, building cars is a routine job; developing a new IT system to capitalize on new cutting-edge robotic production technology is a unique task. Also, long lines of communication cause delay and message distortion, negatively affecting the ability to make fast and effective decisions. Any question would first have to go up the hierarchical ladder to the top of the department, then to the chief of the other department, and then down the hierarchical ladder to the relevant person. The answer must then travel back the same route, subject to politics, and unsolicited meddling.

Task force

The origins of the phrase *task force* go back to the U.S. Navy during World War II. Creating a task force allowed ships that formally belonged to different fleets and squadrons to join for a single specific purpose without reassigning responsibility or requiring the reorganization or repurposing of the fleet. Task forces were temporary fighting units that were disbanded after their objectives were achieved or sunk by enemy forces. Before, formal groups conducted naval operations, but the speed at which the war evolved required more flexibility in resource deployment. In management today, a task force is created to make assessments, recommendations, or devise action plans to address critical issues or opportunities.

Some perceive a task force as extreme project work, but fundamental differences exist. Unlike programs and projects, a task force does not have delegated power to implement solutions. The management is free to accept, reject, or ignore any suggestions or recommendations from the task force. Another element is effectiveness over efficiency; if a company faces a serious production error incurring a massive loss of money, the optimal use of time and resources through careful planning common to projects is of secondary importance.

Incident response teams

Incident response teams (IRT) are initiated to address urgent, non-routine, but solvable problems. The issue at hand may impact business operations, brand reputation, financial standing, damage to property, data confidentiality or integrity, and even lead to a lawsuit or fines from authorities. Consider a ransomware attack that encrypts core business systems, causing massive loss of revenue and introducing the risk of bankruptcy. This is a solvable problem, the IRT can attempt a system recovery or ransomware removal using special tools. However, in the case of a large exfiltration of sensitive data, the horse has escaped from the stable. Locking the door is no longer an alternative. The only option is to limit the damage, and a crisis management team must be established.

Crisis management teams

A *crisis team* responds to emergencies with imminent danger to life, property, or the environment when there is no longer hope for effective and timely remediation of the problem. In crisis preparation, different scenarios can be developed, including preplanned contingency actions. However, expecting the unexpected is the life motto of all crisis teams. Crisis organizations must focus on developing capabilities that can be quickly reconfigured to deal with any emerging crisis. The crisis team must focus on deploying contingency measures to address:

1 Danger to life and property
2 Securing the environment
3 Informing the public
4 Business continuity and recovery
5 Customer relationships
6 Financial stability
7 Company reputation.

Crises managers are mandated extraordinary authority, superseding the standard chain of command in the organization, including full access to necessary resources. In projects, the focus is to balance the effectiveness of actions with efficiency considerations to ensure that the business case remains justified. In crisis management, the focus is purely on effectiveness and speed. When a crisis occurs, time and resource optimization are secondary considerations. Breaking company policies could be justified; even breaking laws could be an option when lives are at stake. However, every leader and team member remains accountable for their actions and decisions and must expect scrutiny from authorities afterward.

Techniques

Step-transition model

A key uncertainty is how the project assignment fits into the bigger picture. The step-transition model visualizes the transformation of the as-is situation to a vision or to-be

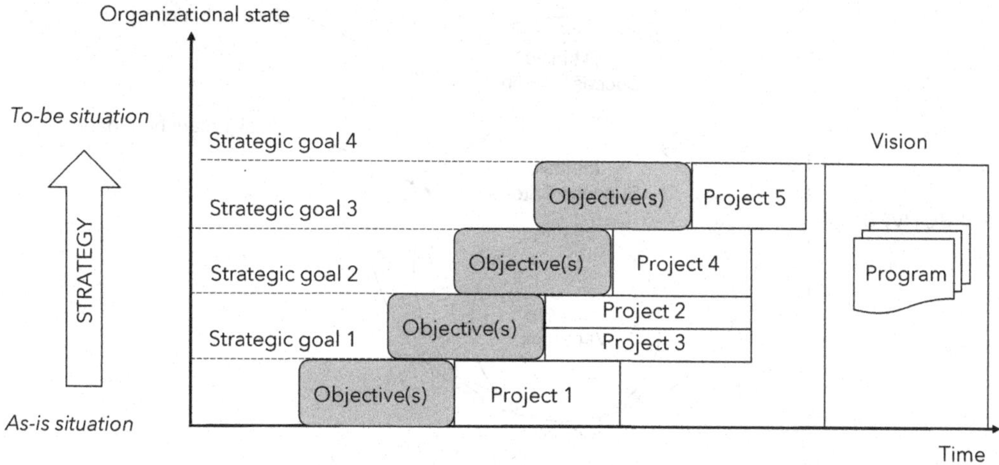

Figure 1.3 The step-transition model provides an overview of other change initiatives.

situation. The master plan to achieve the change is formulated in the strategy, which is broken down into strategic goals supported by objectives. Project organizations are tasked to realize logical groups of objectives. Beware of defining projects at the goal level only, as all projects are time and resource limited. Goals are inherently fuzzy and susceptible to interpretation or stretching by stakeholders pursuing their agenda, increasing the possibility of time and budget overruns. Projects can be gathered into programs for economies of scale or to manage resource dependencies (Figure 1.3).

The diamond of success

Managing uncertainty is a means to an end: Maximizing the chances of project success. Ironically, the definition of *project success* itself is uncertain. Although the concept of project success has been studied for over 50 years, a consensus exists that project success is a subjective, multidimensional, time-, context-, and stakeholder-dependent construct (Ika 2009; Frefer et al. 2018). A sound definition of project success is critical; without one, the effectiveness of different project management methods cannot be established.

During the early years of project management, Gaddis (1959) defined the project work form as 'an organization unit dedicated to the attainment of a goal—generally the successful completion of a developmental product on time, within budget, and in conformance with predetermined performance specifications' (p. 89). This early definition of project success, known as the *iron triangle,* was gradually extended with other dimensions, such as project efficiency, the impact on the customer, direct and business success, and preparing the organization for the future (Shenhar, Levy, and Dvir 1997).

The project achievement can be perceived and modeled as a system. In that context, project success or failure can be regarded as *extreme system states* that vary over time due to *success-driving factors* influencing the *success variables* and the *success criteria* (Cuypers

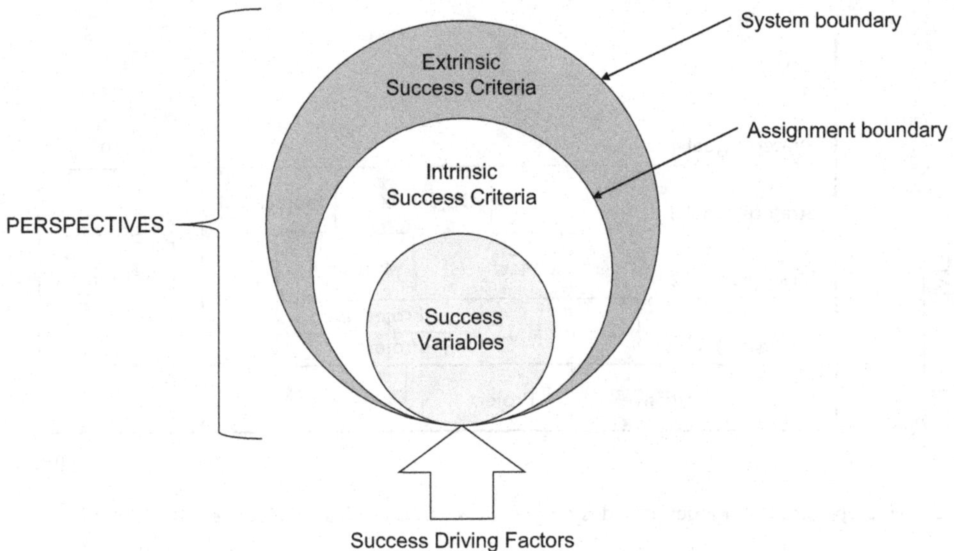

Figure 1.4 The logical model for defining project success (Cuypers 2022).

Source: Reproduced with permission, https://www.doi.org/10.33422/4th.bmeconf.2022.03.01

2022). The project's *intrinsic success* is an evaluation of the project's achievements in the context of the assignment stated in the *business case* and *scope statement*. Projects are the vehicles of change, and the impact can reach far beyond the limits of the initiators' envisaged purpose or imagination. Over time, the extent, scale, and severity of expected and unexpected effects will emerge. The project achievement beyond the original assignment is evaluated using *extrinsic success criteria* (Figure 1.4).

Project achievement is regarded as an *open system,* subject to outside events, trends, and forces resulting from interactions with other systems, which may include but are not limited to:

- The nature and culture of the parent organization
- Contractors and partners
- The project's political, technological, and economic environment.

Success-driving factors can primarily be differentiated according to *awareness*, whether the team is conscious about their existence and *nature*. Second, whether these factors are controllable or uncontrollable.

System elements: A *stakeholder* is any organization, group, or individual affected by a project, positively or negatively, knowing or unknowing. The *project result* is the sum of the domain deliverables that leads to a new or improved version of a product, service, or capability.

Project performance is a snapshot of the team's *effectiveness* and *efficiency*. Effectiveness always comes first; e.g., there can be no project efficiency without effectiveness. In addition

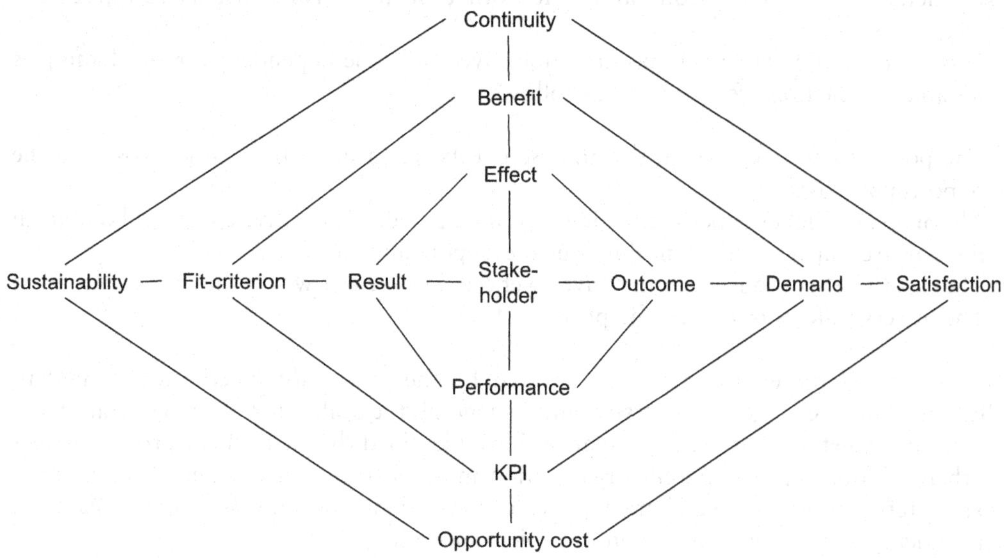

Figure 1.5 The diamond of success (Cuypers 2022).

Source: Reproduced with permission, https://www.doi.org/10.33422/4th.bmeconf.2022.03.01

to *hard dimensions* like productivity, performance includes soft *human factors like* teamwork, problem-solving, and learning ability.

The *project outcome* is the cumulative result of the project performance. The project's *intrinsic success* involves the evaluation of the project's achievements within the limits of the assignment, as stated in the business case and scope statement. Although validation and verification are essential, acceptance of the result ultimately depends on confirmation. A *fit criterion* describes the pre-agreed method, conditions, and acceptance criteria used to determine whether the properties of the accomplished result fit the requirements of the expected result and adequately address the project drivers.

A *benefit* is a positive value perceived from a stakeholder perspective. *Demands* govern the activities deployed to create the deliverables that make up the project result. Demands stipulate mandatory adherence to ethics, laws, regulations, company policies, processes, routines, industry standards, budget at completion, deadlines, material, and resource use.

Key performance indicators (KPIs) are qualitative and quantitative criteria used to gauge the performance of the project team, enabling forecasting of the outcome. A KPI has a target and actual value, and a KPI can be leading or lagging. The project's *extrinsic success* involves the evaluation of the project's achievements beyond the limits of the assignment. *Continuity* refers to the ability of the parent organization to effectively and efficiently deliver products, services, or capabilities that are in demand by society over time. *Opportunity cost* is losing alternatives when a specific project is chosen instead of others. Considering their relative urgency and importance, the cost-benefit ratio must be compared with other project proposals, as resources are scarce.

Satisfaction is a stakeholder-specific, subjective, and time-dependent notion. Examples of possible satisfaction scenarios are as follows:

1 The positive effects outweigh the adverse effects and are worth both the cost and the opportunity costs
2 Although at a higher expense than initially anticipated, the positive effects still outweigh the adverse impact while canceling out the opportunity cost
3 The positive effects outweigh the adverse effects but are not worth the opportunity cost
4 The adverse effects outweigh the positive effects.

The interests of the environment are covered by the *sustainability* criterion related to pollution, climate change, biodiversity, and in general, the ability for future generations to inhabit our planet and thrive. Now that we have identified the elements of project success and their relationship, the parent organization must operationalize the intrinsic and extrinsic criteria tailored to the characteristics of the assignment, and the project operating environment, to create an expression of project success.

Principles

Organizations shape our daily life

Whatever we do, eating, drinking, working, voting, sport, education, organizations affect every part of our lives. Although technical knowledge is highly valued in the job market, combining technical and organizational skills is worth its weight in gold.

Federated organizations enable technology

Organizations and technology are like two sides of the same coin; organizations leverage technology to deliver value to society, while technology is created, deployed, and maintained by a federation of organizations.

Adaptation is a perpetual activity

Organizations are subject to continual inside and outside trends and forces. A profitable market can dry up due to emerging technologies or competing products like Kodak painfully experienced when digital photography took over. Digital cameras erased the celluloid film and the entire industry built around it. In addition to outside forces like technological changes, internal forces from employees may require change initiatives related to working conditions, wages, health, and safety. Although labeled as a standing organization, it is not permanent, and adaptation is a continuous process.

The temporary organization complements the standing part

The standing part of the organization is responsible for realizing the mission, requiring operations, support, governance, development, and management type of activities. Special initiatives may invoke temporary work forms to achieve one-of-a-kind results. Temporary organizations support the efforts of the standing organization, assisting in particular tasks that the regular organization is ill-equipped to perform.

Resource level across the organization

The organization's workload will vary over time; typically, the temporary workforce comes from the standing part. Managing the overall workload versus the capacity over time is a central point of attention. Remember that regular operational activities bring in the money that funds the projects. How much time and effort can you draw from the standing part of the organization without damaging the business? Finally, there is a limit to the amount of change people can absorb all at once, so balancing transformation with periods of relative stability is necessary.

Not every project is a change, nor do all changes require a project

Projects are commonly dubbed the vehicles of change, but not every change requires a project, and not every project represents a change. For example, a customer delivery project will bring in revenue but does not alter the organization's structure, roles, routines, or procedures.

Strategy is a means to an end

Strategic alignment is essential when selecting project proposals, but not an overriding one. Sometimes people suffer from *strategy blindness;* fulfilling the strategy becomes the goal. Remember that strategy is a means to an end, not an end in itself. Provided a project is a response to essential drivers and has a valid business case, the proposal must be judged on its merits irrespective of its strategic alignment.

Strategy is not a given

Organizations can adopt a reactive or a proactive behavior. A *reactive* posture implies that the organization has no long-term plan but responds to impulses and implements solutions with a short-term perspective. Alternatively, the organization can proactively be engaged in long-term strategic planning to shape its future. A strategy is not always a must-have or a prerequisite for projects; some companies operate in stable environments with long-lasting customer relationships, production technologies, logistics, and legislation written in stone.

Doing nothing is not ignoring

Doing nothing can be a sensible option in highly volatile, chaotic, or uncertain situations with no apparent correlation between actions and effects. Our experiences are thought-driven, and consequently, our problems are thought-created. As thoughts continuously change, so may our perception of a problem change over time. A decision to wait for situations to clear up and let views mature takes courage, as a doing nothing strategy can easily be interpreted as weakness or a lack of initiative. Doing nothing is not ignoring, which is consciously failing to give attention to things that need attention.

Artifacts

Glossary

Dull as it may seem, a primary project asset that reduces uncertainty is a glossary with mutually agreed concepts to ensure effective communication. Unconvinced? Try the following experiment. Ask your colleagues which comes first:

- Problem or risk
- Mission or vision
- Effectiveness or efficiency
- Specification or requirement
- Strategy and tactic
- Goal versus objective.

The results may be unsettling; the expected outcome is likely to be around 50/50. An equal number will define goals first, and the other half will start with objectives. Ambiguity in definitions shows through disagreement about the logical sequential relationship. Once aware of the fundamental gap in conception, one cannot help but wonder about the value added of all the time spent in meetings, workshops, and e-mails, discussing the project's problems and activities. To reduce communication uncertainty, the team needs a common language to describe everyday reality. Creating a single source prevents the problem of different authors creating multiple dictionaries with disparate content. Use the one-breath challenge explained in the following paragraph related to as a source of definitions, and establish a mindset of language accuracy.

Document structure

Project documentation forms a hierarchical structure:

1 *The mission statement* states the raison d'être of the organization or the value it provides to society
2 *Vision statement*, a future state of the organization, or an endeavor
3 *Strategy* is the master plan to achieve the vision in the shortest possible time, with minimum effort, and risk
4 The *program blueprint* outlines the capabilities the organization wants to obtain
5 A *feasibility study* provides an overview of the alternatives to achieve a (strategic) goal, including an assessment of success and a recommendation for the optimal solution
6 *Project brief*, a high-level project description including a scope statement (content) and business case (rationale) behind the assignment
7 A *project mandate* initiates a project, establishes the steering committee and core team, and authorizes the use of company resources to create a project management plan
8 The *project management plan* is an umbrella plan describing the methods, tools, and techniques that will be used to control the project dimensions
9 *Project sub plans* contain the contents of the plan, such as stakeholders, deliverables, activities, and a cost budget.

Document templates are integral to project management methods; for some, the documents are the method. Before designing a template, consider its purpose and place it in the documentation hierarchy. Lower-level papers must detail higher-level plans and should not duplicate information or contradict them. Document breakdowns are preferably founded in a logical model such as the step-transition model.

Concepts

Clear, distinct, and concise concepts are prerequisites for logical thinking. Once you go down the slippery path of fuzzy, ambiguous, or sloppy concepts, your ability to reason logically will be significantly reduced. The *one-breath challenge* is a fun and challenging game: Explain the fundamental difference between two concepts aloud in one breath. When you run out of air, your turn is over. An explanation using examples is not allowed. Try the difference between:

- Mission versus vision
- Standing organization versus temporary organization
- Formal versus informal organization
- Urgent versus important work
- Routine versus unique work
- Program versus portfolio
- Task force versus project
- Incident team versus crisis team
- Preplanned versus improvisation
- Scope statement versus business case
- Prototype versus proof of concept.

Questions

1 How is the standing organization structured in your company?
2 Is the organigram updated and available?
3 Does the parent organization have a PMO, and if so, what is the tasking and the responsibilities?
4 Which temporary organization types are used in your parent organizations?
5 Are there any assignments where a different organization form would be more appropriate?
6 How powerful is the informal organization?
7 What method is used to define and assess project success?

References

Cuypers, P.W.M. 2022. "Defining Project Success, a System Thinking Approach." *Proceedings of The 4th International Conference on Applied Research in Business, Management, and Economics* [online] Available at: https://www.dpublication.com/wp-content/uploads/2022/03/26–4275.pdf [Accessed 14 Apr. 2023].

Frefer, A.A., M. Mahmoud, H. Haleema, and R. Almamlook. 2018. *Industrial Engineering & Management* 7: 1.

Gaddis, P.O. 1959. "The Project Manager." *Harvard Business Review*, May-June 1959, 89–97.
Ika, L.A. 2009. "Project Success as a Topic in Project Management Journals: A Brief History." *Project Management Journal* 40, no. 4: 6–19.
Mangram, M.E. 2012. "The Globalization of Tesla Motors: A Strategic Marketing Plan Analysis." *Journal of Strategic Marketing* 20, no. 4: 289–312, DOI: 10.1080/0965254X.2012.657224
Shenhar, A., O. Levy, and D. Dvir. 1997. "Mapping the Dimensions of Project Success." *Project Management Journal* 28, no. 2: 5–13.
Thimmesh, C. 2015. *Team Moon: How 400,000 People Landed Apollo 11 on the Moon*. New York: Harper Collins.

Chapter 2

Methodology

Introduction

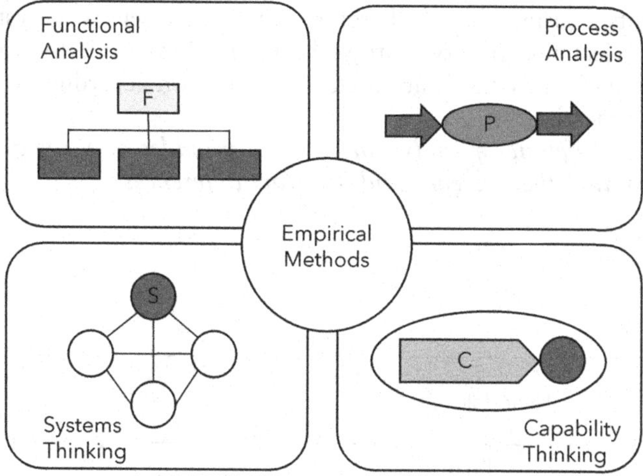

Figure 2.1 Theoretical versus practical approaches.

In 1913, the Danish physicist Niels Bohr proposed a model of the hydrogen atom, depicted as a tiny nucleus surrounded by orbiting electrons, not unlike the solar system (Bohr 1913). Although other models had been proposed previously, the Bohr model could explain and quantify the hydrogen atom's spectral emission lines earlier observed in the experiments conducted by Johannes Rydberg (Rydberg 1889). Models are lenses through which we perceive the world; they are helpful provided they complement empirical knowledge and observations. We create *models* to capture the essence of complex realities, enabling us to understand and explain observed phenomena.

Models are simplified versions of reality; they contain enough information to combine explanatory value with ease of understanding. Simplicity implies omitting details clouding the issue; the explanatory value is lost if a model is equally complex as a real-life entity it represents. This chapter presents the primary modeling disciplines applied to organizations: Process analysis, functional analysis, capability thinking, system thinking, and its complement, the empirical approach. Models are used across scientific fields, professions,

DOI: 10.4324/9781003431961-4

businesses, and industries. Each approach has strengths and limitations and provides a different viewpoint. From a methodology perspective, the question arises: Which method is best suitable to model project uncertainty, and why?

The definition of uncertainty is uncertain; pun intended. Any physicist stating, 'If there is speed, there must be acceleration because of distance traveled' would quickly find himself the target of ridicule for such a vague statement. Time (t), speed (v), distance (s), and acceleration (a) are separate concepts, connected through the formula: $s = v_0.t + 1/2at^2$. Contrary to the hard sciences, project management researchers get away with ambiguous statements such as 'risk is the cause of uncertainty.' The debate on the definition of uncertainty often gets clouded by using perceived synonymous concepts that are used interchangeably.

Like the physics example, uncertainty-related concepts like risk, problem, threat, and opportunity are independent but connected elements forming a system. A change in one element may affect all other elements of the system through direct or indirect paths. A vital strength of systems thinking is providing a holistic view of complex behaviors and the underlying structure of elements causing them. Therefore, this book selects a system thinking approach to model project uncertainty. Although system thinking is the main approach, diagrams typical to the other methods are used in conjunction according to the principle: The more models, the merrier!

Note: Each method warrants a lifetime of study; this chapter provides only the quick and dirty version intended to capture their essence and illustrate differences.

Definitions

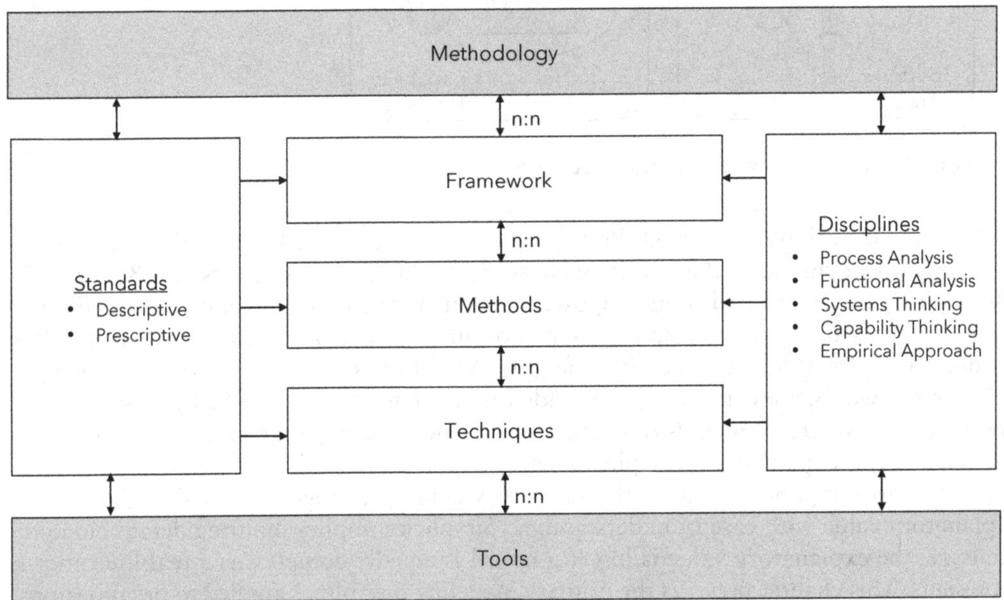

Figure 2.2 Methodology concepts and their relationships.

A *model* is a physical or conceptual representation of a real-life entity intended for visualization, analysis, teaching, study, or research. Another description is a coherent set of assumptions about how an actual world entity works.

The word *analysis* comes from the Ancient Greek ἀνάλυσις, analysis, 'a breaking-up' or 'an untying'; from *ana*- 'up, throughout' and *lysis,* 'a loosening.' Analysis is breaking up a complex topic, system, or substance into smaller parts.

The *methodology* is the structured study of methods to determine their strengths, weaknesses, limits, and application (Figure 2.2).

A *framework* is a collection of methods designed to achieve a goal – for example, the Scaled Agile Framework (SAFe) or the Toyota Production System (TPS).

A *method is* a cohesive set of principles, techniques, and activities to achieve a result or outcome in a structured manner (PMBOK, Agile, PRINCE2, Six Sigma).

A *technique* is a specific way of carrying out a particular task or procedure (Kanban, PERT, Gantt chart).

A *tool* is a device, instrument, machine, or platform designed to operate on materials, energy, or information, adding value to the process (pen and paper, Microsoft Project, Jira, MS Excel).

Note the n:n relationships; for example, the Kanban board technique can be done using yellow notes and a pen, a spreadsheet, or an application specifically designed for the purpose. Also, as frameworks are made up of a combination of methods, the validity of a framework is more challenging to prove than individual methods. For example, SAFe combines several agile and no-agile principles, methods, and techniques into a prescriptive amalgamation, making it hard to identify the active ingredients.

Elements

Functional analysis

Functional analysis is based on the principle that the overall workings of complex systems or phenomena can be explained through decomposition into easier-to-understand subfunctions. For example, the intricate workings of the human body can be explained by

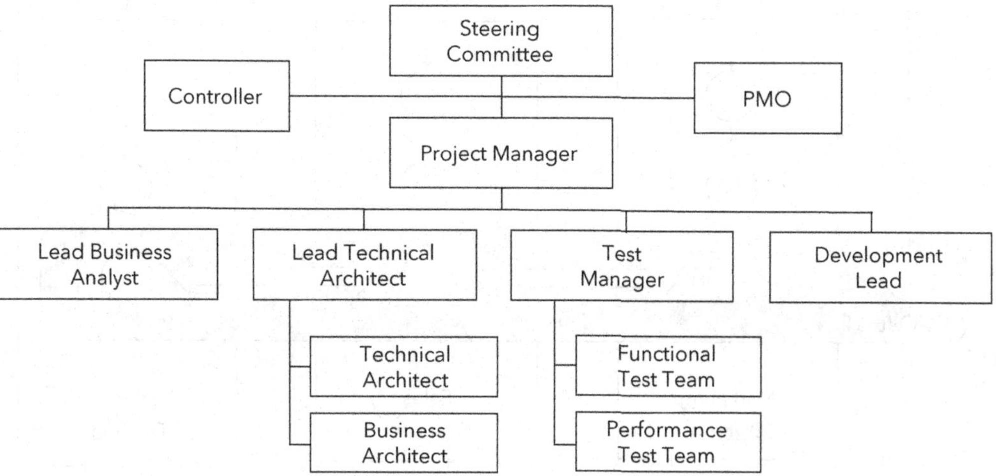

Figure 2.3 An example of an organization chart showing the functional breakdown of a project.

describing the individual functions of the organs, like the heart, lungs, brain, stomach, and liver. Functional analysis is a well-known approach to capturing an organization's nature, design, and workings. The main strengths of functional analysis in management are its appealing simplicity and the ability to create specialized structures exhibiting high levels of effectiveness and efficiency. The drawbacks of a strictly functional approach to organizational design include the following (Figures 2.3 and 2.4):

- Focus on elemental functions can lead to a lack of understanding of the overall structure, loss of perspective, or overall goal
- A lack of flexibility, adaptation, and the ability to improvise when faced with non-routine challenges
- Functional organizations can result in silos that poorly communicate with other silos, which again might lead to an 'us-against-them' perception and an internal competition mentality
- Doing simple repetitive work governed by strict routines can be demotivating.

The need for projects as a work form was partially driven by the inherent weakness of highly functional organizational structures that evolved during the fifties and sixties, namely an inability to perform out-of-the-ordinary work. A functional organization works well in stable environments where specialist repetitive work is involved, referred to as the 'business as usual' or BAU. Projects deal mainly with out-of-the-ordinary assignments where highly functional organizations struggle. Building cars is a routine job; developing a new car model, or setting up a new production line for manufacturing, is a unique task for which the standing organization is poorly equipped.

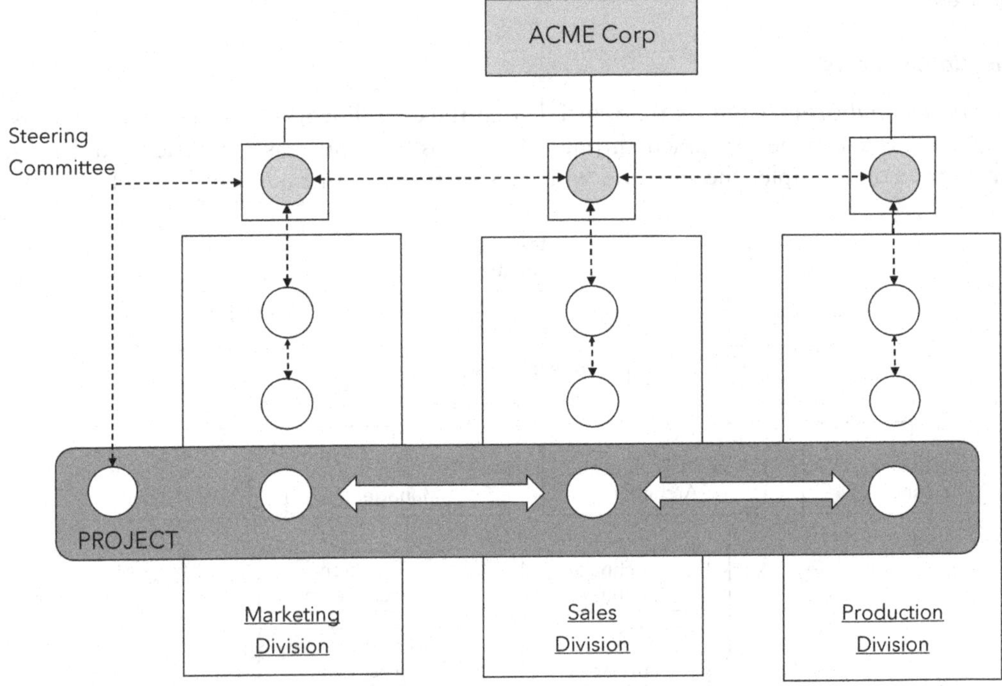

Figure 2.4 Shortened lines of command, control, and communications in a project.

Extended lines of communication in functional hierarchical organizations cause delay and message distortion, negatively affecting the ability to make fast and effective decisions. A question from an engineer regarding the design of the new car model would first have to go up the hierarchical ladder to the head of the design department, then to the chief of the production department, and down the hierarchical ladder to the relevant production person. The answer must then travel back the same route, subject to delays, distortion, and unsolicited meddling. Projects as a work form ensure short command, control, and communication lines across organizational boundaries with minimum bureaucracy to get the job done.

Process analysis

Contrary to a functional approach, *process analysis* looks across organizational units and boundaries, focusing on the transformation and flow of materials, value, energy, or information (Figure 2.5).

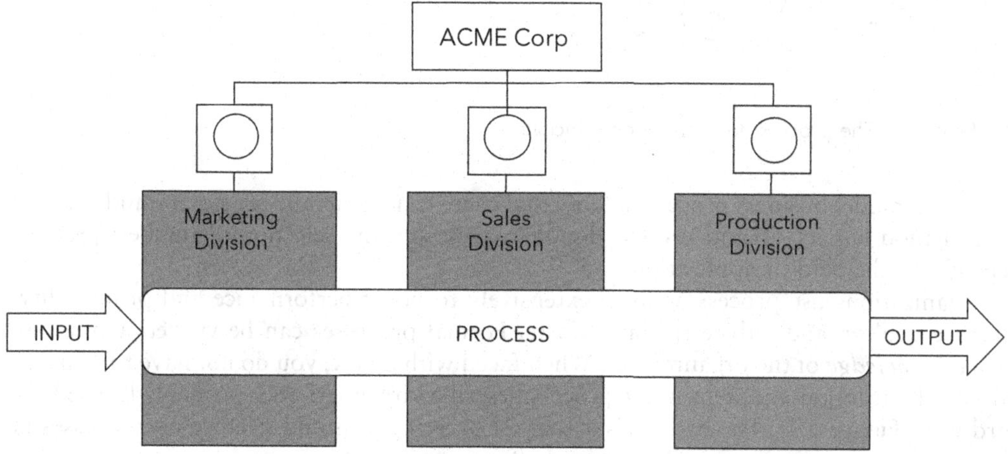

Figure 2.5 The process analysis focuses on the transformation of inputs into outputs.

The common denominator in functional and process analysis is breaking a complex topic or substance into smaller parts for better understanding. In process analysis, the top-level process is broken into more detailed processes at various decomposition levels to understand inputs, outputs, and transformations. Two primary flavors of process analysis exist: *Black box* and *white box*. Only the inputs and outputs are identified in the black box variety, not the inner workings; hence, the name (Figure 2.6).

A fundamental rule in black box process decomposition is that the sum of the inputs and outputs must be equal at all levels. In the illustration, the top levels have one input and two outputs; therefore, the second level must have the same number of inputs and outputs. If you find a new input or output at a detailed level not previously identified at a higher level, add it for consistency.

In *white-box* process analysis, you determine the logic, rules, or algorithms that make the conversion from input to output. Several diagrams, types, and conventions graphically depict the flow of actions, decisions, and events. In management, various methods, such as event-driven process chain (EPC) and business process modeling notation (BPMN), have

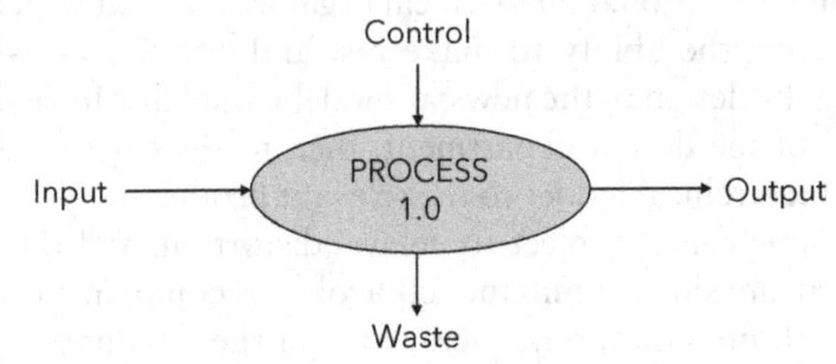

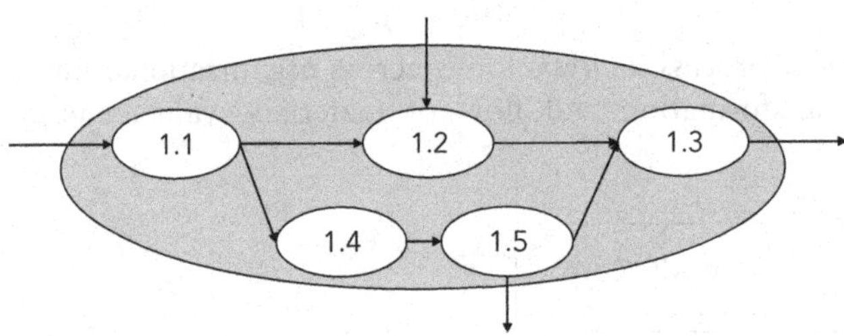

Figure 2.6 The process decomposition principle.

evolved to model business processes. Note that there is no generally accepted standard, and each method has its advantages and disadvantages, and the selection of the best practice depends on the field of application.

Organizations use process analysis extensively to boost performance and profitability, improve quality, and reduce risk and waste. Formal processes can be viewed as the *collective knowledge* of the organization. When faced with a task, you do not have to reinvent the wheel but follow the steps in the process described by others who probably learned the hard way (Figure 2.7). The bad news is that an overemphasis and reliance on processes in organizations can create several unwanted effects, such as:

- Reduced exception handling ability; the established procedures cover most standard events but fail at anomalies or exceptions
- Mental rigidity; a strong focus on developing processes reduces the organization's ability to think 'out of the box'
- Split responsibility: When multiple people are responsible for different processes, the ability to make decisions can be weakened
- Loss of perspective; a process is a means to an end but not an end in itself, where following the process becomes the goal as opposed to getting the job done
- Sub-optimization; locally optimizing individual processes may have a detrimental effect on overall organizational performance
- Decision paralysis; lack of process is used to stall decisions, e.g., 'We can do nothing before we have decided on a proper process'
- 'Fat' organizations; means processes containing non-value-adding tasks or overhead, with people earning a salary performing them
- Lack of motivation; having processes does not imply using them. Why follow tedious and cumbersome procedures if one can take shortcuts?

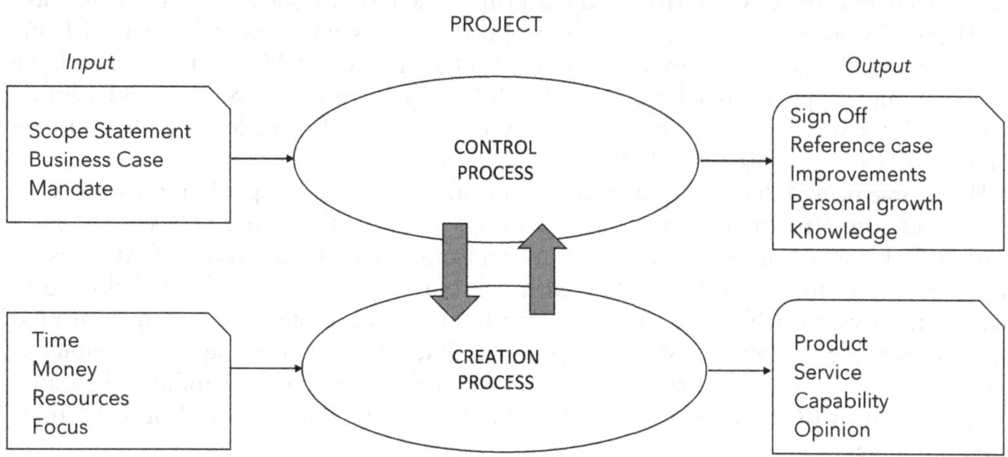

Figure 2.7 A project process model at the first decomposition level.

Capability thinking

A *capability* is the ability of people and their assets to achieve a deliberate result or outcome. In daily language use, the concepts of result and outcome are almost synonymous, with only subtle grammatical or contextual differences. Capability thinking is technology-free, starting with the result in mind rather than the means, and working backwards to a possible solution. This approach reduces the risk of getting locked down into a narrow path while overlooking potentially better alternatives. Rather than taking existing systems or technologies as a starting point for development, the reverse approach stimulates thinking outside the box and can lead to significant breakthroughs.

On 2 April 1982, Argentinian armed forces invaded the British Falklands Islands, around 945 miles east of the Argentinean mainland. The British Royal Navy assembled an expeditionary force to travel over 8,000 miles to recapture the islands. The British fleet would be working well within the operating range of the Argentinian air force, and air support was critical to the mission's success. However, the British task force was hopelessly short of aircraft carriers that could provide landing space for their transport helicopters necessary for the landing and vertical land and take-off jet fighter, the Sea Harrier.

Aircraft carriers are highly complex systems that combine a floating airfield, an aircraft repair and maintenance facility, ammunition bunkers, aviation fuel tanks, and a small village. Designing, building, testing, and fielding an aircraft carrier is complicated, laborious, and typically takes years. British engineers created a solution by converting a merchant ship into a floating airfield. The Atlantic Conveyor was a civilian hybrid container ship modified by welding a steel deck over the container hold that functioned as a flight deck. Containers were placed on the topsides, serving as workshops, spare stores, and accommodation for the flight and maintenance crews. Although not intended as an aircraft carrier, the vessel served as a transport vessel with a flight deck that added the desperately needed additional transport capacity.

The conversion was completed in less than ten days, and the vessel sailed from the United Kingdom with five Chinook and six Wessex helicopters. At Ascension, 14 Harrier fighter aircraft were embarked. On arrival in the Maritime Exclusion Zone around the Falklands, the Harriers were flown off to the carriers HMS *Hermes* and *Invincible*. The Atlantic Conveyor was instructed to move closer to the Falkland Islands on 25 May to disembark the helicopters and supplies at first light. She was attacked by 2 Argentinian Super Etendards that fired 2 AM39 Exocet anti-ship missiles, sinking the vessel, and 12 men lost their lives (Royal Navy Board of Inquiry Report 1982).

The people behind the transformation did not start with how to speed up the process of building an aircraft carrier; they asked themselves: What is the fastest way we can get a floating deck for a Harrier or helicopter to land on? The Atlantic Conveyor story is an example of capability thinking, starting with the result in mind and working backward to find alternatives to achieve it. A key strength of organizations that organize around capabilities is the potential to shift their mission quickly by rearranging core capabilities into new constellations. Project capability catalyzes the other core capabilities: Research and development (R&D), business innovation, business development, and business transition initiatives.

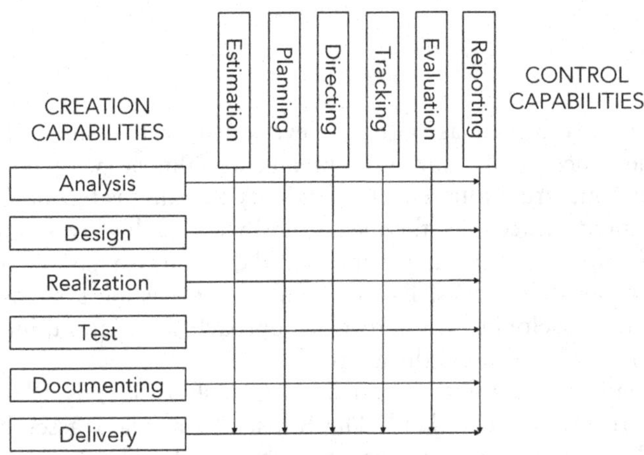

Figure 2.8 **Project control and creation capabilities at the operational level.**

Project capability can be broken down into:

1 Strategic project capability
2 Tactical project capability
3 Operational project capability.

Strategic project capability is the ability to define, select, prioritize, and authorize suitable projects given the needs and issues of the organization. *Tactical project capability* supports the active projects approved at the strategic level to ensure maximum benefits are realized within the shortest possible time with minimum resource use. Tactical project capability means optimizing project sequence, timings, resource assignments, and deconfliction with the organization's 'Business As Usual' part and resolving structural problems beyond the project's mandate or ability to solve. *Operational project capability* is the ability to achieve the expected project results with maximum benefits while minimizing effort, lead time, waste, and uncertainty. Operational project capability breaks down into control and creation sub-capabilities; see Figure 2.8.

Systems thinking

Yellowstone National Park is nearly 90,000 square kilometers, mainly in Wyoming, spreading into parts of Montana and Idaho. Large predators like wolves and cougars were deliberately eliminated in the park's early days. Not being hunted, elk populations started to dominate the landscape, eroding vegetation and starving in winter. In 1995, after careful planning and modeling, 14 wolves from Alberta were released in Yellowstone, followed by another 17 Canadian wolves in 1996. The reintroduction of wolves started a widespread trophic cascade of events, restoring balance in the ecosystem. In biology, a *trophic cascade* is a change that begins at the top of the food chain and eventually works down toward lower species and vegetation. Ultimately, the cascade even affected the landscape's physical geography and the rivers' course (Figure 2.9).

The reintroduction of wolves is a famous example of *systems thinking* and the explanation goes as follows. Although wolves are predators that kill other animals, they also provide life to other species. Not only did the wolves' predation reduce the population of elks, deer, and bison, but they also changed their behavior, avoiding areas where they were easy prey for the hunting wolfpacks. As the regions became less grazed, vegetation regenerated; as a result, insects returned, soon followed by songbirds. As the trees grew, the

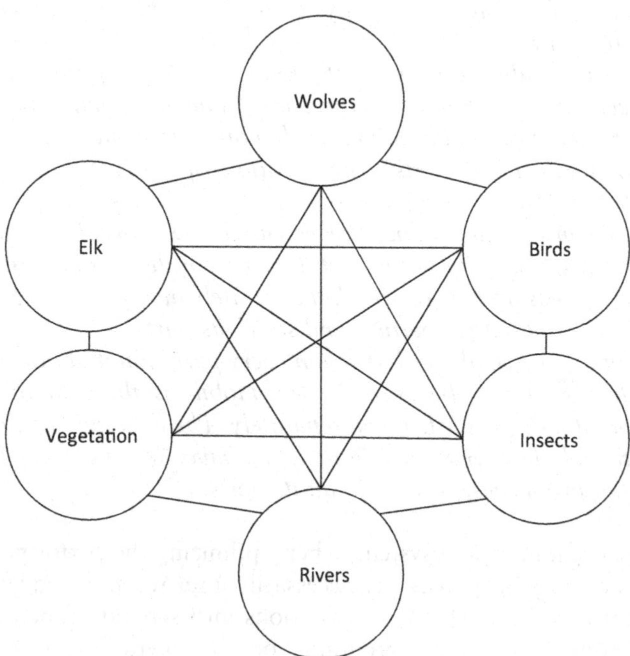

Figure 2.9 A systems thinking model of the Yellowstone Park ecology.

beavers returned, creating micro-ecosystems with their dams, opening the doors for other species, such as fish, reptiles, and amphibians.

As the wolves also killed competing predators like coyotes, the number of rodents like mice and rabbits increased, providing food for smaller predators like birds of prey, weasels, and badgers. Most interesting, the wolves did change not only the ecosystem but also the geography by stabilizing the course of the rivers. As trees grew, their root system stabilized the banks of the rivers, causing them to meander less and halt the banks' erosion. The rivers started to run straighter and faster, subsequently becoming deeper. The riverbanks functioned as new ecosystems to house different species.

The human mind has limitations to what we can grasp regarding size and complexity. A natural reaction is to break things down into smaller parts we can comprehend. Reduction is the foundation of functional and process analysis. The drawback of this approach is that understanding the behavior of the individual components may be harder to understand without its context. The main strength of system thinking is to see the larger picture, as the Yellowstone example illustrates. The behavior of elemental components may seem inadequate or ineffective at an individual level but makes perfect sense on an aggregated level as a part of a more extensive system.

One of the most precise, concise, and amusing descriptions of systems thinking is from a speech by Professor Russel Ackoff. The following excerpt is a partial and adapted transcript:

> *A system has three characteristics; First, a system is a whole that contains two or more parts, each of which can affect the properties or the behavior of the whole. None of the parts has an independent effect overall; how any part affects the whole depends on what other parts are doing. The parts of a system are always connected; between any parts, there is always a direct and an indirect path.*
>
> *Third, if you group the parts into subgroups, no matter how you subgroup them, each subgroup always has an effect on the behavior of the whole, and none will have an independent effect. These characteristics can be summarized in one statement: The whole cannot be divided into two independent parts. The function of the automobile is transportation. None of its parts alone can do that for you.*
>
> *This statement has several consequences; one, the essential behavior of a system derives from how its parts interact, not on how they act, taken separately. For example, life is a property of the whole; there is no part of you that separately lives. Therefore, if a system is dissembled, it loses its essential properties, and so do its parts.*
>
> *If you take an automobile and disassemble it but retain every part, you will not have an automobile but a collection of parts. Because the automobile is the sum of the interaction of its parts, not the sum of the parts taken separately. The defining parts of a system are the properties of the whole, which none of the parts have. When the whole is dissembled, it loses its essential properties, and so do all its parts.*

Ackoff makes an important observation: In any system, when optimizing the performance of the parts, the whole system's performance does not necessarily improve and frequently worsens. When designing organizations, we divide corporations into separate functional departments, production, marketing, finance, and programs, or split operations into discrete processes. Then we run each part as well as possible, assuming the whole will run better. Such is a false assumption because when a system operates as best as possible, none of its parts may be; how the elements of a system fit together determines the system's performance, not how they perform separately.

A system thinking approach has several strengths. First, it provides a holistic view of the domain, the project, and the combined elements. Systems thinking can help the project to create long-term solutions, prevent problems from reoccurring, and minimize the chances of triggering unintended consequences. If your project opens Pandora's box, system thinking can help you select a suitable project strategy to deal with it.

Empirical approach

A classic engineering joke goes as follows:

> *Theory is when everyone knows how things should work, but nothing does. Practice is when everything works, and nobody understands why. When theory and practice meet, nothing works, and no one knows why!*

The previously discussed methods have in common that they are theoretical, as opposed to an empirical approach. The *empirical approach* tests a hypothesis by gathering empirical evidence using direct or indirect observation and represents the logical counterpart of theories. Theoretical approaches aim to make the black boxes transparent using models. In the practical world, only observations matter, and systems are seen as black boxes. For example, consider the following riddle: Five birds are sitting on a telephone wire. A hunter comes along and shoots one. How many birds are left?

The theoretical answer would be five minus one equals four. The empirical observation is one dead bird; the others flew away, scared by the shot. Empirical methods are not modeling techniques but about conducting real-world experiments and learning through observation. The development of herbal medicine was based on trial and error; over the ages, the healing properties of various plants were discovered, and their use was perfectioned. Herbalists knew from experience that it worked but lacked the theoretical knowledge to explain why. In a perfect world, theoretical models explain observations, while experiments confirm the model's validity.

In project management, SCRUM is an example of an empirical approach. The inventors of SCRUM were not academics but experienced IT people with years of knowledge from practicing in the field. They noticed that traditional general project approaches such as PMBOK and PRINCE2 performed relatively poorly in the software development domain. SCRUM is designed to address the specific challenges related to software development while capitalizing on the degrees of freedom unique to computer programming.

For example, welcoming new requirements in software development is relatively easy as you can add new components almost at will and at any time. Adding 20 additional stories to a skyscraper on a whim is impossible unless the foundation has provisions to take the extra weight. Even if the architect had the foresight, the supplemental materials and work would represent a high cost. Like any special tool that will outperform a generic tool, domain-specific methods outperform domain-agnostic approaches.

Empirical methods are time-honored practices developed through trial, error, and observation. Although empirical methods are known to work, they do have a downside. SCRUM consists of a prescriptive set of roles, routines, and ceremonies; follow the recipe, and operating software will emerge, voilà. When it does, life is good. But what if it doesn't? A fool with a tool is still a fool. Is it the incorrect use of SCRUM that causes the failure, or is SCRUM not working for you? In the latter case, making adaptations requires understanding the logic behind the prescriptions: A theoretical model.

Techniques

Context analysis

The *context diagram* is one of the first models to be drawn up in any system development project to identify the number of integrations, interface standards, protocols, and data flows with supporting systems. Systems can be regarded as *open* or *closed*. Closed systems are assumed to have no outside factors affecting the properties of the system. The context diagram may show the trends and forces acting on open systems. In addition, a context diagram will reveal the stakeholders that own and operate the adjacent systems. A critical modeling decision is where to draw the *system's extensive* boundary. One may fail to see the big picture if the border is too narrow. When the limit is set too wide, there is the risk of an information and complexity overload. The *intensive or in-depth boundary* shows the detail of what is included (Figure 2.10).

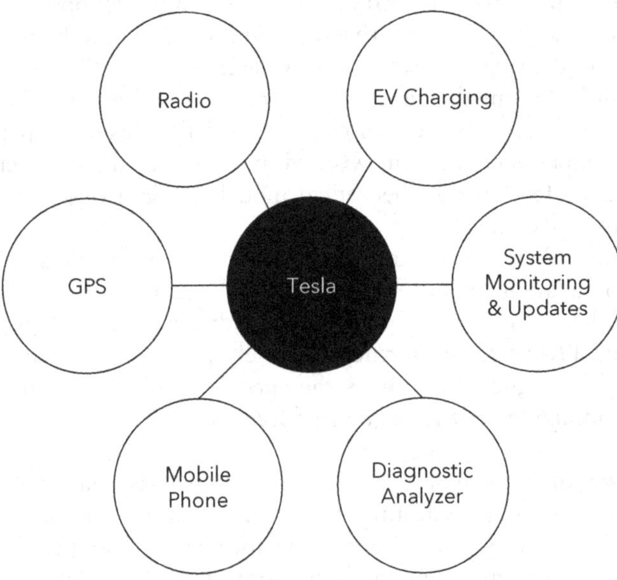

Figure 2.10 Context diagram of a Tesla electric car.

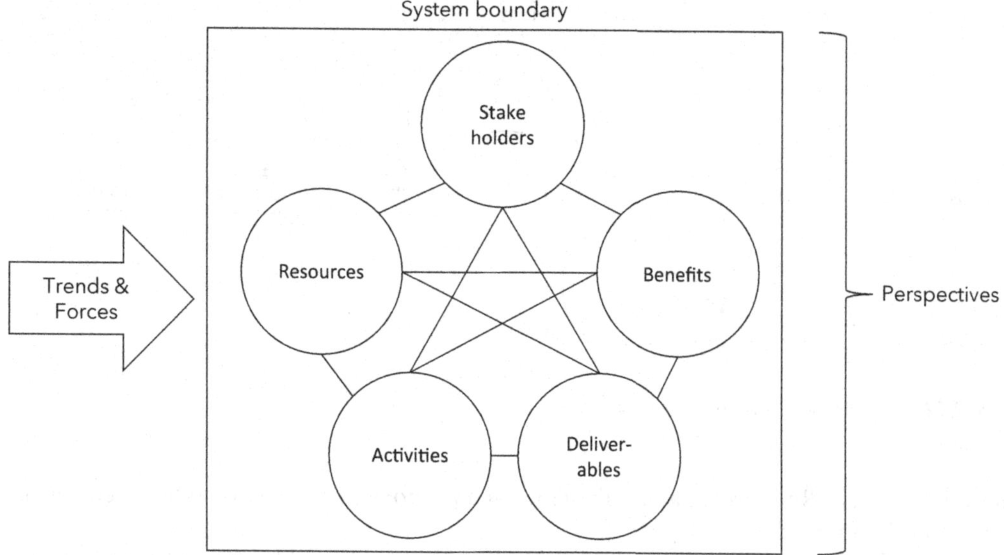

Figure 2.11 A project is perceived as an open system.

System diagraming

A *system diagram* shows the static perspective on a system, consisting of elements, relations, and the system boundary. Each element is connected through direct and indirect paths in a system, while a change in one element can propagate throughout the system. The main elements can be broken down into subcomponents. For example, project deliverables can be broken down into *control* types of deliverables (business case, mandate, project management plan) and *creation* types of deliverables (requirements document, a design, product or service, a test report) (Figure 2.11).

System state analysis

A *state diagram* describes the behavior of systems, usually perceived as a finite number of states, but sometimes this number is a modeling abstraction. Various forms of state diagrams have evolved with individual semantics. The system's behavior is by a series of states and transitions that can occur from one state to another, with intermediate conditions and sometimes end states. A state diagram is where system thinking meets process analysis; the transition from one state to another could be initiated by an event and modeled as a process (Figure 2.12).

Causal loop diagraming

System dynamics can be visualized using causal loop diagrams (CLDs) consisting of variables and links. If one variable strengthens the other, the link is marked with an 's' or a plus sign. The link is marked with an 'o' or a minus sign if variables decrease. Two basic types of

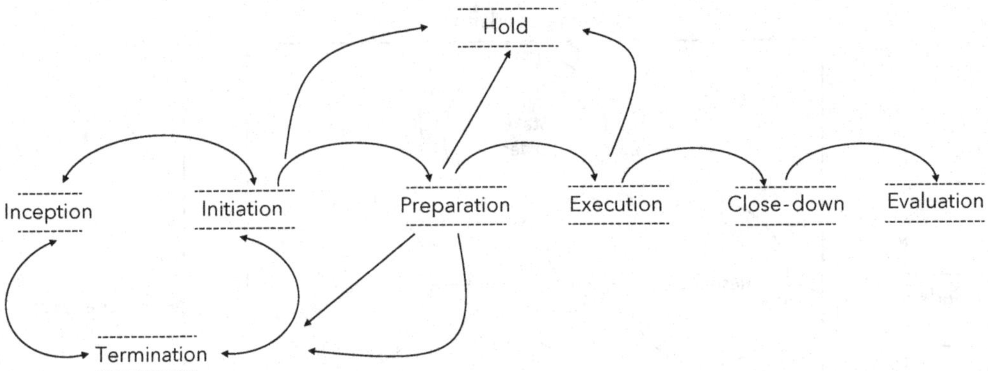

Figure 2.12 Example of a system state diagram.

causal loops exist: Reinforcing and balancing. In a *reinforcing loop* marked 'R,' a change is augmented by more change (Figure 2.13).

On the other hand, *balancing loops* resist change to bring equilibrium and are identified with a central 'B.' Multiple variables and loops can be connected to provide an overall system picture. To determine if the system is overall reinforcing or balancing, count the number of 'o' links. An even number, or none, indicates a reinforcing system. An odd number of results in a balancing system (Figure 2.14).

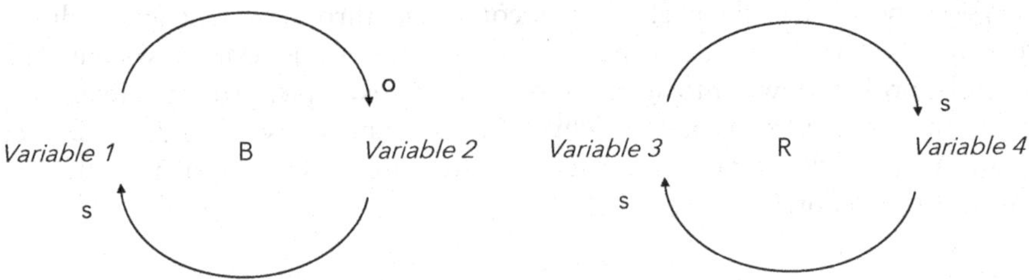

Figure 2.13 Balancing and reinforcing loops.

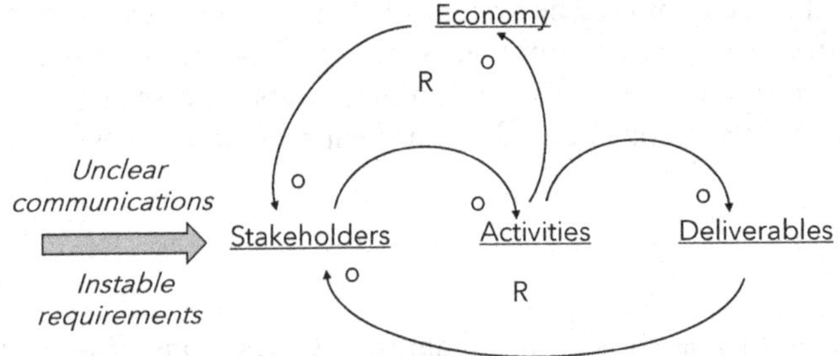

Figure 2.14 A causal loop diagram showing the effects of unclear communications and unstable requirements.

Principles

All models are wrong

All models are erroneous because they are incomplete representations of reality; however, some models are more valuable than others.

The more models, the merrier

The more different types of models you can create, the broadened perspectives you get on the entity and the more complete your understanding.

Keep your models authentic

A typical whiteboard session results in myriad squares, arrows, think bubbles, and annotations while everyone nods: Yes, that is how it should work. Most drawings depict a happy mix of systems, processes, people, decisions, storage, and information flows. The fuzzier the model, the easier it is for people to agree, but on what exactly? For your next session, stick to one modeling convention at a time. Draw a cross on the whiteboard; divide it into equal squares; and create separate processes, systems, functions, and capability models per quadrant.

My model is not your model

You may have inherited a folder structure from a colleague and always struggled to find files. Finding things on your extensive drive poses no problem, as it has been built according to your logic. Accordingly, other people's models seldom appear as logical as yours, even if the same conventions are used. Remember that any model represents 'a' version of the truth, not 'the' truth. Rather than spending time and effort to agree on which model is the best, exploit the individual merits per model and if possible, combine them.

Any model is a means to an end

The purpose of a model is not to be perfect. Any model that results in a constructive discussion does a valuable job. Even if you agree to disagree, the model has a useful function in pointing out the differences of opinion.

Any model is good until a better one comes along

Models are dynamic and must evolve as new information emerges and insight improves. If recent information does not fit, you must adapt the model or create a new one.

Artifacts

Several systems thinking diagrams exist, but the most used are as follows:

- System diagrams
- Context diagrams
- Cause loop diagrams
- State diagrams.

Concepts

Take a deep breath, and explain out loud the fundamental difference between:

- Method and methodology
- Tool and technique
- Business and organization
- System and process
- Functional analysis and process analysis
- Systems thinking and capability thinking
- Theoretical and empirical methods
- Function and capability
- Function and feature
- Element and relation
- Extensive and intensive boundary
- Context diagram and system diagram
- Balancing loop and reinforcing loop.

Questions

1. Does your parent organization have a methodology, to determine the effectiveness, efficiency, and application of project methods?
2. What schools of thought are used in your projects? For example, process analysis or empirical methods?
3. Is the project free to select the best suitable method given the assignment, or is there a mandatory company method?

References

Bohr, N. July 1913. "On the Constitution of Atoms and Molecules." *Philosophical Magazine* 26, no. 6: 1–25.

Rydberg, J.R. 1889. "Researches sur la constitution des spectres d'émission des éléments chimiques." *Kongliga Svenska Vetenskaps-Akademiens Handlingar 2nd series*, 23, no. 11: 1–177.

Royal Navy Board of Inquiry Report, Loss of SS Atlantic Conveyor 1982. Ministry of Defence site Available at: www.gov.uk/mod [Accessed 14 April 2023].

Chapter 3

Project uncertainty

Introduction

Radon is a radioactive natural gas that seeps out of soil and rocks. The U.S. Environmental Protection Agency estimates indicate that the radioactive radon gas that accumulates in houses, schools, and workplaces is the second-largest cause of lung cancer after smoking, causing at least 21,000 deaths yearly (EPA 2022). The levels of radon gas can be controlled using low-cost, practical measures, but managing any threat starts with defining it, as you cannot control what you cannot define. In 1898, five-time Nobel Prize-winning scientist Marie Salomea Skłodowska Curie, better known as Madame Curie, discovered the radioactive element polonium, named after her homeland Poland. Together, with the physicist Henri Becquerel, she developed the theory of radioactivity, for which they received the Nobel Prize in 1903 (The Nobel Foundation 2023).

Before her discovery, there was no concept of radioactivity, and the radiation threat was an unknown-unknown: Invisible, odorless, and deadly. Defining the concept of radiation was the first step toward control. The second step was to make the phenomenon observable, and Geiger counters were developed. The next step was to devise protective measures, like lead liners, to absorb radiation. In the case of radon, ventilation systems pump the gas away from cellars and confined spaces under houses to prevent radon from accumulating. Uncertainty, like radioactivity, is everywhere in our lives; it can never be eliminated but can be reduced. The working premise is that even a slight reduction in uncertainty by making more information available can significantly improve the chances of project success.

This chapter presents a generic concept of project uncertainty. Using a system thinking approach, we will create a model of a project consisting of the elements:

- Assignment
- Context
- Decisions
- Methods
- Scenarios.

By projecting the uncertainty matrix on the system, we can analyze the known-known, known-unknown, unknown-known, and unknown-unknowns aspects of the project. These main elements will be further broken down into components in Chapters 4–8 of Part I. Armed with a definition of project uncertainty, we can focus on reduction in Part II (Figure 3.1).

DOI: 10.4324/9781003431961-5

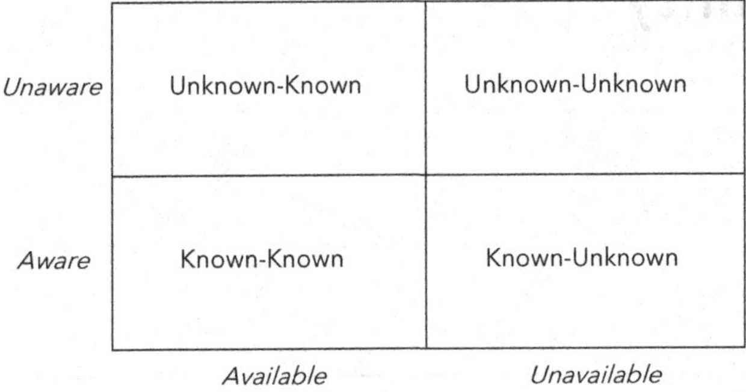

Figure 3.1 Uncertainty is defined as a lack of information awareness or availability.

Definitions

Uncertainty

Imagine being a god capable of knowing everything there is to know about a project, both in the past and future. Complete certainty exists when all relevant information is available concerning every aspect of the project: The assignment, the project context, decisions, methods, and scenarios. Unfortunately, we are not divine creatures, and the world looks quite different for us mortals. First, we do not have all the relevant information, and second, we do not always understand the relevance of existing information or know about its existence. Assume that the rectangle in the above figure contains everything there is to know about a project. From a human perspective, the rectangle can be divided as follows:

- The x-axis represents *information availability,* divided into 'available' and 'unavailable'
- The y-axis represents *information awareness*, divided into 'aware' and 'unaware' of its existence.

The combination gives the following quadrants:

1 *Known-knowns* refers to available information, and you are aware of its existence and relevance
2 There is also unavailable information you would like to have or *known-unknowns*
3 It might be that information is available, but you are unaware of its existence or *unknown-knowns*
4 Finally, there are *unknown-unknowns*: Unavailable information, and you are unaware of its importance.

Consider the following examples illustrating the use and interpretation of the matrix, with an ordinary life event and a project-related example.

Example 1: Problem

a During a meeting at the office, your smartphone slips out of your pocket unnoticed. The problem is an *unknown-known*: The information about the loss is available by simply checking your pockets, but you are unaware. Eventually, you decide to make a call and subsequently discover that your phone is gone. The problem is now a *known-unknown*: You know about the issue but not the solution. Where is the phone? Has it been hacked? How do I get it back? Then, a friendly colleague informs you that your phone has been found and delivered at the reception. Although the matter is not yet solved, the solution is fully defined or *known-known*

b The Sales Department chafed off 30% of the price and timeline for a customer delivery project to close the deal and collect their bonus. The project is unaware that the estimates are unrealistic and the delivery will inevitably go over time and budget. The problem is an unknown-known; the information exists, but the project team is unaware.

Example 2: Risk

- Waking up one morning and looking out the icy window, you see your neighbor gently sliding into a tree with his car. The possibility of crashing your brand-new vehicle on the way to work exists. The collision risk is a known-unknown: Although identified, one cannot know whether an accident will occur. The risk mitigation action of driving slowly leaves residual risk; although reduced, the possibility remains. You call your boss and agree to work from home, avoiding the risk altogether, making this risk a *known-known*
- A construction project uses a worn-out excavation machine, and the risk of a mechanical breakdown is identified. Although aware, the risk represents a *known-unknown* factor, as time will tell whether an actual failure will occur, or the machine holds out. The team decides on mitigating actions, and a mechanic replaces the most worn-out critical parts. Although the risk is reduced, a residual risk of a technical failure remains (known-unknown).

Example 3: Prerequisite

- You decide that the exterior of your house needs a comprehensive face-lift and hire a local constructor to do the work. Changing the house's appearance requires written permission from the municipality to ensure that the change follows the esthetic rules. The prerequisite is an *unknown-known*; the information is available, but you are unaware. A local government inspector drops by and requests to see a permit for the work. Due to the missing prerequisite, the work is stopped
- A department leader starts a project to address an urgent problem in the group. A prerequisite for starting a project in the company is a management approved business case, providing authorization and funding. The Project Management Office gets wind of the under-the-radar project and demands that the activities be put on hold until the required documentation and approvals are in place.

Example 4: Dependency

- When building a house, the foundation must be in place before the walls can be built. Putting on the roof depends on the walls being in place
- Activities A and B are planned in parallel according to the project plan. In reality, starting activity B depends on the completion of A. The relationship is an *unknown-unknow*, and

the dependency becomes clear during execution. After discovery, the plan gets adapted, but the promised project delivery date could not be achieved because of the delay.

Example 5: Assumption

- A man jumps into his car, assuming that the petrol tank is full, although the fuel gauge on the dashboard shows otherwise. The heavy traffic absorbs his attention, and he does not notice the critical fuel state until the alarm light comes on; and the *unknown-known* becomes a *known-known*
- A project manager struggles with estimating the time and cost of what he perceives to be a unique project; the numbers provided by the team members vary considerably. Previously the company did a similar project, and accurate historical data is available in a lessons-learned report buried in the archives, an *unknown-known.*

Example 6: Constraint

- A car's petrol tank is one-quarter full, good for approximately 190 kilometers, a *known-known* constraint
- A department head approves a leave request for an assigned specialist but forgets to notify the project. The project manager schedules the person for an activity on the critical path. The plan gets delayed due to an *unknown-known* constraint.

Example 7: Opportunity

a A group of tourists makes a guided tour through Amsterdam. Everyone in the group looks up at the beautiful facades the canal houses are renowned for. The group passes a 100 euro bill lying on the sidewalk unnoticed. Although the money is visible, the *unknown-known* opportunity is not spotted

b A project implements a new off-the-shelf ERP system. One team member previously worked for the vendor, known to the project manager. The opportunity to use his experience is an unknown-know.

System uncertainty

For any system, the generic uncertainty-related questions include the following:

1 Are all relevant elements within the system boundary?
2 Is the system open or closed?
3 If open, what trends and forces influence the system?
4 Is the system stable, neutral, or unstable?
5 What is the natural variation?
6 What is the resilience of the system?
7 What is the robustness of the system?
8 Are the effects of interventions understood?
9 Is the system tuned for maximum synergy?
10 Is the observer positioned inside or outside the system?
11 Are the observations affecting the system?

If we model a project as a system, we could translate the generic uncertainty-related questions into the following:

1 Which interrelated systems exist outside the project boundary?
2 Is the project operating within a closed or open environment?
3 What outside trends and forces influence the project?
4 Are we in control of the project state?
5 What is the natural variation in the project performance?
6 What is the ability of the project to adapt to adverse events?
7 What is the capacity to withstand negative events?
8 If we make a change, can we foresee the consequences?
9 Is the sum of the project output more than its parts?
10 Are we viewing the project from the inside or outside?
11 Do our measurements and observations affect the stakeholder's behavior?

Project uncertainty

Systems can be studied from different perspectives, such as economic, technical, socio-political, historical, and uncertainty viewpoints. We can model projects as a system, by defining the main elements, such as the assignment, context, decisions, project method, and scenarios. Next, we can model project uncertainty by superimposing the uncertainty matrix over the elements of the system. Information regarding each element gets divided into the four categories of the uncertainty matrix: Known-knowns, unknown-knowns, known-unknowns, and unknown-unknowns (Figure 3.2).

Superimposing the uncertainty matrix over a system model provides a conceptual model of project uncertainty. Still, in practical project management, this approach may be too complex. Working in the field, a practical tip is to distinguish between inherent

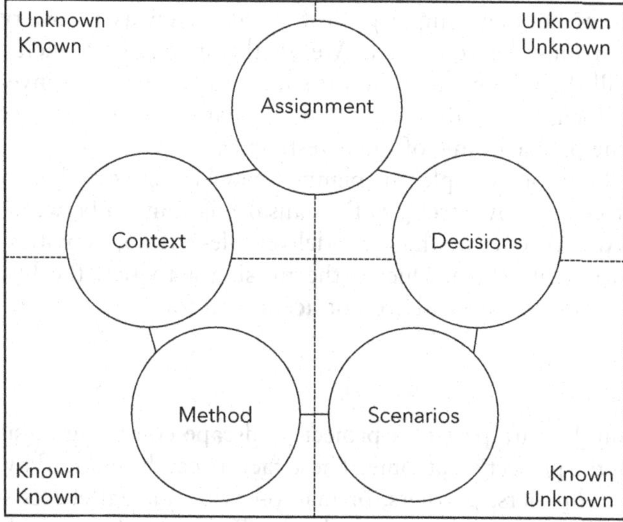

Figure 3.2 Project uncertainty is visualized as a system.

and implicit uncertainty. *Implicit uncertainty* refers to project elements the team is unaware of, for example, undiscovered stakeholders, decisions, risks, or problems. In other words, built-in uncertainty. For example, the project works on a known problem A, while another undetected problem B is causing time and budget overruns. When a risk, problem, threat, stakeholder, or the need for a decision is discovered, ask yourself: What else is out there?

Explicit uncertainty relates to uncertain aspects of known elements. Suppose the team identifies two solutions A and B for a known problem. Explicit uncertainty exists about whether other valid alternatives are being overlooked, which solution is best, and how to get confirmation that we chose the correct one. From a control perspective, the estimates regarding time and cost to implement the solution are working assumptions; their accuracy remains to be seen. Finally, if implementing the chosen solution is not as easy as predicted, what are the criteria for breaking off and going for the next best alternative?

Elements

Assignment uncertainty

Projects are established to carry out unique assignments, meaning *non-routine* work that the standing part of the organization is ill-equipped to handle due to a lack of knowledge, technology, capacity, or a combination of causes. At the highest level of aggregation, the elements of the project assignment are as follows:

1 Stakeholders
2 Benefits
3 Deliverables
4 Activities
5 Resources.

A project starts with stakeholders holding unique project drivers such as needs, risks, problems, and opportunities that must be addressed. Are all the stakeholders including their demands on our radar? Will there be benefits, and if so, are they worth the invested time, money, and organizational focus? From the financial side, what is the monetary value of the anticipated benefits and the payback time of the investment? The envisaged benefits result from the project's deliverables; for example, the planned new IT system will result in faster response times and lower costs. How strong is the causal relationship between the deliverables and the benefits? Are we overlooking any deliverables? If so, activities are missing in our plan necessary to create them. Due to the missing activities, the budget estimates will be too low as the resources needed are not accounted for.

Context uncertainty

Projects do not exist in a vacuum but are part of a project landscape consisting of situational trends and forces affecting the project's outcome. These factors can be induced by the parent organizations, customers, suppliers, partners, or macro-environmental effects such as the world economy, natural disasters, war, or a pandemic. The main elements of the project landscape are as follows:

1 Prerequisites
2 Constraints
3 Inter-dependencies
4 Threats
5 Opportunities.

Decision uncertainty

A project is a unique undertaking for the parent organization requiring unprecedented decisions. The components of decision-making are as follows:

1 Qualifiers
2 Alternatives
3 Rationale
4 Effects
5 Confirmation.

Decision qualifiers are the meta-level aspects of a decision. Decisions can be urgent, important, do-or-die versus reversible, unique, or repetitive. Failure to identify available alternatives can lead to losing precious time that might not be recoverable. What logic do we use to select an option? If we change the rationale, do we end up with another solution? What will the expected effects be, and which unexpected effects might surface? Will the balance between positive and negative impacts be favorable? When will we know that we have made the correct decision? What decisions are inherent to the situation we should concern ourselves with but not address?

Method uncertainty

The right tool for the job is a known aphorism that applies to projects. Most people share the experience of doing home improvement work using inadequate tools. Things start happening in a jiffy when using professional equipment specifically designed for the job. An essential question is whether the project uses the best possible project method to achieve project success. The elements of the method are as follows:

1 Approach
2 Techniques
3 Tools
4 Communication
5 Coordination.

Have we adopted the correct tactical approach? Are we using proper tools and techniques, or are they mainly slowing or dragging us down? Is our communication effective? Are all resources operating in a coordinated fashion? As the project's assignment, context, decisions, and scenarios are a source of constant change, adapting and finetuning the method is a steady effort to ensure that the project works at maximum synergy. *Synergy* is where the whole's output is more significant than its parts' sum. A synergetic team will work faster in any respect, be it job execution, risk identification, or problem-solving.

Scenario uncertainty

A *scenario* is a postulated sequence or development of events culminating into a desired outcome. The elements of the project scenario are as follows:

1 Plan
2 Risk
3 Problem
4 Crisis
5 Measures.

The *plan* is the envisaged desired scenario for the best possible outcome, capitalizing on all known opportunities while minimizing time, effort, cost, and risk. *Risks* are possible unwanted events creating problems; every unsolvable problem is a potential crisis. A *crisis* occurs when limiting the damage is the only remaining valid option, when all actions to solve a problem have failed. Scenario-driven uncertainty is a continuum, starting with a secure state that is abandoned when introducing a risk event; for example, when an aircraft takes off, the risk of crashing becomes a reality. When an engine failure happens, a problem event occurs. If the engine can be restarted before the plane loses too much altitude, the problem is solved. If all attempts to restart the engine fail, a crisis event has occurred, and the only remaining option is to crash land and save as many lives as possible. When facing known risks, problems, and crises, the team can choose to prepare or deploy *measures*:

1 Pre-emptive measures in the risk stage
2 Countermeasures in the problem stage
3 Contingency measures in the crisis stage.

Techniques

Feasibility study

A *feasibility study* aims to create an overview of relevant alternatives and recommend the best choice based on the selection criteria and constraints. The options are evaluated regarding pros, cons, costs, and uncertainty. Consider a feasibility study for an off-grid, zero-emission house based on renewable energy sources: Geothermal, solar, and wind power. The investments for geothermal energy require at least 100 households to participate, and

Table 3.1 Overview of the project elements and components

Assignment	*Context*	*Decisions*	*Method*	*Scenarios*
Stakeholders	Prerequisites	Qualifiers	Approach	Plan
Benefits	Constraints	Alternatives	Techniques	Risk
Deliverables	Inter-dependencies	Rationale	Communication	Problem
Activities	Threats	Effects	Coordination	Crisis
Resources	Opportunities	Confirmation	Tools	Measures

is not feasible. Based on climatic information, the solar alternative is recommended, given the low average wind speeds for the area and the higher cost of wind turbines compared to solar cells. With approval for the recommended option in hand, the next step is to create a scope statement and a business case for solar energy (Figure 3.3).

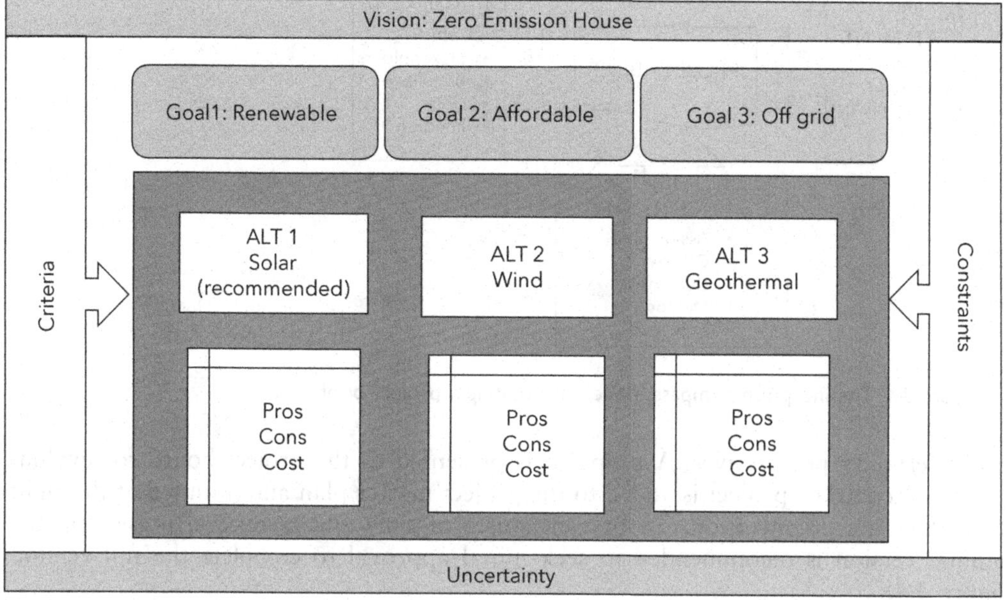

Figure 3.3 A feasibility study to evaluate the solutions for a zero-emission house.

In the *comprehensive approach*, the alternatives are evaluated based on the following:

1 *Technical feasibility* involves asking whether the organization has the technical resources, knowledge, and expertise
2 *Economic feasibility* involves assessing the economic factors in terms of cost, funding, savings, or revenue
3 *Strategic feasibility* evaluates the project alignment with the vision, strategy, or business objectives
4 *Legal feasibility* analyzes the ability to meet compliance, liability, and legal requirements
5 *Operational feasibility* assessing the available resources versus other planned projects, training needs, and customer commitments.

Inception compass

A *project brief* is a top-level document describing the *scope statement* (content) and the *business case* (justification). A *full project brief* includes an evaluation of the strategic

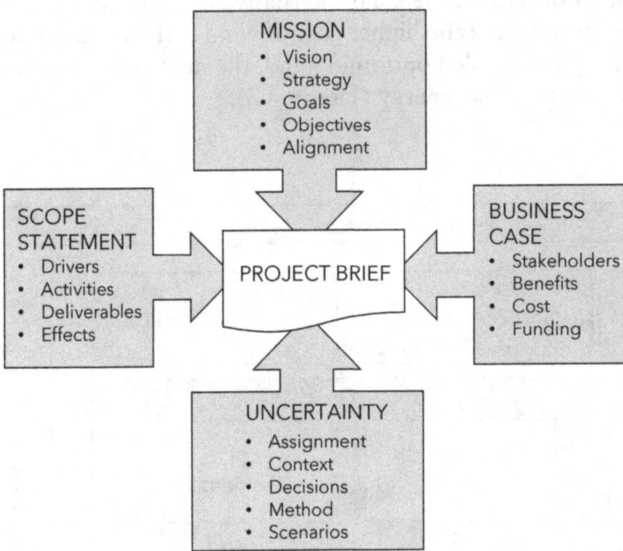

Figure 3.4 The inception compass model for creating a project brief.

and uncertainty perspectives. A proposal is presented to the project board for evaluation. If selected, the project is added to the project master plan and initiated at the right moment in the organization. To prevent waste of time and resources, presenting the minimal version is recommended to seek initial approval to complete the full version (Figure 3.4).

Prototyping

Prototyping is a form of reverse engineering. When the requirements or technical workings are uncertain, a prototype is created to prove the idea can work. A prototype typically has limited features; only the questioned functionality is implemented. Based on the prototype, the actual design is completed, and the requirements are derived. A prototype is often seen as the same thing as a *proof of concept* (POC) because both have similar goals. While the POC is more of a theoretical process where the team checks the idea's feasibility, the team builds a working version when prototyping.

The Norwegian offshore industry has many years of experience building floating concrete oil platforms kept in position by anchors in the deep waters of the Norwegian coast. This technology is used by the Norwegian oil company Hydro to develop a prototype of a wind turbine mounted on a gigantic spar buoy. The Hywind offshore floating wind turbine idea was born in 2001 when two colleagues and friends from Statoil (now Equinor), Dag Christensen and Knut Solberg, participated in the Færder sailing race. During the evening, the wind dabbed off, and as they floated past a navigation buoy, they thought: If we could make a floating buoy one hundred meters high and put a windmill on top, we can produce renewable offshore wind energy. They created a sketch on a napkin and started developing mathematical models for controlling the rotor blades.

Although the idea may seem intriguingly simple, the sea waves induce complicated motion patterns on the turbine, with dynamics in six dimensions. Complex algorithms had to be developed to control the pitch of the blades to allow for this degree of movement. The algorithms were tested on models in a wave basin in 2005 in Trondheim. Another challenge was the tremendous forces from winds, waves, and currents, creating complex dynamics on the moorings. A full-scale 2.3-MW demonstration floating turbine was deployed in June 2009, west of Karmøy in Norway. The turbine still operates today, enduring winds up to 40 m/s and waves over 10 meters. The rest is history. In 2017, the first floating wind turbine park consisting of five 6-MW turbines went operational on the coast of Peterhead, Scotland (Power Magazine 2009).

Mock-up

A *mock-up* is a prototype with no working parts or functions but focuses on the exterior appearance or the product's esthetics. Examples of mock-ups are miniature scale models of houses, boats, or sketches of computer screens (wireframes). The car industry still uses full-scale clay models despite extensive 3D design capabilities to spot flaws not visible in digital renderings. Even Tesla, known for revolutionizing car manufacturing, still uses clay models, which are cheaper and more flexible to work with than any other material. A full-scale model provides a holistic perspective on the design instead of focusing on a minor aspect, a drawback of digital design methods. Also, an entire team can assess and work on different parts of the car while simultaneously in a collaborative process.

Principles

You cannot manage what is not defined

A prerequisite for effective uncertainty management is a practical definition of the phenomenon. Like in the radiation example, the first step is to develop a concept, make it observable and measurable, and then implement control measures. Although total certainty is not likely to be possible, uncertainty reduction can significantly improve the chances of project success.

Uncertainty is a property of the observer

An observer discovering new information about a system does not fundamentally change the system through newly gained insights. Imagine inspecting a running diesel and seeing oil dripping from under the engine. The problem existed before its discovery; becoming aware differs from the matter's existence.

Risk is but one of many sources of problems

Problems are not exclusively caused by risks; unknown prerequisites, dependencies, or constraints that the plan does not cater to will become apparent at some point and cause issues.

None of these factors have a probability of happening like a risk; they were there all along but not on the planner's radar.

Risk management alone is not enough

There are two types of risks, those you know and those you do not. Evaluating known risks is one part of the job; finding unknown risks is the other half. Remember that the risks you are not seeing might be more threatening than those you focus on.

Beware of the evil-spirit syndrome

Any unfortunate event was attributed to an evil spirit in the old days, whether there was a flood, a storm, a draught, a disease, an illness, or a failing crop. Today, the evil-spirit approach haunts project management: Anything that can go wrong is dubbed risk, independent of the cause. Whether the project suffers from poor estimates, flawed plans, wrong decisions, scope creep, budget, and time overruns, risk is the culprit and treated similarly. This is the equivalent of a doctor prescribing the same pill regardless of the diagnosis.

Effective uncertainty management depends on discriminating the various elements causing issues and address with differentiated counter actions.

You will never know what you do not know

A popular but erroneous theory is that uncertainty is zero at the end of the project. Typically, the point is illustrated by graphs depicting an artist impression of a diminishing curve. Uncertainty is not destined to decrease over time. In theory, uncertainty could go up by making mistakes or wrong decisions. Also, due to the unique nature of a project undertaking, you will never know how alternative choices would have panned out.

Consider a project choosing between design solutions A, B, and C and selecting B. The implementation goes entirely to plan within the lead time and cost. The business case targets a 20% saving due to increased efficiency, which is realized. But what would have happened if solution A had been implemented? Could we have achieved 30%? Since projects are unique undertakings, we will probably never know. How to determine the size of the known-unknow quadrant is the essence of the *uncertainty paradox*: 'You will never know what you do not know!'

There are facts, and there are assumptions

Consciously ask yourself what type of information you are dealing with. If there is no possibility or time to get the facts, make a working assumption as a last resort. Any estimate or project plan is a working assumption until confirmed to be accurate.

Having a problem and knowing that you have one are two different things

Note that the problem's symptoms can remain below your detection threshold; alternatively, if they are detectable, they might not be recognized for what they are. The moment of becoming aware does not necessarily coincide with the issue's inception or occurrence. Once a problem has manifested itself, track down the time and origin of the problem. Analyze the lead time for the problem detection and implement measures enabling earlier detection.

Time and cost overruns are symptoms, not risks

A doctor's challenge is to accurately diagnose the underlying cause or causes of the symptoms he observes. A diagnosis is never a given, bad eyesight can cause headaches, but so can bad working conditions leading to a drinking problem. System thinking is helpful; complex behavior can be explained by defining the underlying system structures. Failure to realize projected benefits, rejected deliverables, stress, time, and cost overruns can be symptoms of complex underlying causes.

Artifacts

The relevant artifacts are as follows:

- Feasibility study
- Project brief
- Prototype
- Proof of concept
- Mock-up.

Concepts

Take a deep breath, and explain out loud the fundamental difference between:

- Information awareness and information availability
- Known-unknown and an unknown-known
- Known-known-and unknown-unknown
- Assumption and issue
- Dependency and constraint
- Problem and opportunity
- Risk and uncertainty.

Questions

1 How are feasibility studies conducted in your company?
2 What method is used for developing project proposals?
3 Which authority reviews project proposals?
4 Do you manage any other types of uncertainty than risk or opportunity?
5 Is a decision log mandatory?
6 What methods for decision-making and problem-solving are being used?
7 Is method uncertainty factored in when evaluating a project?

References

Environmental Protection Agency 14 Oct 2022. *What is radon gas? Is it dangerous?* [online] Available at: https://www.epa.gov/radiation/what-radon-gas-it-dangerous [Accessed: April 15, 2023]

Power Magazine 2009. Top plants: *Hywind floating wind turbine, North Sea, Norway.* [online] Access Intelligence. Available at: https://www.powermag.com/top-plants-hywind-floating-wind-turbine-north-sea-norway/ [Accessed: April 15, 2023]

The Nobel Foundation 2023. *The Nobel Prize in physics 1903* [online] Available at: https://www.nobelprize.org/prizes/physics/1903/marie-curie/facts/ [Accessed: April 15, 2023]

Chapter 4

Assignment uncertainty

Introduction

This chapter will look closely at the uncertainties related to the project assignment. A *project* is a temporary workforce tasked to create a unique result delivering maximum benefits for designated stakeholders within specific demands such as cost and lead time. Perceived as a system, the main elements of the project assignment are as follows (Figure 4.1):

- Stakeholders
- Benefits
- Deliverables
- Activities
- Resources.

This chapter will dive deeper into each element and analyze the direct and inherent uncertainties. For example, an *explicit uncertainty* related to a known stakeholder is whether we fully understand the attitude toward the project or there exists a hidden agenda. An *implicit uncertainty* is whether there exist any stakeholders we are overlooking. Finding stakeholders early and identifying their needs and expectations is essential. An undiscovered

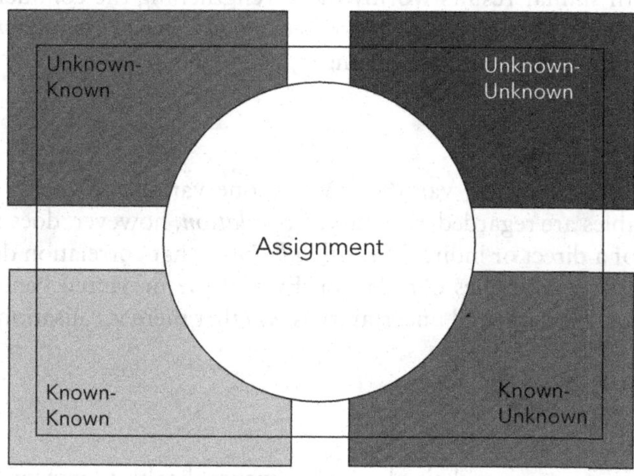

Figure 4.1 Superimposing the uncertainty matrix over the assignment.

DOI: 10.4324/9781003431961-6

stakeholder might expect to reap benefits, receive deliverables, or state requirements towards the project. These unidentified expectations imply that there are missing activities in the plan necessary to create them. Given that the costs of these missing activities are not accounted for, the planned budget is too low. Typically, these absent interests will be uncovered as the project unfolds. Consequently, the plan must be updated, and the project will exceed the initial time and budget limits. Worst case, this cycle is repeated several times, not uncommon in IT projects. As a rule, the later the discovery, the more costly and time-consuming the corrective actions will be.

Definitions

Causation

Causation requires that a change in one variable induces a change in another; in other words, a cause-and-effect relationship exists between action and result. In 1996, Emily Rosa, then a fourth-grader, saw a video of therapeutic touch (TT) practitioners claiming they could detect human energy fields to diagnose and treat disease. Could this be true? Rosa designed an experiment where practitioners were asked to sit at a table and extend their hands through a screen. Emily sat on the other side, randomly selected one of the practitioners' hands by tossing a coin, and held her hand over. The TT practitioners were asked in which of their hands they felt Emily's energy field. The practitioner produced a correct answer on average of only 4.4 times, effectively less than the theoretical performance of a person randomly guessing (50%).

The simple but elegant experiment shows no causal relationship between therapeutic touch and a patient's health. If the practitioner cannot feel the presence of another human being in the first place, how could they cure a disease? The experiment suggests that the claims from therapeutic health professionals are unjustified. The study, which included an extensive literature research, was published on April 1, 1998. George Lundberg, the editor of *JAMA*, aware of the uniqueness of the situation, said, 'Age doesn't matter. It's good science that matters, and this is good science.' The TT experiment has been repeated with similar results worldwide, strengthening the confidence in the conclusion (Rosa et al. 1998). In projects, there must be a causal relationship between the deliverables and the benefits, and the stronger, the better.

Correlation

Correlation describes an association between variables: When one variable changes, the other also does so, and the variables are regarded as covary. *Correlation,* however, does not necessarily prove the existence of a direct or indirect *causal link*. Note that correlation does not imply causation; causation always implies correlation. Even if the measured benefits correlate with the project efforts, a fundamental uncertainty is whether there is causation or mere correlation.

Placebo effect

The placebo effect is when a person perceives their physical or mental health to improve as a result of a dummy treatment, such as a pill with no active ingredients. The placebo effect is caused by the person's belief in receiving treatment and their expectation to feel better. When studying the effects of medicine, a control group is given a placebo to assess the difference between the group getting the actual medicine. In the TT case, any reported benefits by patients could be attributed to the placebo effect. In the project context, using risk matrices has no proven value, but people using them report benefits potentially based on suggestions similar to the placebo effect (Hubbard and Evans 2010).

Elements

Stakeholders

Although technology tends to take the spotlight, without stakeholders, there is no project. A *stakeholder* is any organization, group, or individual affected by a project, positively or negatively, knowing or unknowing (Figure 4.2). Stakeholders can have a *positive* or *negative* attitude toward a project. During one of my projects, I was made aware that a senior manager openly criticized our work. As a much respected and influential person, his negative comments impacted the team's morale. Although I racked my mind, I could not imagine the reason, as the project did not interfere with any of his areas of interest. Later, I discovered that the office spaces had been reassigned to collocate the project. As a result, the senior manager lost the best room in the building he had worked for many years.

Although the office affair was a fluke, take heed of *zero-sum projects,* where the benefits for some stakeholders come at the expense of others: Project failure means victory for the

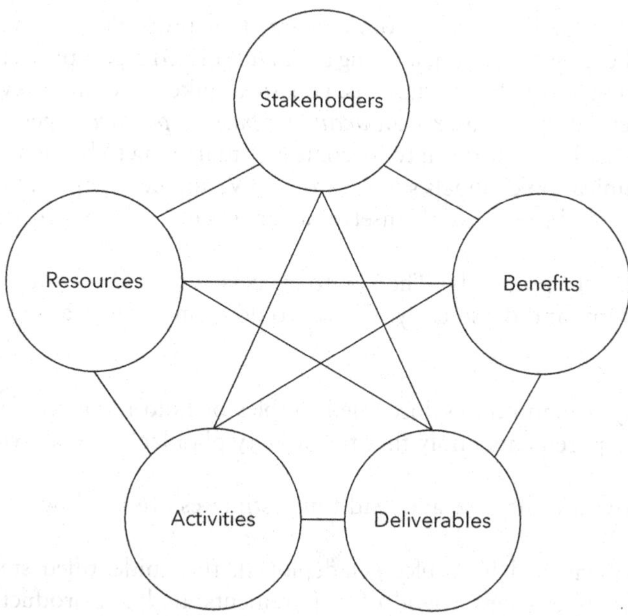

Figure 4.2 The elements of the project assignment subsystem.

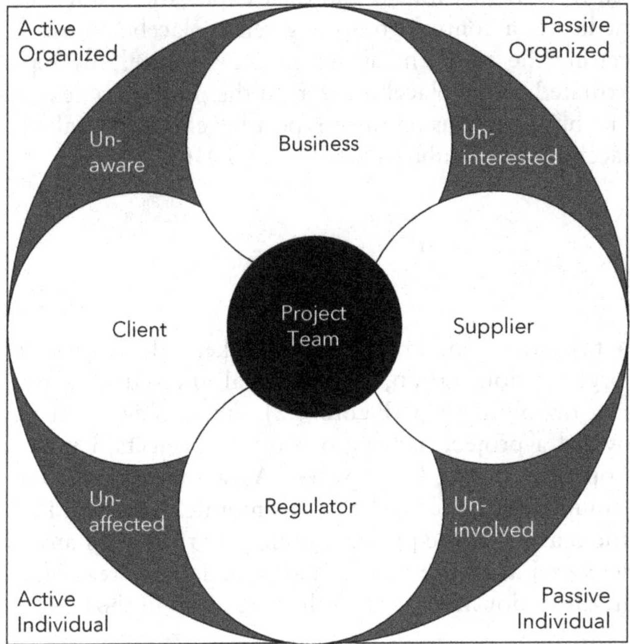

Figure 4.3 The stakeholder discovery map shows a project's generic stakes and attitudes.

negative stakeholders. Stakeholders can be *conscious* or *unaware* of the project's existence or effects. When your neighbor, unbeknownst to you, is doing an unauthorized repair project on his gas heater installation following YouTube instructions, you are a stakeholder in the event of an explosion. Negative stakeholders can assert an *active* or *passive posture*, operating individually or organized. Social media platforms have become a virtual arena to be managed in addition to traditional communication channels such as radio, TV, and newspapers. Look specifically for stakeholders who might perceive themselves as unaffected, whereas they are not (Figure 4.3).

Rita Mulcahey (2018) said it very pointedly: The key to success is to find all your stakeholders, find out what they want, and do so early. Failure to do so may cause a domino effect in the project:

- Overlooked stakeholders may demand undisclosed deliverables or hold requirements
- The missing deliverables or requirements imply that the activity plan lacks the activities necessary to create them
- Due to these unidentified activities, the cost and lead time estimates are too low.

Once the incomplete or unsatisfactory deliverables get deployed, the unidentified stakeholders will become aware, initiating a new round of requirements analysis, production activities, testing, and deployment. Finding stakeholders or requirements through iterations will incur substantial time and budget overruns (Figure 4.4).

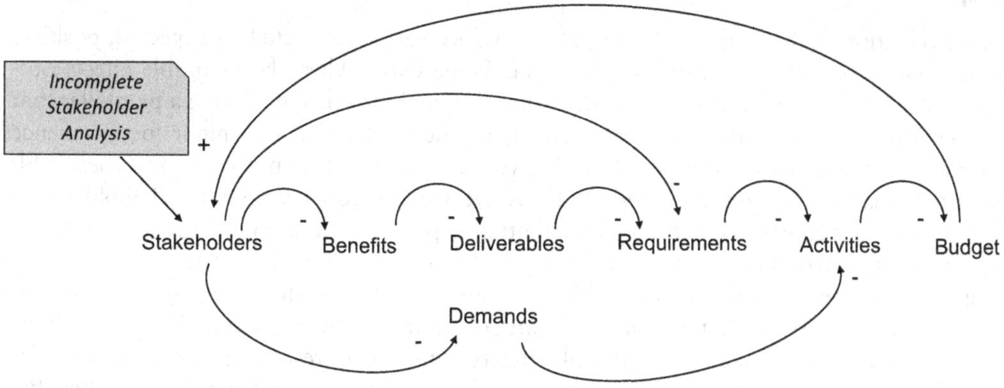

Figure 4.4 Causal loop diagram of the cascading effect of failure to identify relevant stakeholders.

Note the difference between overlooking stakeholders and *emerging requirements*. An agile principle states that it is highly unlikely to uncover all requirements beforehand. New requirements will emerge as the project evolves. In contrast, others will get depreciated or discarded as increments get delivered, as the users gather experience using the system. The same goes for identifying all stakeholders in advance. Acknowledging this principle does not relieve the team from making the best possible effort, as failure to identify the right stakeholders becomes more costly as time passes (Table 4.1).

Projects are often confronted with comprehensive lists containing 'project requirements,' 'business requirements,' 'quality requirements,' and 'acceptance requirements.' Reduce complexity by making a logical split in *demands* that govern activities and *requirements* that shape deliverables. For example, strict safety regulations must be followed during gas welding, like prescribed safety clothing and equipment, due to the intense heat. Although these demands shape the welding activity, they do not determine the nature or qualities of the end product. Demands may involve general adherence to ethics, laws, regulations, company policies, processes, routines, industry standards, or project-specific demands related to budget at completion, lead time, and deadlines.

Table 4.1 Aspects of uncertainty related to stakeholders

Stakeholders	A stakeholder *is any organization, group, or individual affected by a project, positively or negatively, knowing or unknowing.*
Implicit uncertainty	Undiscovered stakeholders, including their needs, expectations, demands, and requirements.
Explicit uncertainty	Negative attitude towards the project Hidden agendas Unknown allegiances Uncovered stakes, needs, requirements, or demands of known stakeholders Unclear roles and responsibilities Degree of engagement Mismatches in vocabulary and concepts Misunderstandings and misinterpretations.

Benefits

The introduction of the project deliverables can induce various expected, unexpected, positive, and adverse effects on the parent organization. *Value* exists when the favorable effects outweigh the adverse effects. Imagine suffering from a severe headache and taking a painkiller that prohibits driving. The tradeoff between remedying the pain versus the minor inconvenience of not being able to use your car implies positive value, as you were not going anywhere with a severe headache anyways. A *benefit* is a positive value perceived from a stakeholder perspective. The stakeholder relationship is essential; a positive effect for one person could be negative for another. Whether a benefit is worth the cost, is a separate matter.

Benefits can be *tangible* or *intangible* and can be demonstrated using *quantitative* or *qualitative* indicators that can be *leading* or *lagging* in nature. A single stakeholder can have multiple stakes in a project, and multiple effects can constitute a single benefit. The stakeholder angle makes benefit evaluation subjective, situational, and time-bound. Benefits might not be measurable until a project has been closed down. Consider a solar farm; to accurately determine the actual power production, four seasons must pass to get actual data (Table 4.2).

Determining the degree of benefit realization requires quantifiable value indicators, a measurement system, a baseline measurement dating from before the changes were made, and measurements preferably after the steep part of the learning curve has been passed. Benefits realization can assume different states during the project; benefits are anticipated and estimated during the inception stage. Once an adequate system is in place, benefits become measurable. Measuring benefits is particularly challenging in the case of business intangibles like improved business reputation, brand recognition, or customer loyalty. A baseline of the as-is situation is a prerequisite to provide evidence of improvement, which may lead to confirmation or rejection (Figure 4.2).

Deliverables

The project result is the sum of its deliverables, represented in a result breakdown structure (RBS). The RBS breaks down the project result into phases (optional), deliverables (mandatory), and work packages (optional). The deliverables can be grouped in stages and broken down to a level where they can be estimated using work packages. A *work package*

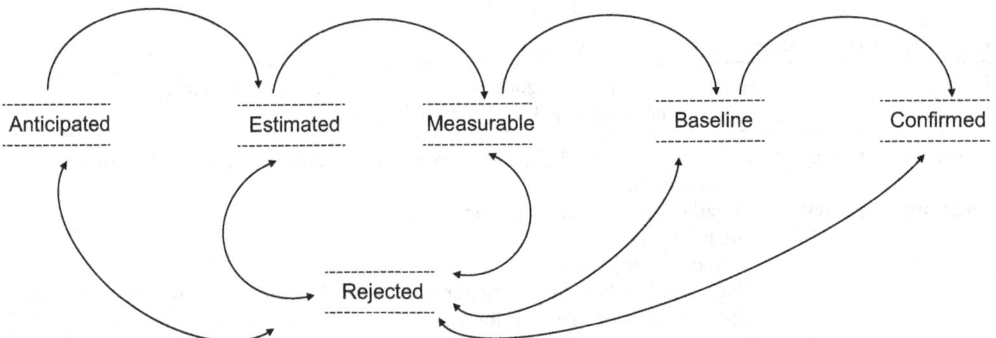

Figure 4.5 A state diagram for project benefits (Cuypers 2022).

Source: Reprinted with permission https://www.doi.org/10.33422/4th.bmeconf.2022.03.01

Table 4.2 Aspects of uncertainty related to benefits

Benefits	*A benefit is a positive value from a stakeholder perspective.*
Implicit uncertainty	Unidentified benefits that potentially could be gained through the project.
Explicit uncertainty	Is there a sound causal relation between the project result and the expected benefits? Are the benefits quantifiable and measurable? Can we establish a baseline for comparison between the as-is and to-be situation? When will we see the first signs of value? Before or after the project has been closed down? Which unwanted adverse effects might emerge? Does the sum of the positive effects outweigh any unforeseen adverse effects? Are the net gains worth the money, focus, and effort, including the loss of opportunity cost?

is a group of activities where the work hours involved can be estimated together as a lump sum. Note that the activities do not need to be logically related, they simply can be estimated together. Projects require *control* and *creation type* of deliverables, which can be of *permanent* or *temporary nature.* Typical control types of deliverables are a project brief, mandate, project management plan, sub-plans, and status reports. The creation (or domain) type of deliverables represents a new or improved version of a/an (Figure 4.6):

1 Product
2 Service
3 Capability
4 Opinion.

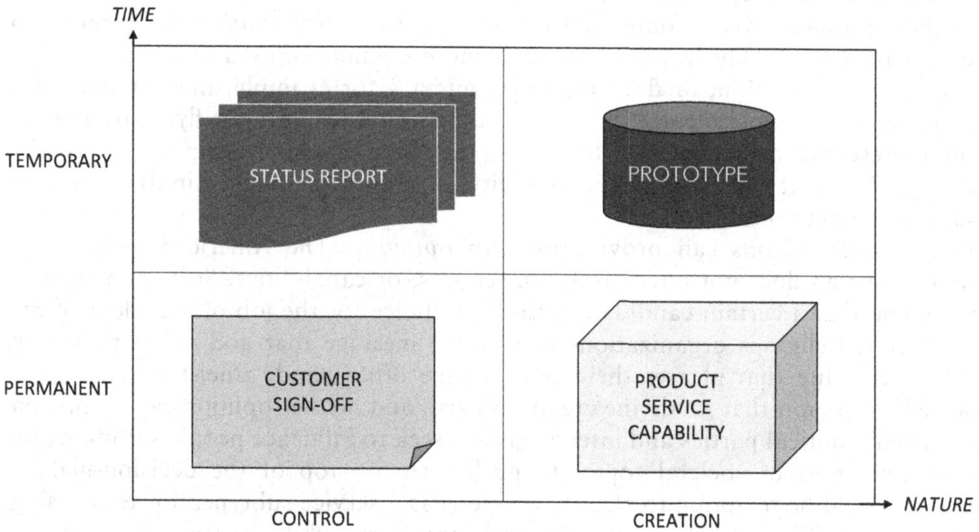

Figure 4.6 Overview of the project deliverable types.

Although often used interchangeably, a product is not a service. Understanding the fundamental difference is important as the challenges differ. Making and selling a product requires logistics, whereas issues related to creating a service tend to be of a capacity nature. Building a product like a table includes shipping the materials to the workshop, storage, transportation to a furniture shop, and finally to the buyer's home. Getting car insurance involves making a phone call to activate the service; the insurance company does not mail a kilo of insurance.

Most products, except those with a limited shelf time like food, retain their value over time. When a carpenter does not sell a table right away, he can do so three weeks later and still make a profit. An empty aircraft seat, however, is a direct loss, as the fuel and crew's wages must be paid regardless of the number of passengers onboard. Another difference to note is customer approval. A product like a table is a tangible object with properties that can be objectively measured. Defining the quality of a service depends on a person's subjective preferences or tastes. For example, what does good music or table service in a restaurant mean, and how is it measured objectively? Measuring the properties of a table, like length, weight, or strength, is considerably less complex and more tangible, although esthetics aspects will always be subjective.

The third type of project result is capability. A *capability* is the ability of people and their combined assets to achieve a deliberate result or outcome. At the individual level, a capability is a user's ability to achieve a result or outcome using a system or tool. A man with an ax or chainsaw can cut down a tree to provide wood for his stove or build a log house for shelter. At first glance, a cutting capability only requires a person and tools. But a chainsaw requires suppliers for fuel, lube oil, and spare parts to sustain cutting capability over time. Although an ax is a much simpler tool, all lumberjacks need food, water, warmth, and shelter to support their effort over a prolonged period. A federation of organizations is required to create an axe; miners delve the ore, traders ship the iron, a blacksmith forges the blade, and a carpenter makes the handle.

In daily language use, the concepts of result and outcome are almost similar, with only subtle grammatical or contextual differences. The word *result* usually refers to the effects of actions. The word *outcome* is more commonly used in a competitive, experimental, observation, or decision-type context – for example, the outcome of a soccer match or an experiment. Note the word *intention.* An aircraft flying tourists to the sun represents a business capability; flying the plane into a skyscraper is a terrorist capability. Note that the features, functionality, or processes involved in flying remain the same; the intention differs.

Finally, organizations can provide us with *opinions.* The American presidential election campaign does not offer products, services, or capabilities. Still, it intends to convince you that a certain candidate is the best choice for the job of president of the United States. Religious organizations convey the message that god exists providing rules for living life that pleases their god. On the other hand, atheist organizations advocate the opinion that no divine creatures exist, and neither opinion can be proven or disproven. Political parties and interest groups seek to influence people's thinking by creating awareness of societal topics to push them on top of the decision-makers agendas. It could be tempting to classify opinions as a service subtype; however, using essential services like school and healthcare is necessary, while opinions are a choice (Table 4.3).

Table 4.3 Aspects of uncertainty related to deliverables

Deliverable	*A deliverable is a tangible or intangible product, service, capability, or opinion created by the project and subject to approval.*
Implicit uncertainty	Overlooked or unidentified deliverables that are relevant to the project.
Explicit uncertainty	Missing requirements Implicit requirements not caught Ambiguous requirements False requirements Missing fit criterion Undefined status of the deliverable.

Activities

To the untrained eye, projects are all about activities; sometimes the activity plan is seen as 'the' project plan. The guiding principle is: Work forward but plan backward. Activities are a means to an end; defining the necessary activities depends on the required deliverables – the question of what we should do starts with answering what must be delivered. The deliverables are described in the RBS sub-plan and the activities in an activity sub-plan. The next principle is cross-correlation: For each deliverable, at least one activity must be planned to create it. The RBS and the activity plan are sub-plans under the project management plan (PMP). The *PMP* is an umbrella plan that describes the procedures used to control different aspects of the project. While the PMP outlines the routines and techniques to be used, the *sub-plans* contain the content, such as an RBS, activity plan, task plan, and budget (Figure 4.7).

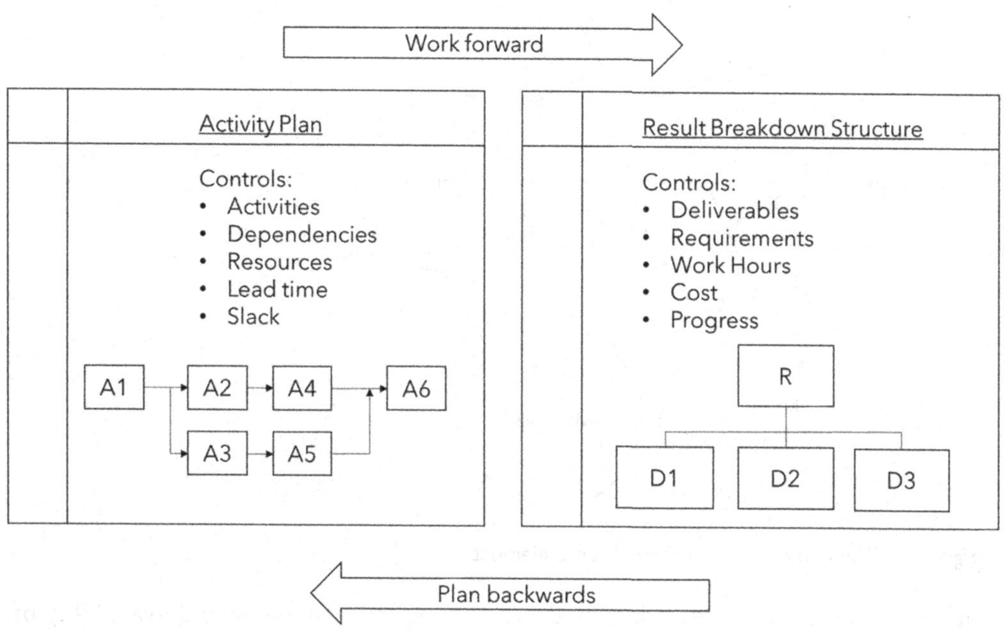

Figure 4.7 The activity and the RBS sub-plan.

Table 4.4 Aspects of uncertainty related to activities

Activities	*An activity groups several tasks representing a measure of work necessary to create a deliverable.*
Implicit uncertainty **Explicit uncertainty**	Missing activities. Unidentified dependencies between activities Unnecessary activities Overhead Ineffective or inefficient activities Scope creep, activities outside of the mandate Accuracy of the required resource and lead time estimates

Activities are often associated with time. There are two perspectives on time, *work hours* and *lead time*, (or *duration*). Work hours are estimated using the RBS, while the project lead time is controlled using the activity plan. For example, painting a room is estimated to take eight hours, while the drying period required is two days. Although the total activity lead time is three days, only the eight work hours incur a cost. Or: An operation is planned to take four hours, conducted by an operating team of eight people, equaling 32 work hours (Table 4.4).

Resources

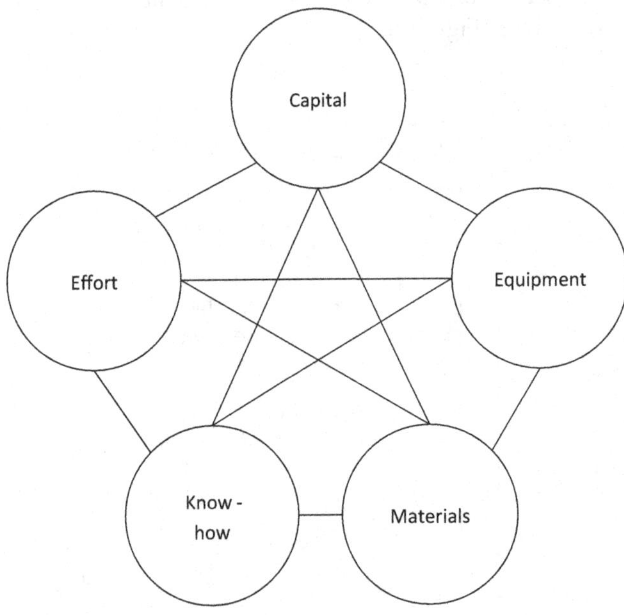

Figure 4.8 The components of the resource element.

The feasibility of the assignment largely depends on an understanding and availability of the required resources (Figure 4.8 and Table 4.5):

Table 4.5 Aspects of uncertainty related to resources

Resources	The means required to create the desired deliverables are funding, materials, tools, effort, and know-how.
Implicit uncertainty	Unidentified imperative resources.
Explicit uncertainty	Resource availability, variation, and constraints Resource quality Resource estimates Variation in resource cost.

1 Funding
2 Equipment, such as tooling and productions systems, including the energy required to run them
3 Materials refer to anything physical that will be used or consumed to complete project deliverables
4 Know-how, practical, and theoretical knowledge, both for the creation and control deliverables
5 Work capacity, or manpower.

Techniques

Project definition matrix

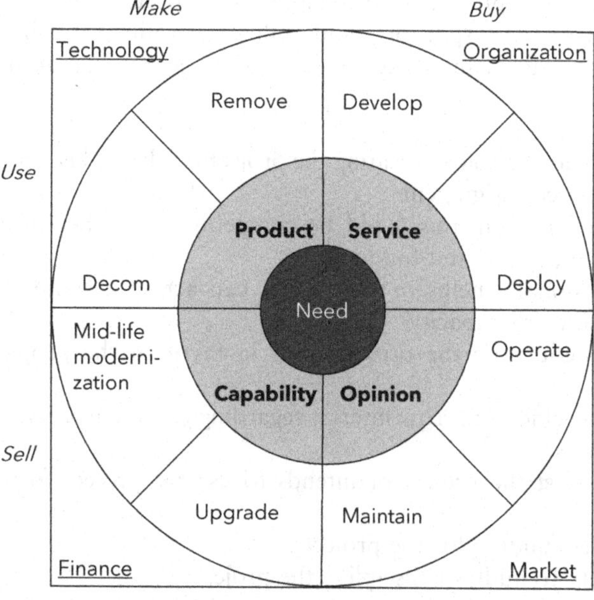

Figure 4.9 The project definition matrix helps clarify the assignment's essential parameters based on the life cycle of the project result.

When an idea for a new project is discussed with management, the inevitable rebuke is to put the essence of the proposal on paper along with some ballpark estimates regarding time, and cost. While the initial focus is often technological on how to get it done, the organization's leaders are interested in the long-term consequences. The Project Definition Matrix is an inception model to help visualize the assignment's essential elements, considering the life cycle of the result or deliverables. Create an elevator pitch about the project by answering the vital questions (Figure 4.9):

1 What are the needs to be addressed by the project?

   a Issues
   b Opportunities
   c Threats
   d Compliance
   e Other.

2 What is the nature of the deliverables; product, service, capability, or opinion?
3 What stages of the life cycle does the project cover?
4 What are the technological, organizational, financial, and market perspectives?
5 What components will be made or bought?
6 What is the intention, own use, or for the market?

Stakeholder mapping

Stakeholder mapping using a sports scheme is a quick and effective way to track people and their roles, stakes, and involvement in a project. In team sports like soccer or basketball, there are players, reserves, referees, fans, sponsors, and followers; sadly enough, also hooligans can be involved. You can classify the stakeholders in a project along that line of thought:

- *Player:* Any person who plays an active role in creating the project results and is a part of the project team through a resource assignment
- *Opposition:* The opposing side or team; this could be competitors or other projects competing for the same resources, focus, and funding
- *Reserve:* Any person that occasionally helps or potentially can act as a stand-in for players, alternatively to increase work capacity
- *Fan:* Any person who will benefit from the project or is in favor of the project in general
- *Follower:* A person who has a specific or narrow interest regarding certain aspects of the project
- *Hooligan:* A person who is against the project or intends to use the project for their private agenda
- *Sponsor:* A person who provides funding for the project
- *Referee:* A person with authority to audit or discipline the project.

Project team members are typically *players*; they are directly responsible for creating the project results and are allocated through an approved resource assignment. A *reserve* is a person who helps on an incidental basis, typically specialists from other parts of the organization, such as procurement, finance, and IT support. They are not allocated to the project, but their services are used on demand using company procedures to request them. A *fan* is a person who benefits from the results or effects or has personal reasons to support the project.

Football clubs can have *followers*, e.g., people who follow a club's performance because they are playing the football pools. Followers differ from fans as they only have a specific interest: Predicting the matches' outcome and winning money. An example of a project follower might be the CFO with a financial interest in the project; or a line manager with someone working on a project who wants to know about the resource claim. Assigning a label is not a 'do-or-die'; you can always make changes based on new insight afterward. Also, some people's roles will change during a project. Thus, a stakeholder register is a living document.

Make a habit of logging any person you encounter during meetings, conversations, and e-mail exchanges. Write down the role, type, and name in a stakeholder registry; for example, enterprise architect, player, John Johnson. In its simplest form, the stakeholder registry is a sub-plan made with a spreadsheet available on the project's document repository. Using filters and keyword searches, they can quickly identify the people they need to answer their questions or get help with problems rather than asking the project manager to introduce a bottleneck. When communicating, filter on a specific group, and customize the content based on their interests and involvement.

Player cards

The player card is a valuable tool to keep track of and connect people, especially when working in virtual teams. A *player card* is a summary of oneself containing a picture and some relevant information. Each team member fills out a player card and puts it in a share or repository. Although straightforward, player cards help start to know one another and lower the communication threshold. A player card can be formal with company mug shots, but adding more personal or hilarious pictures may help break the ice. The more outspoken or funnier the photos, the easier it will be to remember the person on them.

Benefit realization matrix

A *benefits realization matrix* depicts stakeholders, stakes, effects, and value. Depending on the stakeholder, an effect induced by the project can be evaluated as positive, negative, or neutral. A positive value exists when the favorable effects outweigh the adverse impacts. Consider a project to implement a digitally controlled production control system that increases productivity and lowers the fault rate, generating more revenue and fewer customer complaints. For the production manager, this is all good news. From a CFO's perspective, funding the project requires a considerably high-interest loan restricting liquidity. Although improved production implies extra revenue in the long term, the financial burden makes the CFO negatively inclined (Table 4.6).

Table 4.6 A benefits realization matrix (Cuypers 2022). Reprinted with permission https://www.doi.org/10.33422/4th.bmeconf.2022.03.01

Role	*Stake A*	*Stake B*	*Stake C*
User	x	x	
Manager	x		x
Supplier		x	
Perception			
Effect 1	+	?	+
Effect	+	-	
Effect	+	-	
Effect	?	-	
Value ∑	positive	negative	positive

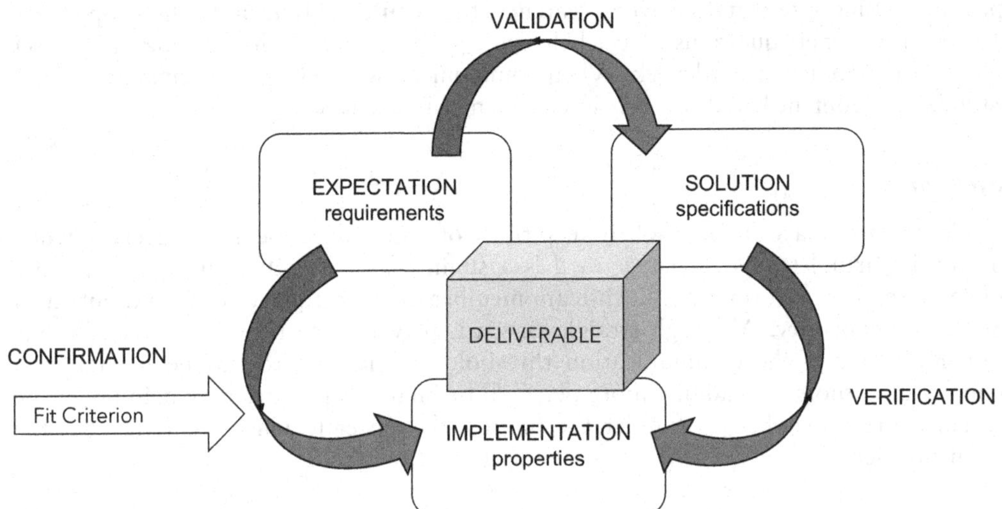

Figure 4.10 The project deliverable sub-assembly (Cuypers 2022). Reprinted with permission https://www.doi.org/10.33422/4th.bmeconf.2022.03.01

Fit criterion

The project result can be broken down into (Figure 4.10):

- The *expected result* is defined by the *requirements* describing the needs
- The *intended result* is determined by the *specifications* of the solution
- The *properties* of the implementation characterize the *accomplished result.*

Requirements can be divided into explicit, implicit, functional, and non-functional types. *Validation* involves ensuring that the specifications of the solution match the requirements. *Verification* ensures that the implementation properties meet or exceed the specifications, also referred to as 'build as designed.' *Confirmation* assesses whether the properties satisfy the needs as stated in the requirements, using a fit criterion. Defining the requirements is half the job; establishing a suitable fit criterion represents the other half. A *fit criterion* describes:

- The method
- The pre-and post-conditions
- The acceptance criteria.

used by the requirement owner to determine whether the properties comply with the requirements. Definition of a fit criterion beforehand removes the uncertainty of how deliverables will be evaluated. Applying a fit criterion must be simple, inexpensive, and conclusive. My favorite example is a building inspector who uses a marble on the bathroom floor to determine if the slope of the tiles inclines towards the drain. Any excess shower water will disappear if the marble rolls toward the drain. No water splashing or mopping up is required for a test. The same marble is used to determine if the kitchen top is mounted level; if flat, the marble should be lying perfectly still anywhere on the countertop. Cheap, simple, and fits in your pocket.

A single fit criterion can cover multiple requirements and help clarify relations. Consider a speed requirement for a car, for 150 kilometers per hour. The speed can be measured using the speedometer, a laser speed gun, on a racetrack using time, with an onboard GPS, and so on. Imagine a 155 km/hour top speed is measured using a police-type speed gun. The car is ribbed for all excess weight, like the spare tire, while the fuel tank is almost empty. Do you approve? The requirement should be rewritten as a top speed of 150 on a flat road, with four 75-kilo passengers onboard, a full fuel tank, and 100 kilos of luggage.

Budgeting

Although commonly referred to as 'the' budget, there are different views on the project economy (Figure 4.11):

1 Business case perspective
2 Planning perspective
3 Realization perspective
4 Funding perspective.

The *business budget* covers the commercial part of the project and describes how a project will make or save money for the organization. A business budget can have a long-term perspective, covering not just the project's duration but other stages of the product life cycle, including operational, upgrade, retirement, and aftercare stages with the associated costs and revenues.

Note the difference between the product life cycle and the project life cycle. A *product life cycle* covers all phases of the product from the invention, prototyping, pre-production, primary production, spare parts manufacturing, and finally, retirement.

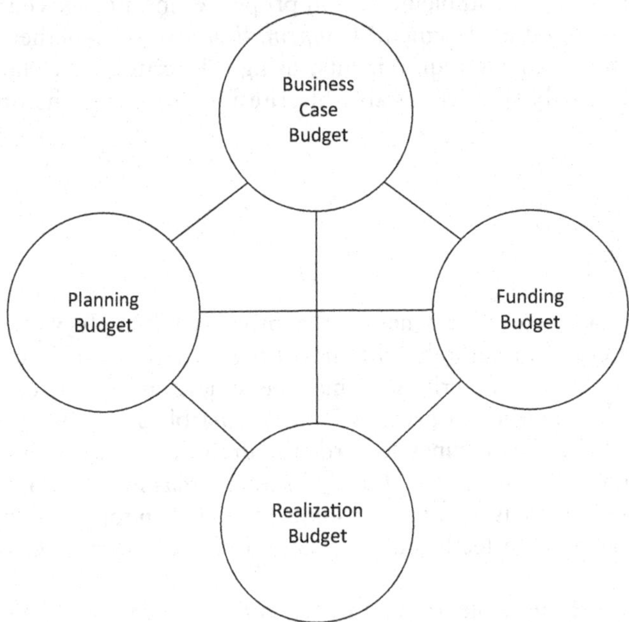

Figure 4.11 The components of the budget element.

Typical *project life cycle stages* are inception, initiation, preparation, execution, close-down, and follow-up. Tip: Avoid the name 'planning' as each stage requires continuous planning and replanning effort.

A single *product life cycle phase* can consist of multiple projects; for example, in the design phase of a new car, there could be several projects to design different parts of the vehicle. If the project is a delivery project for a customer, the business budget will typically show the project cost, project sales price, and expected profit. A reserve can be included for warranty or guarantee work, mid-life upgrade, and decommissioning. The required investment, profit, savings, and payback time are key numbers if the project is an improvement or investment type.

The *planning budget* shows the planned periodical cost based on the activity plan, the cumulative periodic cost line, the management and contingency reserve, and the planned invoicing (Figure 4.12):

- *Cost estimate per deliverable* = Sum of the cost components + uncertainty cost elements specifically related to a deliverable or activities directly related to creating the deliverable
- *Planned value* = Cumulative cost estimates per time-period
- *Budget at completion* = Total Cumulative Planned Value
- *Cost baseline* = Budget at Completion + Contingency Reserve
- *Project budget* = Cost Baseline + Management Reserve.

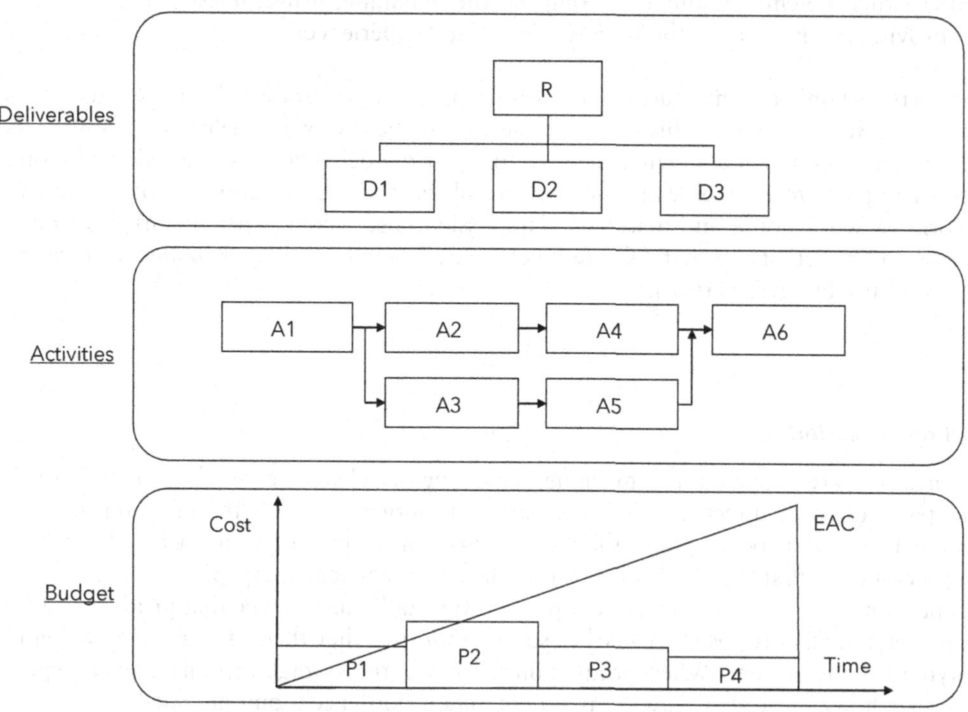

Figure 4.12 Transforming deliverables into activities, periodical, and cumulative costs to determine the Planned Value.

The *funding budget* shows how and by whom the project's expenses will be paid. In addition, the expected and actual cash inflows, cash outflows, and remaining funds are calculated. A project can be funded with own money, by customers, partners, through a loan, or by crowdfunding. When financing is required, the interest costs must be included in the business case. The funding budget takes actual cash flow into account; there are different points in time when:

- A deliverable has been approved, triggering a payment
- The invoice is added to the budget when it has been sent
- The approval for the amount is given
- The accountant enters the payment
- The bank transfers the money
- The amount is received and available.

The *realization budget* calculates the earned value (EV) and the actual cost (AC) incurred during project execution. The realization budget also forecasts the cost required to complete the remaining project deliverables, estimate to complete (ETC). Updating the realization budget involves:

- Assessing the status of deliverables
- Calculation of the actual creation cost involved

- Forecasting the effort required to complete the remaining deliverables
- Improving estimation capability based on gained experience.

In projects, the only true measure of progress is approved deliverables. Even if an activity is reported as 80% complete, this does not mean that the EV of the deliverable is 80% as well. Despite a completed activity, there is no EV if the deliverable is rejected. Therefore, use activity plans to control lead time and a result breakdown structure to control cost in the form of work hours and materials. Tip: Assign cost accounts per (main) deliverable rather than per activity so that AC can be compared with the initial estimates to trace the sources of any budget overruns.

Principles

Local optimization

Organizations are like fine-tuned machines; changing one element can induce changes to all other parts through direct and indirect paths. Adopting a system thinking approach is essential to prevent local optimization that moves problems elsewhere. Consider a production company that makes plastic bottles. The existing machine capable of making 1,000 units per hour is soon end of life, and a project to install a newer type that produces 9,000 bottles per hour is proposed. A market survey indicates that there is a growing demand justifying the investment. When production increases, the storage capacity and transportation capability must also grow to avoid creating a bottleneck, pun intended.

All plans are working assumptions

There are two types of information in projects: Facts and assumptions. An activity plan represents the desired scenario through which objectives or goals could be achieved. It must be regarded as a working assumption until the plan panned out. In the meantime, proof must be gathered to confirm that the plan is (still) sound. An explicit uncertainty is that the plan may be flawed; the implicit uncertainty is that the team overlooks a smarter approach.

Do not take causality for granted

Consider a group of 500 patients that were given medication with the following results:

- After two days, 76% were healthy
- After three days, 84% recovered
- After five days, all patients were declared fit.

Would you conclude that the medicine in question works based on this data? Possibly. Then a new test was conducted involving a control group of another 500 patients who were given a placebo. The patients recovered at approximately the same rate. Does that make you change your mind? Suppose we extend this example to project benefits. After introducing a new IT system, revenue increased by 25%, and the project was claimed to be a success. Without a control group in project situations, how can we prove a causal relationship exists between introducing the new system and the benefits? Could the increase result from natural variation, another trend, or a force the project is unaware of, and could it be a mere correlation?

The iron triangle fails in the case of weak casualty

In academic, scholar, and practitioner circles, the question of determining project success has been an ongoing debate for several decades. A commonly used method is the so-called iron triangle; a project is considered successful when delivered according to scope, cost, and time. Suppose the causal relationship between the results and benefits is weak. In that case, project success, according to the iron triangle, is insignificant, as the intended benefits will fail to emerge.

Beware of zero-sum game projects

In game theory, a *zero-sum game* represents a situation involving two parties, where a win for one side goes at the expense of the other. In other words: The gains for one player are the loss for the other and vice versa. For example, a production automation project would result in layoffs in the production force. A successful implementation would mean that today's workers will lose their jobs making them negative stakeholders. Zero-sum situations can be obvious or more subtle in nature. The successful adoption of a new banking app will eventually cause local bank offices to close their doors as there is less need for personal interactions.

Requirements are dynamic

Requirements are a common source of uncertainty. Requirements can emerge, evolve, or depreciate over time. Requirements may be stated ambiguously or implicitly. Expect the degree of requirement interpretation to vary across stakeholders depending on the profession, education, and experience. Also, their meaning and interpretation may change over time based on emerging insight.

Look for implicit requirements

Implicit requirements are not stated directly but represent expectations written between the lines. Put yourself in the stakeholder's shoes by going through different usage scenarios to uncover unspoken views and promises. When all the requirements regarding the roof type, angle, ladder to the chimney, and color of the tiles are meticulously stated, the implicit requirement is that the roof does not leak.

A fit criterion reduces uncertainty

Stating requirements is half the job; defining a suitable fit criterion to confirm the requirement has been met is the other half. Defining and landing an applicable fit criterion reduces uncertainty, as the team knows how a deliverable will be evaluated, enabling them to test beforehand and make any necessary corrections. Note that a fit criterion can be established when a requirement is stated; no designed solution or implementation is required. The requirement should be dropped if a requirements owner cannot say a practical fit criterion. For instance, the classic requirement is 'the product shall be easy to use.' How exactly can you prove this? What is easy for some might be difficult for others.

Establishing the fit criterion does not require a solution

Requirement owners will typically attempt to dodge the fit criterion question by saying: Show me a solution or an implementation, and I will tell you whether it works for me. Consider a speed requirement of 150 kilometers an hour for a vehicle project. Agreeing to use a laser gun to measure the speed does not depend on whether an electric motor or a combustion engine will be implemented. If no suitable fit criterion can be established, the requirement is either ambiguous or the requirement owner does not know what they want.

Tasks are not small activities

Distinguish between tasks and activities, where a *task* is a one-person job. It is not uncommon for people to work part time on projects and have one foot in the standing organization; alternatively, you deal with specialists involved in multiple projects. They do not have the time to orient themselves about the big picture; they only want to know what to do for the day. Breaking down activity plans into task plans, for example, using Kanban boards helps to provide the per-resource perspective on the work at hand.

Artifacts

A practical tip is to establish draft versions of the various plans right away at the start of the project. Project planning is messy, resembling a pinball being bumped back and forth. As events unfold, the uncovered information can be processed and captured immediately in the appropriate sub plan. A *project working log* is a valuable place to temporarily store data as you come across various information such as issues, risks, problems, decisions, prerequisites, and constraints. Transfer the items into the relevant plan or location later. Other key *control artifacts* that capture the project assignment are as follows:

- Project brief
- Project mandate
- Project management plan with sub-plans, for example:
  - Stakeholder register
  - Benefit matrix
  - Result breakdown structure
  - Activity plan
  - Communication plan
  - Test plan
  - Task boards
  - Budget
  - Uncertainty register
    - Issues
    - Risk
    - Decisions
    - Prerequisites
    - Constraints
    - Dependencies
- Status reports
- Project change requests.

Essential *creation type of artifacts*:

- Requirements document
- Solution design
- Bill of materials
- Design decision log
- Test report
- List of known errors.

Concepts

Value and benefit
Effect and stake
Product and service
Requirement and demand
Requirement and specification
Property and requirements
Verification and validation
Project life cycle and product life cycle
Planned value and earned value
Assumption and presumption.

Questions

1 How are stakeholders discovered and tracked in your project?
2 Is the stakeholder register up to date?
3 Which authority assesses benefits after the project closes down?
4 What benefit realization methods are used?
5 Are deliverables defined and tracked in a separate plan?
6 How are requirements identified and tracked?
7 Is progress determined based on activity or through approved deliverables?
8 Is a board or authority responsible for integrated resource management across projects and the standing organization?
9 What type of budgeting techniques are used?

References

Cuypers, P.W.M. 2022. Defining Project Success, a System Thinking Approach. Proceedings of The 4th International Conference on Applied Research in Business, Management, and Economics [online] Available at: https://www.dpublication.com/wp-content/uploads/2022/03/26-4275.pdf [Accessed 14 Apr. 2023].

Hubbard, D., and D. Evans. 2010. "Problems with Scoring Methods and Ordinal Scales in Risk Assessment." *IBM Research and Development* 54, no. 3.

Mulcahey, R. 2018. *PMP Exam Prep*, 8th ed., Edmonton: RMC Publications Inc.

Rosa, L., E. Rosa, L. Sarner, and S. Barrett. April 1, 1998. *Journal of the American Medical Association* 279, no. 13: 1005–1010.

Chapter 5

Context uncertainty

Introduction

Projects do not exist in a vacuum but are conducted within the context of the parent organization, sometimes in combination with partners and suppliers. The chances of project success are affected by trends and forces originating from the project landscape or *project context*. The project surroundings can constitute a political, economic, or power wrought minefield that needs to be carefully navigated. Projects are designed to improve the organization, inversely, various stakeholders will attempt to modify the project outcome to suit their interests better, sometimes at the expense of the organizational benefits.

An improved understanding of the project's context increases the chances of success. Developing situational awareness starts with analyzing the parent organization's mission, vision, strategy, and operating environment to understand how the project fits into the bigger picture. An accurate understanding of the situational factors enables the team to develop tactics and plans to deal with positive and negative influences. The situational factors can be divided into (Figure 5.1):

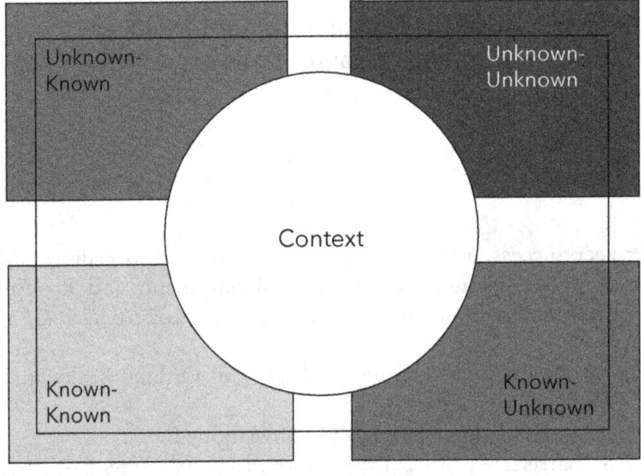

Figure 5.1 Uncertainty related to situational factors.

DOI: 10.4324/9781003431961-7

1 Prerequisites
2 Constraints
3 Inter-dependencies
4 Threats
5 Opportunities.

Definitions

The *parent organization* is the organization that commissions the project. A project can be a cooperation between peers or a hierarchical structure with a customer, main contractor, and suppliers.

The *organizational environment* is the parent organization's setting, characterized by relevant political, economic, logistic, and juridical factors.

The *direct world* is where suppliers, customers, regulators, and fifth parties operate, while macroeconomic, technological, and political trends and forces are part of the *indirect world*.

The *project context* consists of the parent organization, partners, suppliers, regulators, and customers, including political, social, and economic trends and forces relevant to the assignment.

Elements

Prerequisite

A *prerequisite* is a mandatory precondition for a project or activity to proceed and can be of a practical, feasibility, safety, or law-related nature. An example of a prerequisite could be a license or certification required to do hazardous work, for example, working professionally with dangerous materials such as asbestos. Without a license in place, the work cannot start or will be stopped during an inspection. Note that approved project funding is a prerequisite; the budget limit is a demand. If the project cost is similar to the maximum available funding, it represents a constraint. Example: The company has bank approval for a $4 million loan to finance the project (prerequisite); the budget is $3 million (demand). If a project change is required adding another million, the budget becomes a hard constraint (Figure 5.2).

It could be argued that prerequisites are elements of the project assignment itself rather than the context. However, doing similar projects in different countries or locations will result in having to meet different prerequisites. Consider a project to set up a meteorological station in the Arctic, the Sahara desert, and the jungle of South America. A prerequisite in the Artic and desert is keeping the team safe from the cold and the heat. Paying a drug lord could be a prerequisite for safe project execution in a cartel-controlled jungle. Although the assignment is the same, the prerequisites vary according to situational factors (Table 5.1).

Inter-dependency

An *interdependency* refers to another party's capability, capacity, or deliveries to complete the project. For example, a project can be a part of a program, where the deliverables from one project provide the foundation for another project. Suppliers or subcontractors may provide

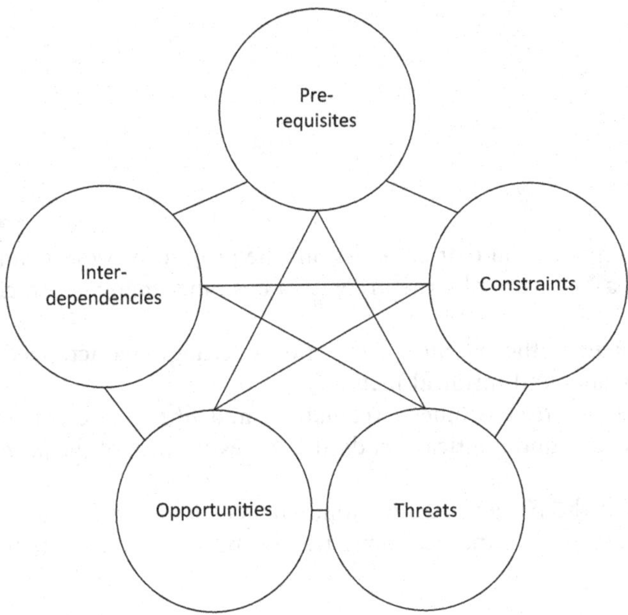

Figure 5.2 The elements of the project context.

Table 5.1 Aspects of uncertainty related to prerequisites

Prerequisite	*A prerequisite must be gained or achieved for a project to proceed with the next activities from an economic, procedural, practical, safety, or law-related perspective.*
Implicit uncertainty	Unforeseen prerequisites that emerge during project execution.
Explicit uncertainty	The ability to get the identified prerequisites in place.

parts, knowledge, or skills critical to complete a project deliverable. Inter-dependencies can be hard or soft; for example, a supplier with a monopoly or unique patent for a vital component representing a hard interdependency. While inter-dependencies are external; *dependencies* are relations at the task or activity level internal to the assignment. An activity that must be completed before the next action can start constitutes a dependency. Standard PERT-type dependencies are (PMBOK, 2017):

1 Finish-to-start
2 Finish-to-finish
3 Start-to-start
4 Finish-to-finish.

The foundation of a house must be completed before construction of the walls can begin represents a hard dependency. If an activity is preferably done first but could potentially be done in parallel potentially at the expense of quality or cost, is a soft dependency.

Table 5.2 Aspects of uncertainty related to inter-dependencies

Inter-dependency	*An interdependency refers to another party's capability, input, or deliverables to complete the project.*
Implicit uncertainty	Hidden interdependencies that are not accounted for in the planning.
Explicit uncertainty	The outcome of the interdependency and impact on the project The ability of the project to negotiate adverse effects.

Compressing a project schedule by running normally sequential activities in parallel is also known as fast tracking (Table 5.2).

Constraint

A *constraint* is a predicament or condition restricting a project's options to achieve its objectives. Resource availability, ethical standards, laws, maximum strengths, or system output are all examples of constraints. A constraint can be hard or soft; for example, a team member might be unavailable due to planned holidays. In theory, time off can be revoked with the promise of financial compensation or to make it up later. The maximum loan a company can get to fund a project, or the maximum lifting weight of a crane, would be hard constraints.

Take a step back, evaluate your project with your team, and consciously ask yourselves: What constraints are we subject to in this project? Even without a specific project assignment in mind, you can create a list of generic constraints applicable to project activities. Any project is susceptible to constraints imposed by:

- Ethics
- Laws
- Cultural norms regarding behavior
- Governmental and enterprise policies
- Mandatory company routines, for example, related to procurement
- Internal systems, for example, for writing hours, expenses, and costs
- Engineering standards
- Interface protocols.

Note 1: Requirements are not constraints; a requirement is a property of a deliverable you must create, while a constraint is a factor effectively limiting your alternatives to doing so.

Note 2: Demands are neither constraints as they govern the activities; for example, the demand to use a specific operating routine is not similar to the maximum output or capacity of a machine used in an activity (Table 5.3).

Table 5.3 Aspects of uncertainty related to constraints

Constraint	*A constraint is a predicament, circumstance, or condition restricting a project's options or possibilities to achieve its objectives.*
Implicit uncertainty	Undetected constraints limit project operations, deliverable creation, or benefits realization.
Explicit uncertainty	Misguided planning related to constraints Inadequate resource leveling.

Table 5.4 Aspects of uncertainty related to threats

Threat	A threat *is an opposing force, trend, or condition that impedes or interferes with achieving project goals or objectives.*
Implicit uncertainty	Subsurface or undetected threats unbeknown to the team.
Explicit uncertainty	Erroneous effect and impact assessment of the threat Lack of proactiveness in negotiating the threat Late response.

Threat

A *threat* is an opposing force that impedes or interferes with achieving project objectives. A threat differs from a risk; a threat is an enduring adverse influence, while a risk refers to a possible event resulting in a problem. When laying bricks during the summertime in Spain, the intense heat poses a threat; sunburn, dehydration, suffering from heatstroke are possible events with a negative impact, i.e., risks. The danger from the sun is omnipresent; a stroke is a potential problem that might happen irrespective of the heat. While risks are always adverse, threats are subject to perception. A storm on the coast may threaten small boats at sea; others will see an opportunity to surf big waves. A raging war threatens people's lives; others may see the urgent needs associated with conflict as an opportunity to make money by doubling the price of food (Table 5.4).

Opportunity

An *opportunity* is a trend, force, or condition that works in favor of the achievement of project goals or objectives. Known opportunities are capitalized upon as part of the plan, emerging opportunities through improvisation. There exists an ongoing academic discussion whether opportunity should be considered a positive risk. The first common sense answer is that the concept of positive risk is confusing; in everyday language, the word *risk* has a negative association. Second, there is a difference between an opportunity emerging and becoming aware.

When a person spots a $100 bill on the sidewalk, noticing the money is not a positive risk event as the money was already there. Spotting the opportunity or failure to see it is independent of the opportunity arising. In contrast, a risk will find you when your number is up, aware or not, like in the radon example, but you can choose not to pick up the money. Also, opportunities are not necessarily probabilistic; a window of opportunity can exist for a particular time and be recurring or deterministic in nature. For example, during each fall, the Passat winds around the Canary Islands will blow to the west, facilitating an Atlantic crossing for sailboats (Table 5.5).

Table 5.5 Aspects of uncertainty related to opportunities

Opportunity	An *opportunity* is a positive trend, force, or condition that works in favor of the achievement of project goals or objectives.
Implicit uncertainty	Overlooked opportunities.
Explicit uncertainty	Failure to exploit an opportunity in part or fully.

Techniques

Strategic planning

A strategy is a winning approach enabling victory or realize a vision based on unique insight into the situation, a competitor, or an enemy. A strategy serves as a protective layer around the organization, capitalizing on opportunities, exploit internal strengths, conceal weaknesses while shielding it from threats.

Strategic planning starts with analyzing the 'as-is' situation and creating a vision of the 'to-be' situation. The next step is to create a master plan to achieve the 'to-be' situation in the shortest possible time, with minimal effort, risk, and waste. Then, the strategy is broken down into strategic goals, representing significant steps or increments. Finally, goals are broken down into measurable or binary defined objectives, achieved or not. The objectives are gathered into logical groups forming assignments for the standing or temporary organizations.

SWOT

SWOT analysis stands for strengths, weaknesses, opportunities, and threats. This simple yet effective technique is useful to analyze the situation of the parent organization and its environment, providing input to formulating a vision and a strategy. Understanding the project context starts with understanding the organizational mission and strategy to achieve the vision. *Strategic alignment* is the degree to which the project objectives contribute to achieving strategic goals. SWOT analysis is also useful at the project level to identify relevant contextual factors influencing the chances of project success.

Context analysis

A *context diagram* is valuable model for mapping the system under discussion (SUD) operating environment. The diagram shows the system under discussion in the center and the surrounding systems as satellites with one or two-way arrows indicating the flow of information (Figure 5.3).

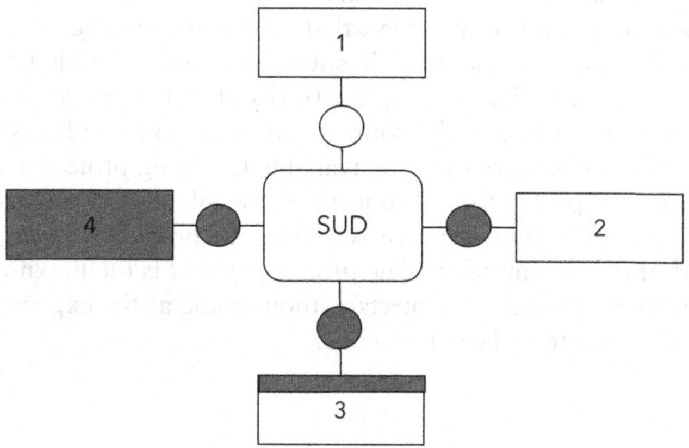

Figure 5.3 A context diagram identifies secondary actors and integrations.

Use the diagram not only to identify secondary systems, but also stakeholders related to systems, interface requirements, constraints, and dependencies. The context diagram is also helpful in visualizing the scope of work for integrations. Four basic situations exist:

1 A straightforward connect to the external system using an existing interface
2 Modify the interface to hook up to an external system
3 Partial modification of the external system, including the interface
4 Redo the inner workings external system entirely, including the interface.

Integrated resource planning

A prerequisite for any project is resource availability of the right type, quality, and quantity. The integrated resource schedule shows the resource needs and free capacity over time for the standing organization and temporary workforces, harmonizing inputs from:

- Sales pipeline
- Customer orders
- The production plan
- The maintenance plan
- Holiday schedule
- Human resources training and development program
- The project master plan
- Program and portfolio plans
- Project plans.

Scheduling capability provides a combined resource outlook for all temporary organizations and the standing part of the business. A permanent tactical level body is responsible for resource-leveling across the organization with the authority to prioritize. Resources can be reassigned to other projects based on changed priorities or to solve urgent problems. If required, the tactical level can put projects on hold if a lack of sufficient or qualified resources makes project execution impossible. In some organizations, the PMO is the custodian of integrated resource planning and acts as a facilitator between operational and support managers, resource owners, human resource managers, program and portfolio managers, and project owners.

Integrated resource scheduling creates an overall plan that shows all ongoing projects detailed per stage or phase and the assigned resources. Resource shortages, double bookings, or conflicts will be coordinated depending on project priority at a strategic level and situational needs. Another key benefit of integrated resource planning is to provide insight into the free capacity. *Free capacity* is resources that are available for doing project work. The strategic level can authorize new projects depending on the available free capacity. Finally, a historical analysis of the integrated resource schedule can provide a basis for determining the project payload of the organization. The *project payload* is the maximum amount of resources the organization can use for projects without going at the expense of customer focus and the ability to generate sufficient revenue.

Business financial planning

Financial planning provides a spending plan for the business based on expected income and expenses. The business budget identifies available and required capital, spending estimates, and predicted revenue. Financial planning provides the framework for business activities and is a yardstick for determining the organization's financial goals and future situation.

Principles

The parent organization arranges the prerequisites

I have worked for companies where the responsibility to get the necessary prerequisites in place was assumed to be a job of the project manager. Project manager activities involved begging for funding and scavenging for people to operate the project. Presumably, this practice was one part laziness from top management combined with a cynical approach where the most robust projects would come out as winners. Establishing a business case and a mandate, thus securing time, budget, and resources, is the responsibility of the management, not the project.

Avoid under-the-radar projects

Under-the-radar projects are unauthorized assignments not formally backed up by management. These projects eat time and resources at the expense of official undertakings. As they are uncoordinated and illegitimate, the effects of one project could counteract other formal initiatives. Without formalities like approved business cases and mandates, the danger of under-the-radar projects increases, negatively affecting the organization's workings.

Scheduling capability is key to coordination

Company-wide scheduling capability is essential to coordinate resource needs across projects preventing overload and turnover. Work overloads typically happen in organizations where people are dedicated and loyal. They hesitate to say 'no' as their work ethos is to make the impossible possible. Others might not understand their limits and get overworked, stressed out, and depleted of energy. Alternatively, they say 'yes' to any request for fear of losing their job, bonus, or promotion. An important principle is that unless a person is free, adding work to an entirely booked person automatically means taking other tasks away.

Projects are not always about strategy

In some organizations, everything is about strategy; however, critical, or urgent projects do not always require a strategic component to be valuable. A long overdue maintenance project is necessary regardless of the organization's strategy. Similar when the main project driver is new laws and the need for regulatory compliance.

Artifacts

Mission statement

An organization's *mission* is to provide value to society. For example, NASA's mission is to explore the universe. A *mission* statement is a short, concise, and inspiring sentence that captures the reason for an organization's existence. Understanding the parent organization's missions is the first step toward discerning how the project fits into the bigger picture.

Vision statement

A *vision* is a view of the organization's future or an endeavor. A *vision statement* is an inspiring one-liner that helps the team focus on the goal. During the 1960s, NASA's vision was to put a man on the moon before the decade's end. The current vision is to send humans to the Red Planet before 2030.

Program charter

When a project is part of a program, the *program charter* provides information about the goals and objectives, including interdependencies with other projects. The *program plan* will shed light on the timings of the different projects in the program and their interdependencies (Figure 5.4).

Strategy

Analyze the organizational strategy to determine the strategic alignment and situational factors affecting the course of the project.

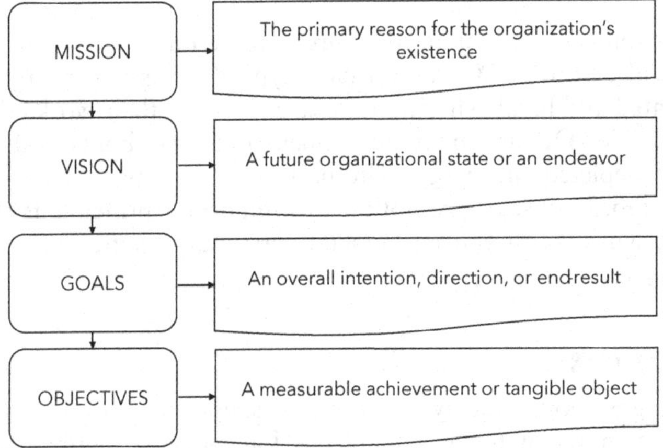

Figure 5.4 The relation between mission, vision, goals, and objectives.

Project Master List

The project master list, an overview of all unique initiatives, can provide indications of interdependencies or opportunities to learn from past or ongoing project initiatives.

Integrated resource schedule

Integrated resource planning assigns resources across the temporary and standing organization, considering customer obligations, production schedules, maintenance efforts, training needs, and holiday rotation. The schedule shows the assigned resources and available free capacity.

Project brief

A prerequisite is an approved *project brief* consisting of a scope statement and a business case, alternatively, the strategic and uncertainty perspectives on the project.

Mandate

Project managers are not resources or budget owners. A *mandate* is needed to authorize using company resources to achieve the project objectives. The project sponsor signs the order, enabling the project owner to initiate the project, establish a steering committee, and authorize the project manager to take command of a core team to produce a project management plan that realizes the business case.

Program plan

The program plan shows the projects, timing, resource allocations, budgets, and interdependencies between the various projects.

Concepts

Organizational environment and project landscape
Mission and vision
Strategy and tactic
Prerequisite and constraint
Threat and opportunity
Goal and objective
Dependency and interdependency
Scope statement and business case
Constraint and demand
Mandate and project brief
Project master list and integrated resource planning.

Questions

1 Does your parent company have a written mission and vision statement?

2 Is a strategy formalized and communicated?
3 What context analysis techniques are being used?
4 Which prerequisites, constraints, inter-dependencies, threats, and opportunities are present in your current project?
5 Does your organization have an updated project master list?
6 Is there a written and approved scope statement and business case for your project?

Reference

Project Management Institute 2017. *A Guide to the Project Management Body of Knowledge*, 6th edt. Pennsylvania: PMI.

Chapter 6

Decisions under uncertainty

Introduction

Decision making is a crossroads of scientific fields: Operations research meets statistics, engineering, neuroscience, economics, and psychology. But it is not always about science; intuition and luck sometimes play their part. Although project work involves constant unprecedented decision making, surprisingly, decision making is not a separate recognized knowledge area in project management methods like PRINCE2, PMBOK, or SCRUM. The good news is that an extensive body of knowledge exists regarding decision making under uncertainty. Due to its multi-disciplinary nature, decision making represents a vast field of expertise and a multitude of different techniques (Figure 6.1).

This chapter is not intended to provide a comprehensive overview; a wide range of excellent books on the topic is available. This chapter focuses on establishing a twofold concept of decision uncertainty. Traditionally, making *decisions under uncertainty* has the spotlight; how to choose the best possible option. However, the essential worry of every project manager is how to discover imperative *decisions hidden from sight*. Undiscovered *urgent decisions* that are overdue cost additional time and money every

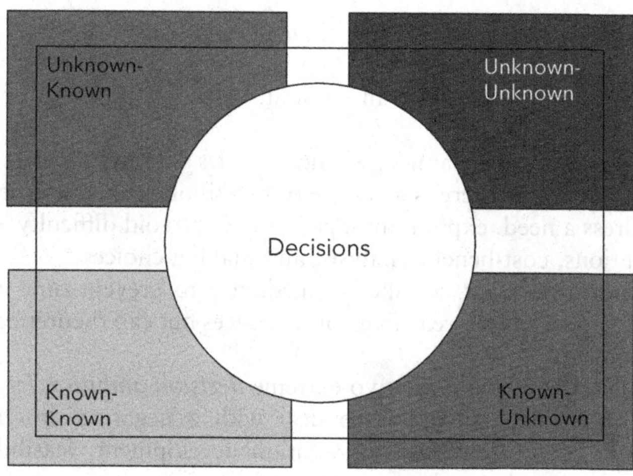

Figure 6.1 Decisions under uncertainty.

DOI: 10.4324/9781003431961-8

minute they are delayed. *Important decisions* have far-reaching consequences which still have slack before they have to be landed. But at some point, all important decisions become urgent ones.

Projects require decision making in various areas: Organization, resources, planning, design, engineering, finance, training, communication, and team building. As projects are about non-routine work, the decisions are typically unprecedented. On the one hand, taking time to make the right decision is desirable; on the other hand, all projects are on the clock, implicitly the decision-making process, too. In this chapter, we will focus on uncertainty related to the components of decision making, being the decisions:

- Qualifiers
- Alternatives
- Logic
- Effects
- Confirmation.

Implicit uncertainty refers to decisions we should be concerned with, given the situation in the project, but are not on the team's radar. Timeliness is essential; because of the project end date constraint, all decisions have the latest point when they must be resolved to avoid time overrun. Once the decision window closes, some alternatives might no longer be viable, or the cost to implement them has increased exponentially.

Explicit uncertainty relates to the known decisions; what are the drivers, alternatives, choice-making logic, effects, and means to confirm that the selected decision indeed is the correct one. If a decision has two identified possible solutions, it is tempting to focus on which one is the best. The essential questions from an uncertainty perspective are: Which possible other alternatives are we overlooking? If we change the decision logic, would we make a different choice? What selection biases affect the decision outcome? Which unexpected effects of the chosen solution might occur? When and how can we get confirmation that the right decision has been made?

Definitions

An *assessment* evaluates a property and determines an amount, value, or appraisal of an inclination.

A decision is a choice or a judgment. For example, a judge decides whether a person is guilty and decides on the penalty. Whether there is a chance of repetition is an assessment.

Decision making aims to address a need, exploit an opportunity, or avoid difficulty and involves judgment, exploring options, cost-benefit analysis, and making choices.

An *urgent decision* is a decision that must be taken immediately to prevent time and budget overruns; an *important decision* has far-reaching consequences but can theoretically be postponed until the latest moment.

Maximizing an outcome or merely satisfying are two extreme *decision ambition levels.*

Problem-solving: The goal of problem-solving is to deal with a negative situation involving symptom analysis, root cause identification, solution development, feasibility analysis, and commitment to deploy an alternative.

Generic problem-solving *ambition levels* are to:

- Dissolve
- Solve
- Resolve, or
- Absolve.

Elements

Decision qualifiers

When deciding, a natural reflex is to seek the best solution. But before diving into the nuts and bolts, take a step back and analyze the decision from a meta-level perspective. A *decision qualifier* is the impetus, principles, criteria, and values that govern a decision (Figure 6.2 and Table 6.1):

- What is *driving* the decision, a threat, an opportunity, a risk, or a problem?
- Is the decision *urgent* or merely *important?*
- When important, what is the latest point in time *the decision must be made*?
- Is the decision a matter of *do-or-die* or *reversible?*
- Is the aim to *maximize* or *satisfy?*
- Is the decision project *internal* only, or are there *outside* parties involved?
- Who is the *decision owner,* and who are the other *decision makers?*
- What are the laws, policies, ethics, and procedures that *govern* the decision?
- Is the decision *unprecedented,* or can we learn from *similar* cases?
- Do *routines or guidelines* exist, or are we *making our own?*

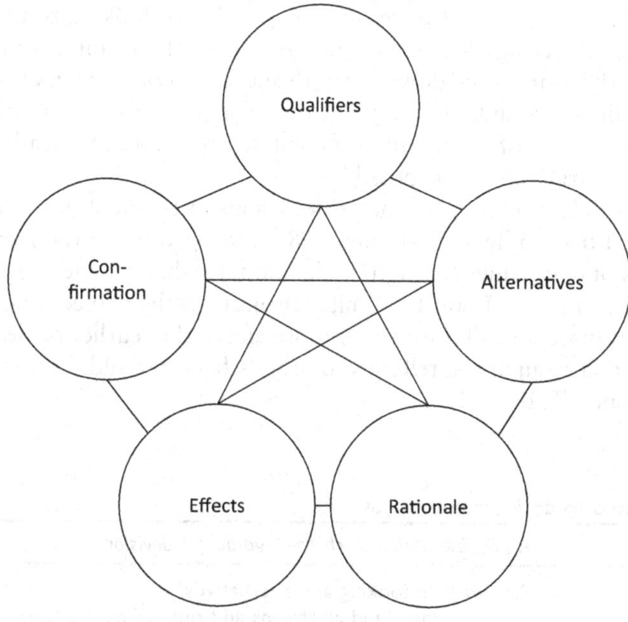

Figure 6.2 The elements of decision uncertainty.

Table 6.1 Aspects of uncertainty related to decision qualifiers

Qualifier	*A qualifier is the impetus, principles, criteria, and values that govern a decision.*
Implicit uncertainty	Meta-level aspects of the decision unbeknown to the team or the decision maker
Explicit uncertainty	Do we understand what is driving the decision? Is the decision urgent or just important? What is the latest point in time the decision must be made? Is there a precedent we are unaware of? Do we have the authority or quorum to make the decision? What guidelines are we overlooking?

- Is the decision *formal* or *informal?*
- What information to log, where, for *traceability?*
- Who should be *notified of the outcome?*

Alternatives

A popular approach to generating alternatives is brainstorming with a group, proposed by Alex Osborne (1953); however, there is little evidence regarding its effectiveness (Mullen, Johnson, and Salas, 1991). A meta-analytic review of over 800 teams indicated that individuals are more likely to generate original ideas when not interacting with others. Brainstorming is expected to harm productivity in large teams when teams are closely supervised and performance is oral rather than written. Another problem is that groups give up when they notice their efforts are not producing much.

Developing alternatives requires creativity, expertise, knowledge, thinking skills, and synergy between the team members. The explicit uncertainty aspect is overlooking solution candidates. What options are we not seeing? When working in groups, the facilitator must ensure that the team thinks in width before going down in depth and starts comparing. Diving into the nitty-gritty details of a likely candidate may go at the expense of exploring other relevant solutions. Assess the possibility of combining different solutions. Theoretically, if solutions A and B exist, could a hybrid version be possible?

Consider the need for outside help from experts or professionals in the field, but more importantly, what can be learned from others. With almost 8 billion people on the planet pursuing happiness and millions of companies trying to make money, what are the chances that the decision you are facing is unique? Look for similar projects in the project master list, access the lessons learned database, or talk directly to those engaged in earlier projects. Although they might have switched companies, telling war stories from the old days is an irresistible pastime for most people (Table 6.2).

Table 6.2 Aspects of uncertainty related to decision alternatives

Alternative	*A possible option or choice regarding a decision.*
Implicit uncertainty	Are we overlooking any alternatives?
Explicit uncertainty	Do we understand all the ins and outs of each alternative? Is the qualitative data based on facts or estimates? What is the accuracy of the quantitative aspects? What qualitative aspects are relevant?

Rationale

In his 2011 New York bestseller *Thinking Fast and Slow*, psychologist and Nobel Prize winner Daniel Kahneman describes a dichotomy between two modes of thought (Kahneman, 2011):

- System 1, which is fast, instinctive, and emotional
- System 2 is slower, more deliberative, and more logical.

The book delineates rational and non-rational motivations or triggers associated with each type of thinking process and how they complement each other, starting with Kahneman's research on loss aversion. In the book's first section, Kahneman describes how the brain systems form thoughts:

> *System 1* is fast, frequent, automatic, spontaneous, unconscious, emotional, and stereotypic, and is involved in types of decisions like determining whether an object is closer than another, complete missing information, localizing the source of a sound, simple math like 3 + 3, routine jobs like driving a car on an empty road, understanding simple sentences.
>
> *System 2* is slower, more conscious, deliberate, infrequent, logical, calculating, and is responsible for recognizing sounds, solving 21×34, running up the stairs, providing someone your telephone number, counting the number of B's in a text, reverse park, assess the validity of complex logical reasoning, adjust behavior in a social setting.

The theory is founded in decades of Kahneman's research, mostly in collaboration with Amos Tversky. Kahneman describes experiments that examine the differences between the two thought systems and how they arrive at different results even given the same inputs. Their research suggests that people are overconfident in human judgment, although simple algorithms tend to beat experts as biases do not influence them.

The human rationale is susceptible to *bias*: A disproportionate preference for or against a particular idea, action, or thing driven mainly by prejudicial, unfair, or closed-minded reasons. People can develop biases for or against individuals, groups, political, or belief systems. When using computer-aided or statistical algorithms, a bias represents a systematic error resulting from a limited or unfair sampling of a population, corrupted data, or inaccurate processes leading to faulty results. Kahneman covers the influence of several biases, such as framing choices and a tendency to replace a complex question with an easy one. The System 1 and 2 mechanisms combined with biases illustrate the vulnerabilities of human decision making.

A wide range of decision-making mechanisms and cognitive styles exist, and the first word of caution is that individual team members may apply different types of logic when arguing for or against a team decision. From an uncertainty perspective, the essential questions to ask related to logic are:

- What is the accuracy, completeness, and reliability of the information the decision is based on?
- What biases are we subject to?

Table 6.3 Aspects of uncertainty related to the rationale

Rationale	*The logic applied to making the decision.*
Implicit uncertainty **Explicit uncertainty**	Alternative selection logic that is more suitable is overlooked Do we use the selection logic correctly? What biases are influencing our decision? If we change the logic, would we make another choice?

- What assumptions are we making to fill in the gaps?
- What type of logic is applied?
- What other decision logic could be applicable?

And finally: If we use another type of logic, would we make a different decision? (Table 6.3)

Effects

Decisions alternatives will likely incur both expected and unexpected effects, good and bad. When making a decision, explicit uncertainty exists and relates to effects you are aware of and those no one foresees. To discover the full range of impacts, put yourself in the shoes of all the known different stakeholders. Next, envision the effects of a decision from different angles, such as:

- Compliance
- Juridical
- Ethical
- Security
- Economic
- Technological
- Political
- Organizational
- Environmental
- Safety
- Sustainability.

When imagining potential effects, refrain from classification in terms of positive or negative to avoid colored thinking (Table 6.4).

Table 6.4 Aspects of uncertainty related to the effects of an alternative

Effects	*Results, consequences, or impact of a decision alternative.*
Implicit uncertainty **Explicit uncertainty**	Which unexpected effects might occur? What is the degree or magnitude of the effects? How do we quantify the effects? What is the accuracy of the quantification? Confusing positive effects for negative, and vice versa? Which stakeholders are affected by the effects?

Confirmation

A popular belief is that uncertainty is reduced as the project unfolds, and complete certainty exists at project close-down as everything is supposed to be known. You may have come across diagrams depicting high project uncertainty at the start, followed by an artist impression curve going to zero toward the project end. The first problem with these diagrams is the units. The horizontal axis represents time, but what is the unit of uncertainty on the vertical? Second, what measurement data set is it based on? The final argument against this theory is the uncertainty paradox: You will never know what you do not know. Given the possibility of overlooked alternatives, decision logic, or lacking confirmation, you would never be able to tell if smarter decisions had been possible.

Making and implementing a decision is one thing, but how and when will you know you made the right choice? *Decision confirmation* is vital for a timely reversal and is essential for learning. Consider a sustainable energy project for a house. Wind, solar panels, and a combination of wind and solar options are being considered. Return on investment projections for each option is based on weather data, work cost, materials, and historical power prices.

Suppose the solar power option is selected. When and how will we know that the actual power generated by the system matches the projected output power? The theoretical answer is when all seasons have passed, but data from 3–5 years would provide a better measuring basis to consider natural variation in the weather. The meta-level confirmation aspect is whether we made the right choice. Would the combined solar and wind option have performed better? You will probably never know (Table 6.5).

Techniques

Various decision-making schemes exist; some are scientifically proven, while others are made famous through business gurus or best sellers. Project decisions can be of control or creation nature and are often intertwined. Common decision types are listed in Table 6.6; refer to the source for their application. Some common project-specific techniques are covered below in this paragraph.

Rolling wave planning

Waves appear to consist of water moving forward, but the physics of a wave involves particles moving in a cyclic pattern. We use the cyclic revisiting principle in rolling wave planning as an analogy. *Agile Rolling Wave planning* is a multilevel, incremental, and iterative planning technique to harness project uncertainty. All planning is subject to the *law of diminishing returns;* conducting detailed planning too far ahead in time is a wasted

Table 6.5 Aspects of uncertainty related to decision confirmation

Confirmation	*The when and the how to establish that the correct decision was made.*
Implicit uncertainty	Unexplored confirmation methods and data.
Explicit uncertainty	False confirmation Late or never confirmation.

Table 6.6 Overview of decision-making techniques

Name	*Application*
Mind Mapping	Specifying alternatives
Affinity Diagramming	Cause and effect
Analytic Hierarchy Process	Manage complex decisions
Conjoint Analysis	Market research
Cost-Benefit Analysis	Financial decision making
Decision Tree	Hierarchical decomposition
Trial and Error	When all else fails
Game Theory	Strategic decisions, negotiations
Heuristic Methods	Rule-of-thumb approach
Influence Diagram	Decision network
Linear Programming	Maximization of a linear function subject to constraints
Multiple Decision Criteria Analysis	Evaluation of options against a set of defined business criteria
Multi-voting	Reducing options
Present Value	Financial decision making
Net Present Value	Financial decision making
Scientific Method	Hypothesize and test

effort. As unexpected events play out, overly detailed plans soon become outdated. At the same time, stakeholders demand long-term projections regarding time, cost, features, and quality, covering the complete assignment (Figure 6.3).

Rolling wave planning is a balancing act between satisfying the need for information on the one hand and minimizing control overhead on the other. The planning focus shifts from high-level long-term to low-detailed short-term in a cyclic motion. In other words: Plan for

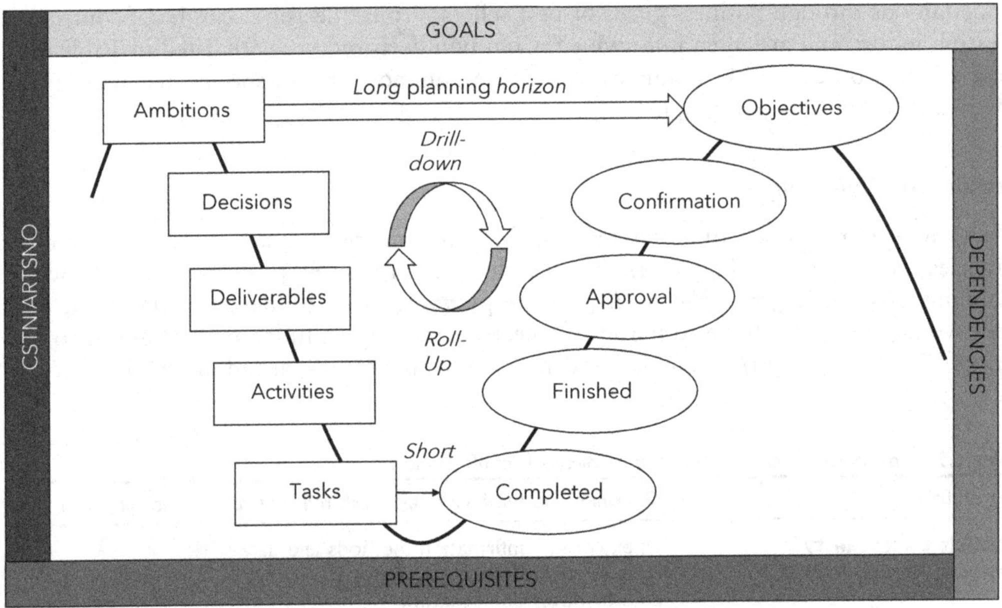

Figure 6.3 Rolling wave planning is a multi-level adaptive planning approach.

what you know, make provisions for what you can expect and improvise for everything that suddenly turns up. This is done using multi-level incremental planning cycles and adaptation as results occur. Ambitions stated as objectives, or alternatively in the form of epics, are broken down into a hierarchical set of plans, each with a specific focus, time horizon, update frequency, and level of detail:

a A milestone table or calendar plan with epics or objectives
b A decision network or decision tree with alternatives
c A PERT chart at the deliverable level and a result breakdown structure
d Gantt charts and PERT chart at the activity level
e A task list or Kanban board at the individual level.

Completed tasks are rolled up to finished activities; activities result in approved deliverables, accepted deliverables confirm decisions, and the right choices lead to achieved objectives. Evaluate the effect of deviations at a lower level on the higher-level plans and adjust for the impact. Horizontal adjustments involve adjusting the number of planning cycles required to achieve an objective and the lead time. For each task being done, the control question must be: Does this effectively contribute to achieving our goals?

Decision trees and networks

Decision tree analysis visually outlines a complex decision's potential outcomes, costs, and consequences. The diagram breaks down all possible options that branch out like a tree with branches, hence, the name. The probabilities are estimated of the different options, and the financial consequences are calculated. The decision tree is a helpful diagram to explore all possible options in width and depth (Figure 6.4).

A *decision network* logically combines decisions and logically visualizes their dependencies into a network graph. Independent choices are displayed in parallel, interdependent decisions in sequence. Based on activity and cost estimates, the lowest and highest cost

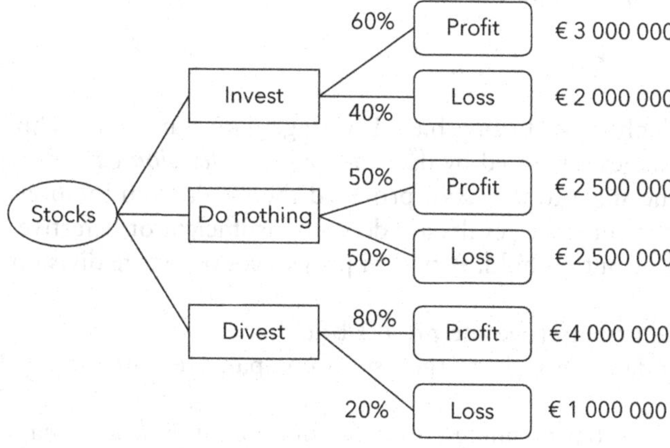

Figure 6.4 A decision tree for a stock market decision.

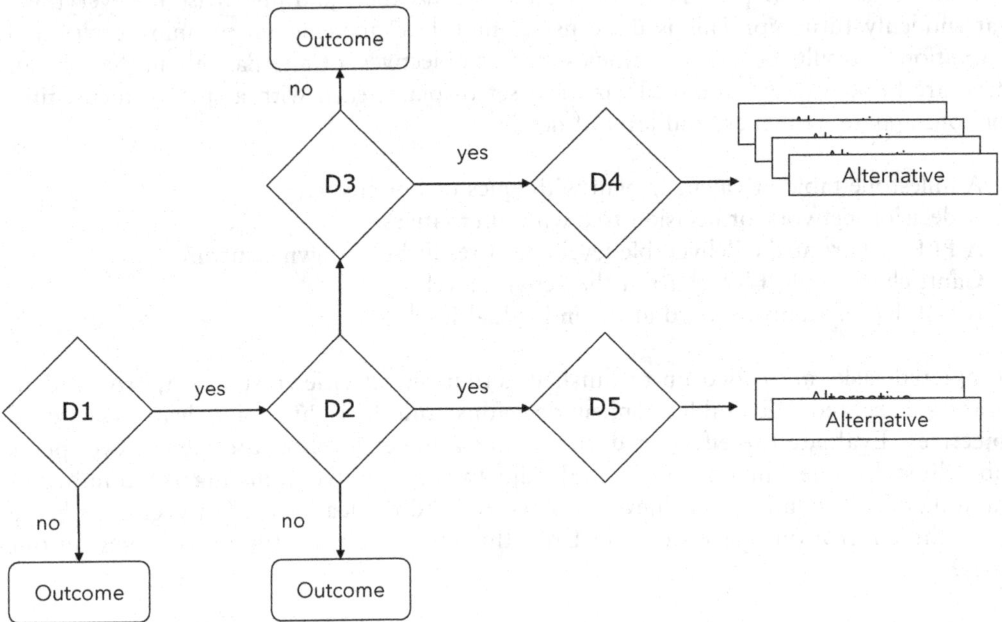

Figure 6.5 A decision network.

paths can be calculated as input for determining buffers or reserves. The anticipated route through the decision network determines the deliverables captured using an RBS. Decisions determine the project's deliverables, which are created through activities (Figure 6.5).

In the sustainable housing example, the decision to go hybrid requires solar panels and a wind turbine. The decision on the location and orientation of the house comes after the power decision. For the solar option, a south-facing roof is best; the optimal place for the wind turbine is away from the house, which determines the position of the building. Once a power solution is selected, the suppliers and the garden's layout can be chosen in parallel.

Stage gate transition

The answer to how to eat an elephant is: In tiny bits. The stage gate transition technique divides the project into control stages separated by decision gates. A *decision gate* is a conscious decision to move from one stage to the next, provided the result from the previous stage warrants doing so. If the current stage results are deemed insufficient or defective, the stage is either extended, redone, or put on hold. A typical project control stage division is:

- *Conceptualization*, the decision to approve the project brief
- *Initiation*, approving the mandate authorizing the use of company resources to realize the assignment
- *Preparation*, completion of the initial planning effort by approving the project management plan

- *Execution*, in accordance with the plan and acceptance of main deliverables
- *Close-down*, the decision to stand down the project organization
- *Follow-up*, the assessment of whether the project achieved the assignment in accordance with the business case.

Proactivity is the key to making this technique work, identifying the decision makers, conditions, and acceptance criteria beforehand. Each decision gate is also a natural point to review whether pursuing the assignment is still valid, given the new information on status, progress, conditions, and organizational priorities.

Responsibility assignment matrix

The RACI matrix describes the roles and responsibilities related to decisions and deliverables. RACI is an acronym for:

- *Accountable* refers to the person who has ultimate responsibility for a decision
- *Responsible*, the person or persons with a duty to respond to decisions and are involved in doing related work
- *Consulted*, typically subject-matter experts whose opinions are sought, primarily through two-way communication
- People are *informed* about status, progress, and actions through one-way communication.

Note that contrary to responsibility, accountability cannot be shared. The initial RACI matrix is created during the project preparation stage and updated as the project evolves. The RACI matrix can be a decision or deliverable-oriented type.

Pre-mortem

A pre-mortem is a technique where the project team mentally leaps forward in time, imagining that a decision has failed, and then works backward to determine the possible scenarios, causes, or circumstances that lead to unwanted effects and outcomes. The technique counters group thinking and reduces biases such as overconfidence, faulty heuristics, and a planning or logical fallacy. The pre-mortem expands on the acknowledged concept of prospective hindsight (Mitchell, Russo, and Pennington 1989), in which participants look back to identify problems and erroneous decisions before they occur.

Principles

Any decision is as good as the information it is based on

The quality of the information directly affects the decision. In theory, one only makes decisions based on known-known information, which are independently verified as facts. In practice, the decision maker must deal with:

1 Unreliable information: erroneous or outdated intelligence

2 Contradicting information: information from different sources that are inconsistent
3 Information noise: where it is hard to tell what is relevant and what not to take into account
4 Ambiguous information: dubious information that is hard to interpret
5 Complex data: entangled information that is hard to discern meaning, implication, and relevance
6 Incomplete information, essential parts of the puzzle are missing.

Beware of irreversible decisions

Once the ejection seat on an aircraft is activated by the pilot, there is no turning back. Carefully evaluate whether the decision is do-or-die or can be reversed. In an irreversible situation, a wrong decision might affect the feasibility or undermine the project's right to existence. Even if reversible, bad choices will take time, money, and effort to reverse, negatively affecting the chances of success within set demands.

Not all decisions are made unanimously

In most cases, like creating ground rules, decisions should be anchored throughout the team with a unanimous vote. However, there is no time for elaborate decision rounds during a crisis when swift action is key.

Lack of promptness is the kiss of death to any project

An agile principle is postponing decisions as long as possible to keep options open. As time goes by, new information may emerge. Although putting off a decision awaiting more or better information is often tempting, do know the difference between when to postpone and when to act. If a motion to delay is made, ask the meeting which essential information we will have available later. If none can be expected, then act.

Any important decision becomes an urgent one at some point

Important decisions can theoretically be postponed, but every important decision becomes urgent at some point. You can put off brushing your teeth today, tomorrow, and maybe next week. But eventually, you will end up in the dentist's chair. Determine the latest point when a crucial decision must be made, make a note, and act decisively when it's time.

Do not paint yourself in a corner

Some decisions drastically reduce the remaining solution space. Like the game of chess, look ahead, analyze the sequence of decisions, and evaluate various scenarios to prevent ending up in a corner with few or no options. Decision networks are essential to provide visibility, allowing for a proactive control of the project.

Decisions are working assumptions

Any decision is a working assumption until proven to be correct. Note the earliest time for confirmation, the method, the person assigned, and whom to notify, and a plan B for when things do not work out.

A design does not cover the open decisions

The technical design of a product, a house, or a system tells you what decisions have been made, not what is left open. Keep a separate log of open design decisions to keep track of the design completeness.

Artifacts

Project working log, or a dedicated *decision log,* to track which decisions were made, by whom, when, the rationale, confirmation method, time, and responsibility.

A *decision support document* outlines a decision, its background, nature, alternatives, pros, cons, and a recommendation from the project team to facilitate the decision-making process for the project owner or the steering committee.

A *project change request* documents the decision to change project assignments, objectives, deliverables, or activities, including the effects in terms of lead time, cost, resources, and uncertainty.

A *variation order documents* the changes made to a contract, in case of a customer project governed by a contractual agreement.

Concepts

Decision versus assessment
Decision making and problem-solving
Alternative and a solution
Cause and symptom
Cognitive bias and statistical bias
Maximizing versus satisfying
Post-mortem and pre-mortem
Unreliable information and contradicting information
Decision tree and decision network technique.

Questions

1 What are the open decisions in your project?
2 Who is the decision owner?
3 What is the latest point in time they must be made?
4 How and when can they be confirmed as correct?
5 Which decision-making mechanisms do you use in your organization?
6 Which other algorithms and logic could be helpful to your team?

References

Kahneman, D. 2011. *Thinking Fast and Slow*, New York: Farrar, Straus, and Giroux

Mitchel D., J. Russo, and N. Pennington. 1989. "Back to the Future." *Journal of Behavioral Decision Making* 2, 25–38

Mullen, Johnson, and Salas. 1991. "Productivity Loss in Brainstorming Groups: A Meta-Analytic Integration." *Basic and Applied Social Psychology* 12, no. 1: 3–23

Osborn, A.F. 1953. *Applied Imagination: Principles and Procedures of Creative Problem Solving*. New York: Charles Scribner's Sons, 1953. OCLC 641122686 [6]

Chapter 7

Method uncertainty

Introduction

The stone statues on the beaches of Easter Island have been an enigma for hundreds of years. What was their purpose? One giant statue is 10 meters high and weighs about 73 metric tons. How did the islanders move the gigantic rocks from the quarry to the seashore? Earlier theories proposed that the statues were transported horizontally about five kilometers from the quarry at Rano Raraku to the shore. The sheer workforce required to carry or pull the stones led scientists to believe the island was more populated during 1400 and 1600 AD when the stones were carved, followed by a decline in today's numbers. This theory leaves another question: What was the reason for the fall in the number of inhabitants?

According to legend, the moai walked to the beach. Researchers compared the features of the stranded stone figures lying along the road with those on the coast. First, they noticed the unique shape of the bottom of the statutes that did not make it to the beach. Also, they observed that the eye sockets were shaped to hold ropes. They theorized that the islanders had transported the moai standing up by wiggling the statue. When moving a heavy object like a washing machine, pivoting it on the corners is more manageable than lifting it. A 4-ton road-type replica was built, and in November 2011, a group of volunteers gathered at Kualoa Ranch in Hawaii and gave it a try. An extra rope at the back was attached for safety, managed by a rear team to prevent the moai from falling over, and two ropes to the side to induce a wiggle.

Initially, there was a disappointment; the statue fell over numerous times and had to be rightened using a crane. After a long day of fruitless attempts, the volunteers were about to give up, but after some coercing from the researchers, they promised to give it another try. The next day, something magical happened; the teams got the hang of the wiggle, and the moai replica started to move forward. Their skill progressed rapidly, and the team managed to move the statue in 40 minutes over 100 meters, with a crew of only 18 people. Even uphill and downhill slopes up to 6 degrees were possible, including a 180-degree turn (Lipo 2012).

The moai experiment is an example of synergy: The output of the people and systems equals more than the sum of the individual parts. Assuming that one person can carry 50 kilos, a four-ton statute would take at least 80 strong workers. That is excluding the weight of the solid rig otherwise needed to carry a moai. So, if the overall goal is to create synergy, how to determine which project method is best? Here is a thought experiment. A CEO consults the four most experienced project managers about the preferred method for a given assignment. Each manager suggests a different alternative: PMBOK, PRINCE2, SAFe, and SCRUM are proposed. Not knowing whom to believe, the CEO decides to do an

DOI: 10.4324/9781003431961-9

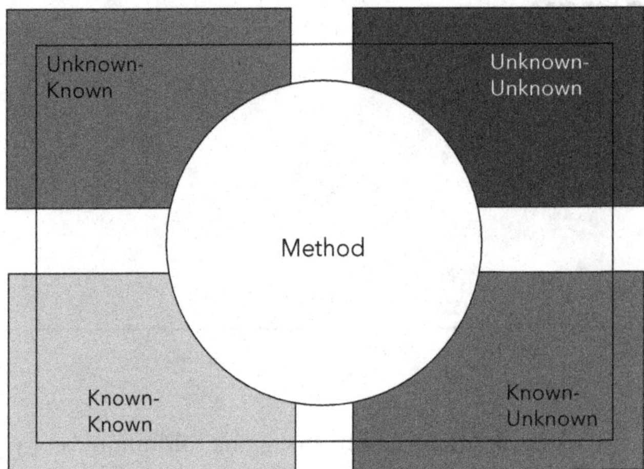

Figure 7.1 Uncertainty related to the choice, implementation, effectiveness, and efficiency of the method.

experiment: Four teams will work on the same assignment all using a different method. The team delivering the best quality for the lowest cost in the shortest time is the winner.

Does the experiment provide irrefutable proof of method superiority? There are many variables influencing project success; situational trends and forces, management support, leadership, luck, team composition and chemistry are some of them. Given the abundance of factors affecting success, does winning prove the existence of a causal relationship between the method and success? Doing the project four consecutive times using different methods is not an option, as the lessons learned will favor any later attempts significantly as uncertainty is reduced by the first attempt. The *methodology* question is: What meta-level method to use to prove which project method works best? In this chapter, we will look at the uncertainties related to the effectiveness, efficiency, and application of the project method, broken down into (Figure 7.1):

- Approach
- Coordination
- Communication
- Techniques
- Tools.

Definitions

The *project methodology* is the systematic and structured study of project methods, focusing on the following questions (Figure 7.2):

1 What (meta) methods are relevant to determine the effectiveness, efficiency, and application of project management methods?
2 What portfolio of project methods can we choose from?

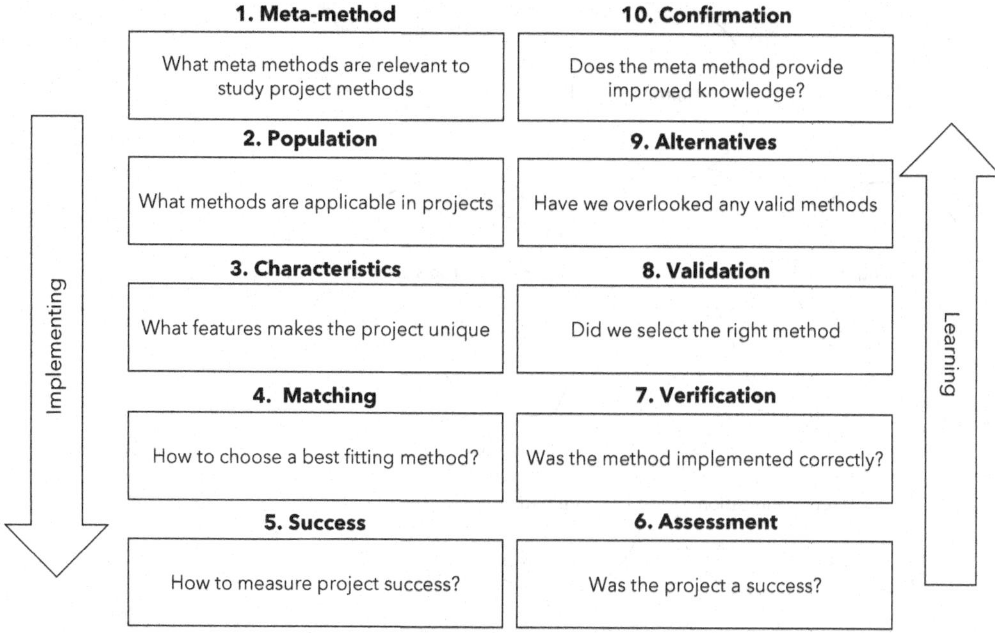

Figure 7.2 The HYVES project methodology model.

3 How to determine the distinguishing features of an assignment?
4 How do we select a best matching project method given the situational factors and the characteristics of the assignment?
5 How do we define and measure project success?
6 How do we determine whether the project was a success?
7 Was the method implemented correctly?
8 Did we select the proper method?
9 Have we overlooked any relevant alternatives?
10 Are the meta-methods accurate and valuable?

Elements

Approach

The *project approach* is the tactical scheme or gambit deployed to achieve the aim given the characteristics of the assignment, available means, and situational factors. Although used interchangeably by some, the method and approach are not synonymous. One can select a different tactical approach within the same method, for example (Figure 7.3):

- Incremental
- Iterative
- Adaptive

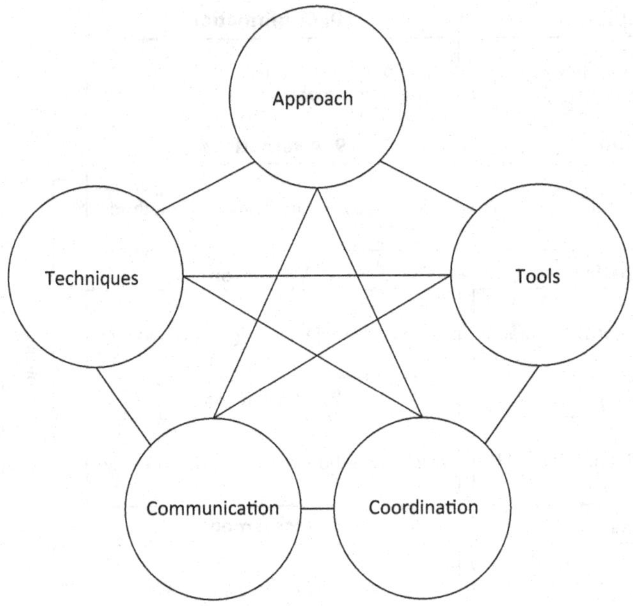

Figure 7.3 The elements of the method.

- Sequential
- Parallel, or
- A combination of the above.

for different project stages, or types of deliverables. A gambit could be to start with some easy assignments to let the team settle in. Another tactic could be focusing on the most challenging task immediately; if successful, a fundamental uncertainty is removed, and estimates can be updated. A critical tactical decision is the location and organization of the team; different professions will require other organizational approaches and means of communication. Note that the project approach is not similar to the project strategy. Technically, strategic thinking occurs at the organization's top, where one can set a vision, devise a strategy, and assign strategic resources. In projects, the objectives and available resources are given (Table 7.1).

Table 7.1 Aspects of uncertainty related to the approach

Approach	*The approach is the tactical scheme deployed to achieve the aim given situational factors and available means.*
Implicit uncertainty	What other relevant approaches are we overlooking?
Explicit uncertainty	Are we using the right approach? Is the approach correctly implemented? How can we know that the current approach is correct? When do we switch methods?

Project techniques

Selecting the appropriate techniques (Figure 7.4):

- Analyze the characteristics of the assignment
- Identify specific team traits, like specialism, location, time zone, and the ability for self-management
- Evaluate the project context
- Examine the technological features
- Define intrinsic and extrinsic success
- Select performance indicators
- Model the custom project method from a
    - Functional
    - Process
    - Systems
    - Capability
    - Empirical perspective.

Select appropriate tools and techniques that best match these properties that the team is comfortable with (Table 7.2).

Tools

As a former colleague and wooden boatbuilder was fond of saying: Using the right tool is half the job. Also: A good plan is half the work. So, provided I plan well and use the right

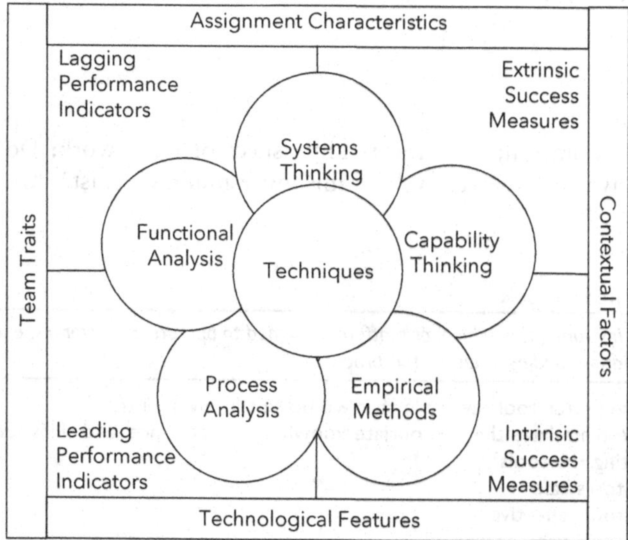

Figure 7.4 Matching project techniques with the characteristics of the assignment.

Table 7.2 Aspects of uncertainty related to techniques

Techniques	*A specific way of carrying out a particular task or procedure.*
Implicit uncertainty	What potentially better techniques are we overlooking?
Explicit uncertainty	Does the team have the appropriate level of knowledge and skills?
	Do the techniques provide value?
	Are the techniques used correctly?
	Are the tools efficient?
	What can we do to optimize and tune?

tools, there is no work for me to do! From a process perspective, projects use control and creation type subprocesses to deliver the required results. *Creation types of tooling* are used for analysis, design, development, testing, and delivery, such as cranes, trucks, computer-aided design applications, software development, and test tools. Microsoft Project is a typical *control tool* for planning and reporting. Often mentioned in the same breath, a tool is not a technique. A Gantt chart is a technique; the means to create a graph could be pen and paper, MS Excel, or MS Project. The Kanban board technique can be made on the wall with yellow stickies or dedicated applications.

The standing organization will typically provide generic management tools, such as applications to log hours, logistics, procurement systems, and communication systems like e-mail. The project offers the necessary specialist tools for the project's duration; note that introduction, training, deployment, and running costs of these tools are part of the project activity plan and cost budget. From an explicit uncertainty perspective, the question arises whether the current systems are used to their maximum potential, implicitly whether better tools exist. Note that in systems thinking, the maximum output is not necessarily achieved when each subsystem operates at top performance; it is about the fit between the parts and their tuning (Table 7.3).

Communication

Another uncertainty that rarely comes up but affects any aspect of team work: Do we understand each other? Or, inversely, what level of misunderstandings exist? Are we

Table 7.3 Aspects of uncertainty related to tools

Tools	*A device, instrument, machine, or platform designed to operate on materials, energy, or information, adding value to the process.*
Implicit uncertainty	Are there better tools available that we do not know about?
Explicit uncertainty	Does the team have the appropriate knowledge, experience, and skills for operating the tools?
	Are the tools safe?
	Are the tools effective?
	Are the tools used correctly?
	Are the tools efficient?
	Can we tune to improve performance?

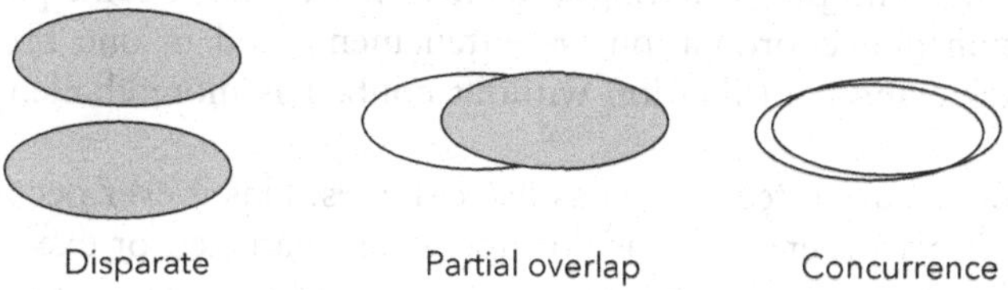

Figure 7.5 The concept spectrum.

communicating effectively and efficiently? *Effective communication* is about getting the message across; *efficient communication* is about the time, effort, and resources it takes to do so. When two people meet at the coffee machine and eagerly discuss a promising project proposal, creating a shared vocabulary is the primary priority. Again, effectiveness comes before efficiency. Effective communication relies on the consistent use of a shared terminology and a continuous effort to update and maintain it throughout the project. During the different phases, the focus will change, for example, moving from analysis to design, implementation, and testing, and the need for new terminology will manifest itself (Table 7.4).

Defining clear and shared concepts is also a key to organizational and group learning. The meaning or content two people put into a word can overlap entirely or partially. Full disparity tends to get quickly uncovered by people raising their eyebrows in confusion, followed by a request for clarification. The trickiest situation is partial overlap; people can engage in endless discussions without noticing that they only understand their version of what is being said, utterly failing to see the other person's angle. After the meeting, each person will have a different memory of the conversation (Figure 7.5).

Coordination

Coordination involves supervising and guiding the different teams to work together effectively and efficiently. A popular definition is letting the left hand know what the right hand is doing. If you want to experience what coordination is, tie one of your feet together with a colleague and try to walk the office hallways together. Coordination is not necessarily doing the same thing simultaneously; in the moai example, the right-hand team must

Table 7.4 Aspects of uncertainty related to communication

Communication	*The imparting, interchange, or transmission of thoughts, opinions, or information by speech, writing, or signs.*
Implicit uncertainty **Explicit uncertainty**	What is not being communicated? Do we share the same concepts? What is the intention of the communication? What is the context? Are we communicating effectively? Are we communicating efficiently?

give more rope when the left-hand team pulls. Getting soldiers to march at the same pace is *synchronization*. Communication and coordination are often mentioned in one breath, although separate concepts. Achieving coordination without contact is more challenging but not impossible.

Nature provides fantastic coordination feats, such as bee colonies. Has it ever occurred to you that every bee in a hive is a worker? There is no supervisor, manager, or executive type of bee in a hive. No single bee has authority over the other, and even the queen bee works every day of her life. A beehive can consist of up to 60,000 individuals at the height of summer organized as a team of teams. The teams work together with maximum independence and minimum need for coordination or interaction. Bees have no long distance communication like mobiles or radios; they can only exchange messages face-to-face with the help of pheromones and visual means. And yet, without any form of direct leadership or technology, work gets done throughout spring, summer, and autumn. Bees build their hive, care for their offspring, gather nectar, scout for promising flower fields, and ultimately secure a future for their species.

Teams will go through different states of cooperation and coordination (Figure 7.6):

- *Confusion*: People wonder why they are invited to the project or why it exists in the first place; typical body language is leaning back, crossed arms, and skeptical looks
- *Squabble*: The team discusses random sideshow topics but nothing relevant to the assignment; discussions are trivial rather than professional
- *Disagreement*: The team bickers and argues about the project's why, what, and how; opposing ideas are discussed
- *Alignment*: There is an agreement on goals, roles, responsibilities, and work methods
- *Collaboration*: People act to what has been agreed upon and work together; ground rules are established and adhered to, and effective coordination mechanisms and communication channels are in place
- *Synergy*: The team's output is more than the sum of the individual inputs. Team members motivate, challenge, and complement one another and enjoy achieving their goals and having fun doing it.

Walking the moai is an example of *synergy:* When the team's output exceeds the sum of the individual results. The explicit goal is to make the project a success. The implicit goal is to

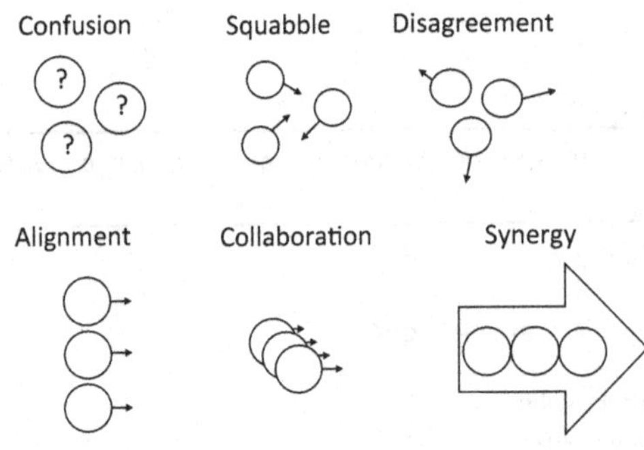

Figure 7.6 Team states.

Table 7.5 Aspects of uncertainty related to coordination

Coordination	*Allocation and distribution of tasks and activities to ensure harmonious execution.*
Implicit uncertainty	Which undiscovered factors are affecting our coordination?
Explicit uncertainty	Are we operating at maximum synergy? What changes will improve coordination?

create maximum synergy. When the team achieves top synergy, the desired results can be obtained faster, with less cost, effort, and rework, and not forget lower frustration and anxiety. Synergy goes beyond what is traditionally known as teamwork; it involves people, practices, communication, coordination, and systems. Defining synergy is easy; in practice, synergy is hard to measure and even harder to create if it is not naturally there. Fantastic teams occasionally come together as if by magic, but building most project groups means starting from scratch (Table 7.5).

Techniques

Logical project control model

Any time spent for control goes at the expense of the hours available for creation. Selecting a fitting method is about achieving the aim of the assignment with the minimum required but responsible level of control. There are two basic alternatives; use an existing method such as PRINCE2 and tailor it to the characteristics of the assignment and context. Alternatively, design and implement a custom method. In the latter case, the primary question to ask is: What aspects of the project do we want to control? The first step is to create a logical control model, displaying the elements, and their relationships. Next, define the element control attributes and meta-data. Then, select the appropriate tools, techniques, communication, and coordination mechanisms (Figure 7.7).

Student-mentor relationships

The team's ability to learn quickly is a prerequisite for success, as you mostly get one shot to get it right within the given demands of time and budget. There are many knowledge areas to master: Technology, tools, skills, software, project management techniques but also team skills. Excellent project managers deliver the right results within the set demands,

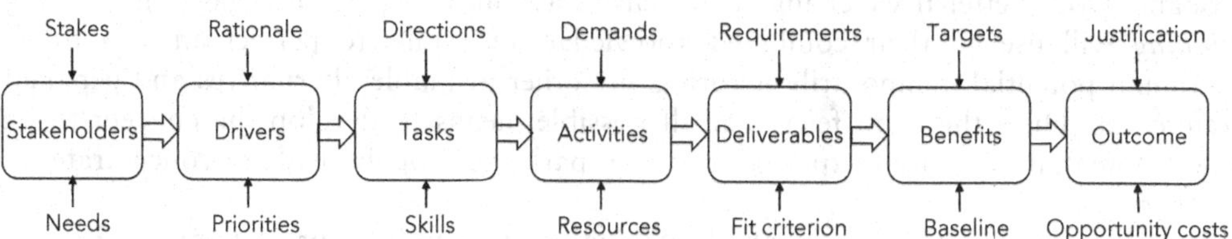

Figure 7.7 Example of a logical control model.

develop their teams, and lift people to new levels throughout the project experience. Rather than being burned out on meeting deadlines, they should be eager to take on the next assignment, armed with new skills, knowledge, and motivation.

Engaging in student-mentor relationships is an effective means to transfer knowledge and skills. Provided they are voluntary, based on trust, and there is a match or chemistry, these relationships can be very satisfying for both parties and may continue after the project has been shut down. Sometimes these relations last for life. In a student-mentor relationship, both parties have a challenge. The students' problem is to master skills and acquire knowledge; the mentor's assignment is to find the most effective and efficient ways to teach these skills and expertise, given the abilities of a student. If the student does not understand, the mentor must be creative to find ways to explain until the student succeeds.

Apart from knowledge, another essential part and benefit of mentorship is developing mental preparedness and resilience. Project work does not often go without significant disappointments and setbacks. The stress caused by deadlines and long hours can result in personal conflicts, anxiety, depression, strained relationships on the homefront, or sometimes divorce. A mentor acts as an emotional safety valve by putting matters in perspective and proportion. The long hours and the short moment of success are quickly forgotten, but personal growth lives on, becoming an asset in the next project.

One-breath challenge

As introduced earlier, the one-breath challenge is a fun way to create awareness about ambiguous terminology, establish shared concepts for effective communication, and build a central project glossary. The glossary, formal or informal, is the foundation for effective communication.

Switching thinking patterns

Critical team practice is the ability to switch between thinking patterns in debates. *Creative thinking* is developing an original idea from scratch or combining existing elements novelly. *Critical thinking* is deciding whether beliefs, opinions, and courses of action are correct, partly right, or false. It also involves assessing the merits, disadvantages, or feasibility of solutions or alternatives. Critical thinking is common as it comes easily to most, but remember that someone must be creative first and conceive an idea allowing others to engage in critical thinking (Figure 7.8).

Opposing thinking is about generating alternative ideas countering another idea. *Creating thinking* is about analyzing the merits and weaknesses of an idea in an unprejudiced and impartial way and proposing further suggestions for improvements. There is a vast difference between saying, 'This will never work because' and 'This will probably work better if we change this element as follows.' A team engaged in *creating thinking* will use all their combined knowledge and skills to perfect an idea to its maximum potential, temporarily ignoring any other available alternatives and personal preferences. Once the team feels that all possible means to develop the concept to its fullest potential have been explored, they can park the thought aside to concentrate on another.

Creating thinking is the rarest of all thinking patterns and is more common in Eastern cultures than in the West. It requires respect, politeness, humility, open-mindedness, and an

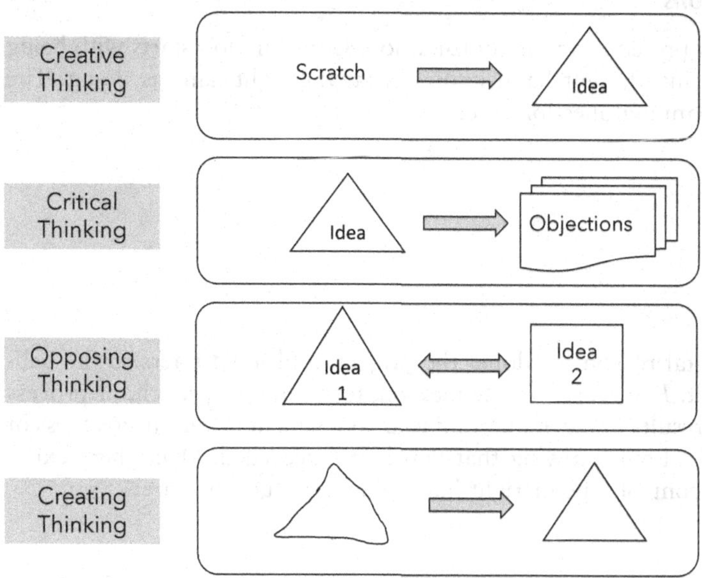

Figure 7.8 Basic thinking patterns.

atmosphere of trust. No team member should be afraid to propose ideas for fear of being criticized, ridiculed, or opposed. Projects require all types of thinking; neither is better in principle. What thinking pattern is best depends on the situation. Creative thinking will help develop ideas, opposing thinking develops alternatives, and critical thinking scrutinizes each idea for actual value while creating thinking will help perfect ideas.

The team's skill is to recognize these thinking patterns and break out of a thinking mode if it is no longer productive. Consider the following discussion:

John: *I think I may have an idea for fixing the database problem; we can simply reinstall the software and add the last working configuration of the standby server without the patch we applied to the primary server (creative thinking).*

Joe: *Nope, that is way too much work. I suggest we report this to the database supplier and let them fix it (opposing thinking).*

John: *That will take weeks, and we do not have the time (critical thinking).*

Joe: *Reinstallation is a waste of time; remember the last time we spent trying for days without any result (critical thinking).*

At this point, the discussion is locked in a spiral of critical thinking where each party attacks others' ideas while defending their own. This type of debate can go on forever, with both sides digging in their heels with the potential of ending up in animosity. John and Joe can break out of this loop by using their combined creativity to develop alternative ideas. Then, engage in creating thinking where both try to correct the solutions' flaws until they are perfect. And finally, commit to the best one. As both sides were positively involved in improving the idea, there was little risk of loss of face or resistance.

Left- and right-hand questions

Effective communication is a prerequisite for coordination. Coordination starts with being on the same page and ensuring the left hand knows what the right hand is doing. The creation type or left-hand planning questions are:

- *Why* are we doing this?
- *What* must be delivered?
- *How* can it be done?
- *Will* it work?
- *Does* it work?

Why refers to the fundamental reason for doing the project, and *what* refers to the deliverables making up the result. *How* refers to the method, technique, approach, or process needed to create the desired result. The *will* question is an assessment of the effectiveness of the solution. Finally, *does* is about knowing that you have succeeded. Once there exists agreement on the logic, the control type or right-hand planning questions are:

- Who?
- Does what?
- When?
- Where?
- With what tools and materials?

Starting in the correct sequence is essential. Our technologically orientated society primarily focuses on the 'how' question. Remember that a sensible answer to the 'why' and 'what' questions is required before worrying about the 'how.'

Ground rules

Ground rules represent shared values, such as awareness, openness, commitment, trust, and attitudes that function as oil in a machine in the relationships between people working tightly together. Ground rules can be established *informally* or *formally and are voluntary* to follow or *enforced* through peer pressure. Kogon, Blakemore, and Wood (2015) suggest four foundational leadership behaviors for what they call 'unofficial project managers.' They define unofficial project managers as team members who usually work on projects without formal project powers. Despite lacking official power or project training, they make decisions that directly affect the scope, time, and cost. The authors point out that unofficial project managers often do not have any formal authority. Still, they suggest that the following behaviors are critical to obtaining a robust informal degree of influence:

- Demonstrate respect
- Listen first
- Clarify expectations
- Practice accountability.

Although presented by the authors as behavior designed to increase informal authority for non-leaders, these are indispensable work attitudes applicable to any person taking part in a project, irrespective of their role. These attitudes are fundamental to creating a work atmosphere where synergy can bloom. Note that these behaviors are related and reinforce one another. Because you respect others, you listen first. You may have your opinion, but so do the other team members. A project has many sides; no single person can grasp them alone. Clarifying expectations is a logical result of listening first, which is the basis for practicing accountability. People can only be held accountable if the expectations regarding their actions or results leave no room for interpretation. Finally, you demonstrate respect to others by keeping yourself accountable and completing the circle.

Tribal spirit

Although the word tribal may sound medieval, modern people are still part of many tribes, depending on the setting. When biking to work, you put on your biker's clothes and outwit the members of the rivaling tribe: The ignorant and polluting car drivers. When we go to a football match, we dress up in the colors, and chant Queen songs about becoming champions. Some modern tribes have a stronger identity, visibility, and coherence than others, but all tribes provide individuals with a sense of purpose, identity, belonging, respect, and security. Building a strong tribal attitude, is a key to effective communication, and engagement.

The basic building blocks of a tribe are names, symbols, practices, a vision, and a story. The external tribal signs are typically symbols, flags, a motto, and traditions. The internal makings of a tribe are about creating a tale of a journey that people can believe in and connect to. Ancient tribes recounted their history through stories told and re-told over the campfire. These stories eventually transformed into tales about the tribes' heroic past and a journey toward a better future, described by a vision. Once tribal behavior gains a critical mass, shared cultural values evolve that elicit synergetic behavior, and any newcomers will be assimilated, adding to the momentum.

Tribal practices are the routines, procedures, formalities, and ceremonies the team adopts to complete the daily work. Social rituals include patterns for:

- Joining and adjourning
- Celebration and grieving
- Revival and rejuvenating
- Rewards and acknowledgments.

Over the course of a project, team members come and go, as there will be different staffing requirements during the various stages and phases of the project life cycle. The function of the joining ceremonies is to introduce new members to the team, make them feel welcome, and lower any barriers. Adjourning is not only a matter of having a one-on-one debrief between the project manager and the team member. Saying goodbye to the team is not always easy, but an adjourning ceremony with the entire unit can make it easier to deal with. It is a time to show the leaving person gratitude, tell war stories, and recall inspiring or funny moments. It can also be an opportunity for people to speak their minds freely.

Various management books stress the importance of celebrating success or victories. Equally important, however, is sharing grief, or licking your wounds together. Sharing feelings in the light of failure and disappointment is not an intuitive thing to do. We do not like to talk about our emotions out of fear of looking incompetent or weak. Dwelling on it is not good, but acknowledging and being open about it has a refreshing and bonding effect on a team. Projects are temporary, but some projects might last for prolonged periods. The time between significant milestones and the taste of success can be extended. Often overlooked, social ceremonies that revive and rejuvenate team spirit are therefore of critical importance, helping to restore focus and create a tenacious attitude.

Principles

Tailoring is not methodology

In books, papers, and research, methods like PRINCE2 and Agile are consistently referred to as methodologies rather than methods, by project practitioners, academics, scholars, and researchers. The *methodology* is the systematic study of methods, their strengths and weaknesses, including their application. The methodology is about the meta-method question: What method will we use to determine which project management method works best given the assignment? All methods can be *tailored* to the assignment, but changing the gap size on a variable spanner does not change its fundamental workings, and becomes a socket wrench. Similarly, selecting a subset of the available PMI processes does not change the process based nature of the method.

Methodology is not plural for methods

Agile is a family of methods with shared principles and related features, like families of plants and animals in biology sharing similar characteristics. Agile based methods include: Scrum, Chrystal, Dynamic Systems Development Method (DSDM), Extreme Programming (XP), lean product development, Kanban, and Feature-Driven Development (FDD). The plural of methods is not methodology, however.

You will probably never know

The ultimate methodology question is: Could we have succeeded better, provided we had used another method? Given that projects are unique and cannot be repeated while changing a single parameter to study its impact, you will never know what could have been possible. *Duplication* is critical scientific principle. When independent researchers repeat experiments with similar results, faith in the conclusions is strengthened. Projects being unique assignments can never be duplicated under similar circumstances, nor can a *control group* be established. For this reason, research in project management mainly relies on interviews and questionnaires, adding statistical methods to find a correlation in the results. But correlation is not causation, and the validity of most project methods is merely a presumption.

Communication effectiveness is another concern regarding interviews and questionaries as a research method from a methodology perspective. Playing the one breath challenge with collegues can be a sobering experience; failure to define the difference between fundamental concepts like goal and objective, or requirement and specification, makes you wonder about the validity of the answers. Adding the fact that there exists no common agreed upon definition of project success, one cannot help but wonder about the interpretation of the answers to the question whether the selected project method had a positive contribution to achieving the aim.

Projects rely on direct and indirect control

Control can be achieved through direct and indirect mechanisms. *Direct control* manages the creation effort to realize the correct results within predefined limits. *Implicit control* is about achieving maximum synergy between the project team and other stakeholders. When the project team reaches a state of full synergy, the correct results can be obtained faster, with less effort, rework, or frustration. By controlling synergy, one implicitly has control over the other areas of the project.

Engagement alone is not enough

Synergy must not be confused with stakeholder engagement. *Stakeholder engagement* is about commitment and active participation. The fact that people are engaged does not automatically mean that they also work together in the best possible way. Imagine a strongly engaged stakeholder with limited team skills, creating havoc in the team through their clumsy actions or poor peoples skills. Engagement is the start, synergy is the goal, encompassing both team members and systems.

Synergy has no end state

The synergetic states will vary depending on the setting, conditions, topic, and team configuration. A group can reach maximum synergy, but this can change when a new team member enters the scene. Team states are dynamic, so a team can progress or fall back to a lower level depending on the topic, group, or course of events.

There exists no 'quick fix' for synergy

I enjoyed working for a boatbuilding company that made beautiful hand-crafted mahogany runabouts. People were awed by their high gloss finish, and a common question was which varnish was used. The exclusive finish resulted from a systematic series of steps, shaping the wood, coarse sanding, fine sanding, epoxying, and polished high-gloss varnish. The curious thing was that varnish highlighted any imperfections in the previous steps. The high gloss was no add-on but the result of a process. Creating synergy is like the layers of an onion; each coat builds upon the previous one, and there is no single quick fix that does it all.

The illusion of communication is genuine

Suppose you have done the one-breath challenge described in the paragraphs at the end of the previous chapters. In that case, you may have become aware of how easy it is to be misunderstood or misinterpret what is being communicated. It is tempting to assume that when all people in the room have a higher education, come from the same country, and work for the same company; everyone is automatically on the same page. That is a mistake: Never assume that you understand one another. Constantly seek confirmation that the message is understood.

Getting an acknowledgment is the sender's responsibility

When situations get hectic, it is easy to miss something in the turmoil of messages going over various communication channels. The originator is responsible for getting an acknowledgment that a message has been received; without a confirmation from the receiver, it should be considered as not sent.

Do not confuse your ambitions with your talents

When you find yourself in a leadership position or aspiring one, remember that you can only be a leader due to the fact that others are willing to follow you. Question your intentions by asking yourself: Am I taking the lead for my personal benefit or the best of the team? Do not confuse the ability to manipulate or dominate people with leadership. The primary concern of any leader should be to maximize synergy, not to impose their will or ideas on the team.

Artifacts

Project Management Plan

Glossary

If someone had told me some years ago that a boring document like a *glossary* was one of the most critical tangible artifacts, I probably would have laughed and dismissed the idea. Getting it right the first time starts with effective communication, founded on shared concepts that are used consistently. A glossary is a living document, preferably on a wiki, maintained throughout the project by the entire team (Figure 7.9).

Team contract

The *team contract* is a set of agreed-upon guidelines, norms, values, and guidelines which a team consciously uses to help individuals decide how to behave. Team ground

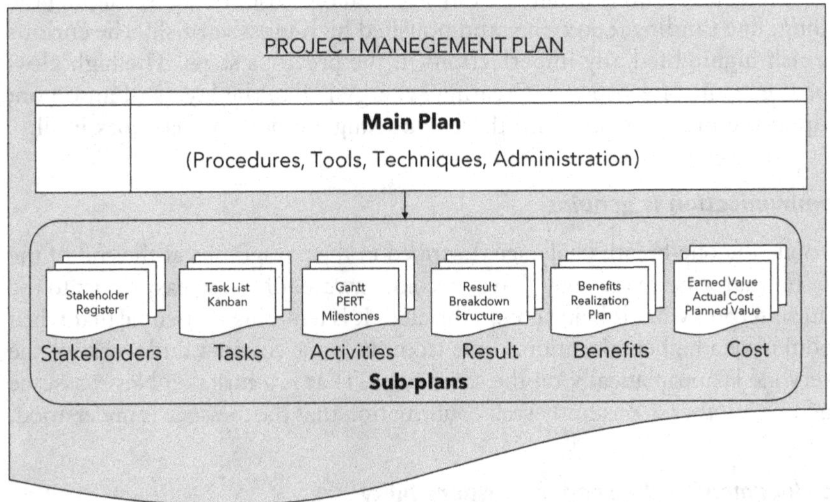

Figure 7.9 The project management plan and sub-plans related to the control model.

rules define the desired behavioral model of how individuals communicate, participate, cooperate, support each other, and coordinate tasks. Ground rules are initially created during the first team sessions, maintained, revised, and enforced throughout the project. Ground rules must be clear, written, consistent, and unanimously agreed to. Following the approved agreed regulations is everyone's responsibility.

On and offboarding checklist

As a project manager, take your time to welcome and say goodbye to every team member in an individual conversation. Apart from formal topics, this is a great way to get to know the person's particular situation related to work, like kids in kindergarten who must be picked up at the end of the day and other factors that dominate work life. Use a checklist to ensure that basic needs are covered, like access to files, writing hours, system access, and expenses. Such a conversation is also a great time to answer any questions about the project and explain how the person's particular involvement, knowledge, and skill can contribute to the project. An onboarding conversation makes people feel welcome, and an offboarding discussion makes them feel valued.

Concepts

Method and approach
Teamwork and synergy
Left-hand and right-hand questions
Communication and coordination
Control systems and creation systems
Mentor and a teacher
An iterative and incremental approach
Big-bang and pilot
Pilot and test
Tribal language and official language
Creative and creating thinking
Opposed thinking and critical thinking.

Questions

1 How was the method for your current project selected?
2 Were there any alternative methods considered?
3 What could be definite reasons for changing the method?
4 What is the current tactical approach?
5 Are there any other options?
6 Is there a central glossary, or does each author create their own?
7 Is there a project plan or a project management plan?
8 Has a team contract been established?

References

Lipo, C.P., T.L. Hunt, and S.R. Haoa. 2012. "The Walking Megalithic Statues (Moai) of Easter Island." *Journal of Archaeological Science*

Kogon, K., S. Blakemore, and J. Wood. 2015. *Project Management for the Unofficial Project Manager* 1st edn., Dallas: BenBella books

Chapter 8

Scenario uncertainty

Introduction

Doctors diagnosing patients might face a complex picture of symptoms caused by different underlying health issues. To find effective treatment, they must unravel the puzzle of genetic factors, diseases, infections, lifestyle, work, and living conditions that may be the culprit. Various sources may cause a composite picture of signs that must be disclosed, and each source of trouble must be addressed individually and effectively. Likewise, project managers must distinguish between multiple uncertain elements to determine their combined effect on project performance and desired outcome.

In the old days, anything that went wrong was attributed to an evil spirit. Whether the misfortune was a fire, flood, or a disease, some heinous spirit was behind it all. Risk is the modern day equivalent of evil spirit; it is a common denominator for whatever might go wrong, or has gone wrong in projects (Figure 8.1).

Finding the true reason for deviation from the plan requires a higher granularity than simply dubbing anything that goes wrong a risk. Suppressing the risk of going over time

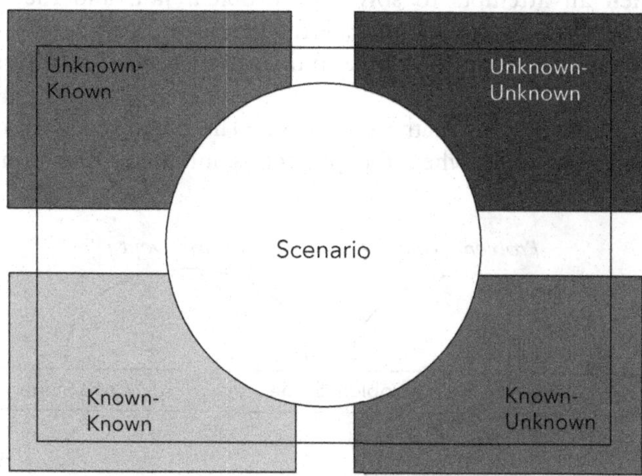

Figure 8.1 Uncertainty related to scenarios.

DOI: 10.4324/9781003431961-10

and budget puts the horse behind the wagon, as time and budget overruns are symptoms, not the problem itself.

It is hard to see risk for what it is without considering the other sources of uncertainty discussed in the previous chapters. Therefore, scenario uncertainty is chosen as the final topic to avoid the evil spirit fallacy. This chapter focuses on uncertainty related to the desrired project scenario and undesired events causing deviation from the plan. Keep in mind that there really is no need for adverse events for a plan to fail. The project plan could be botched and bound for failure from the beginning for multiple reasons: Poor decisions, flawed methods, or optimistic estimates. Any unidentified prerequisites, constraints, dependencies, or undisclosed stakeholder needs and demands not incorporated into the plan, will cause the plan to desintegrate. This chapter will examine the elements that make up scenario-driven uncertainty:

- Plans
- Risks
- Problem
- Crisis
- Measures.

Definitions

Stages

Various stages characterize *event-driven uncertainty*. In the *secure stage,* no actual risk exists. A canoe on the shore has no chance of turning over or sinking, these risks are purely conceptual. Launching the canoe is a *risk event*; the dangers of rolling over or drowning are introduced into the situation. Then, one of the paddlers leans over to the side, the boat flips over; a *problem event* has occurred. They hold on to the boat attempting to push it toward the shore. But the current proves too powerful, and the paddlers start getting cold and exhausted. A *crisis* occurs when all attempts to solve the problem fail, and the only remaining option is to reduce the damage. Unable to save the canoe and cargo, they can preserve their lives. Eventually, they abandon the canoe and start swimming to the river shore (Figure 8.2).

Risk, problem, and crises are *abstractions* in the safe stage. The perceived risks of a project proposal become *actual risks* once when the project is initiated. Risk sounds

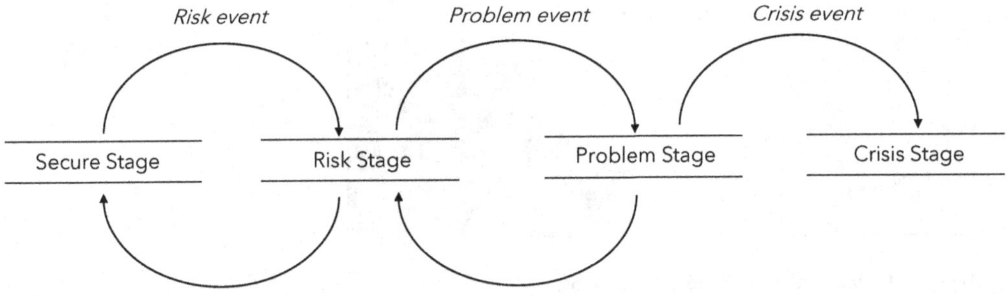

Figure 8.2 Stages of the risk continuum.

ominous, but the risk stage often coincides with a system's normal operating phase. The risk of a crash is introduced when an aircraft takes off and starts its routine flight. The chances of a plane crash have been steadily declining over the last 20 years, and in 2008 the probability of taking a flight during which a given passenger suffers death is equal to 0.0000005% (Jozwiak et al. 2015). Risk is an integral part of driving a car and flying an airplane. Running any project is subject to risk, even if things go according to plan. Explicit uncertainty revolves around the question whether the any of the identified risks will happen or not, and the amount of damage incurred. Inherent uncertainty exists about the presence of risks below the team's radar.

Pre-emptive measures in the risk stage involve avoidance, mitigation, or transfer actions. Countermeasures are deployed when a risk has become a problem. *Countermeasures* either addresses the problem or create a *workaround* that reduces the problem to an acceptable level. *Contingency measures* are actions designed to reduce the extent of the damage when fixing the problem is no longer an option. The chosen posture is a function of risk appetite, risk tolerance, resource availability, and economics.

Thresholds

Identification threshold: Any risk, problem, or crisis can be reasoned about, provided it is conceptualized. Before Madam Curie established the radon concept, identification and detection were impossible (Figure 8.3).

Telltales are any signs or measurements indicating that a risk is present. For example, static electricity in the air suggests the possibility of a lightning strike.

Awareness threshold: The risk telltales, problem symptoms, or crisis signs are recognized.

Cognition threshold: The pattern, cause, consequences, and extent are understood.

Reaction threshold: The lead time required to deploy pre-emptive, counter, and contingency measures addressing identified risks, problems, or crises.

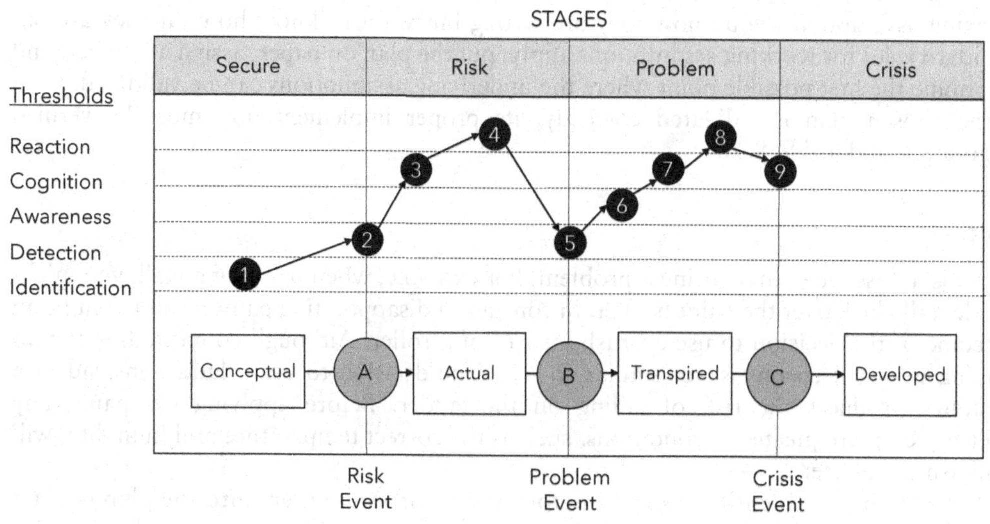

Figure 8.3 Stages and thresholds.

Symptoms are any signs or manifestations indicating the presence of a problem; for example, when you get a flat tire, your car will heel over and becomes sluggish on the wheel.

Having a risk, a problem, or a crisis and knowing that you have one are two different things. In a best-case scenario, the risk is discovered right away. In a worst-case scenario, risk, problem, and crisis events remain below the team's detection threshold. Even if the signs are visible, they might be missed leaving the team unaware. The low-fuel indicator on the dashboard is easy to overlook when driving in dense traffic requiring the driver's full attention to what is happening outside. Also, note the possibility of a delay between a problem occurring and the first signs becoming visible. In the above figure, an example of event-driven uncertainty scenario goes as follows:

1 In the secure stage, a conceptual risk fails to be identified
2 A risk event is introduced into the situation, unaware to the team
3 The team eventually recognizes the risk, and the decision to deploy pre-emptive measures is made
4 Mitigation actions designed to reduce the probability of the risk becoming a problem are in place
5 Despite mitigation actions, a problem does occur
6 The team becomes aware of the symptoms
7 The problem is understood
8 Remedies to the problem are initiated
9 Failure to solve the problem, the only remaining option is to reduce the damage; a crisis is a fact.

Elements

Plan

The *plan* is the preferred scenario of how events should unfold in time. All plans are working assumptions, making any plan a known-unknown. Estimates are special cases of working assumptions; you know they are wrong but want to know how far they are off. Standard rules for working assumptions apply; put the plan on paper, assign an owner, and determine the first possible point where the underlying assumptions can be validated. Even if the chosen plan is validated correctly, its proper implementation must be verified (Figure 8.4 and Table 8.1).

Risk

A *risk* is a possible event causing a problem. For example, when painting a wall, you might accidentally kick over the paint bucket. In contrast, a disappointing paint result might be an outcome of the decision to use a brush instead of a roller. Although connected, note that making wrong decisions is not similar to risk. The decision to use a ladder instead of a scaffold introduces the risk of falling off the ladder. Before applying the paint, any unidentified prerequisites or conditions, such as the correct temperature and humidity, will diminish the allure.

Again, failure to identify relevant factors and incorporate them into the plan is not a risk, as a prerequiste has no probability of happening. Either you read the paint

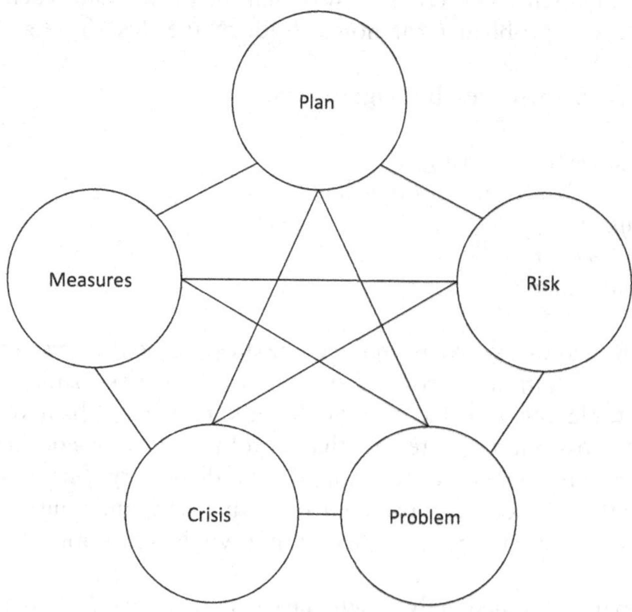

Figure 8.4 The elements of scenario-driven uncertainty.

Table 8.1 Aspects of uncertainty related to the plan

Plan	*The plan is the desired scenario of how the project will play out in time*
Implicit uncertainty	What better plans are we overlooking?
Explicit uncertainty	Will the plan work as intended?
	What is the robustness of the plan?
	What is the resilience of the plan?
	When to adapt the plan?
	When to abandon the plan?

instructions, or you do not; you *decide* to create the right conditions, or take a shortcut and skip the preparations work. There is no paint god tossing a coin whether the job will succeed or not. In the scenario where the paint manufacturer made a mixing mistake causing the paint not to cure, the problem is already a fact. Becoming aware when it fails to dry, is not a risk occurring, the problem event already took place at the factory. If the paint comes in two parts, making a mixing mistake would be a risk. Risk management is about how the plan could go wrong, uncertainty management is reasoning about what already has gone wrong and how to find out. Doing a small sample paint test would uncover the issue in this case.

Note the word possible in the definition; risk is a *potential problem* due to a possible event. There exists a chance of occurring, but not a given. A future adverse event that is bound to happen, regardless of what you do, must be regarded as a problem and no longer a risk. When all signs and indicators tell you there is no way that the project can reach the deadline in two weeks, you have a problem right now, although the deadline has not arrived yet.

How to evaluate risk? Risk is characterized by (Figure 8.5):

1 The *probability* of a problem event occurring
2 The *likelihood* of discovering that a problem event has occurred
3 The first order-effects or *impact*
4 The second-order effects, or *recovery*
5 The third-order effects or *consequences.*

Note the word *problem-event* instead of risk event. In the context of this book, a *risk event* introduces the risk element into a situation; a *problem event* is when the risk instantiates, and the problem becomes a fact. Having a problem is one thing; knowing you have one is another. *Likelihood* refers to the possibility of detecting that a problem event has occurred. Probability and likelihood are strictly synonyms according to the dictionary, but it is essential to distinguish between the chance of a problem occurring and knowing it has happened. When driving, the signs of a flat tire are apparent, but would you notice if your rear lights stop working?

Some problems become apparent immediately when they occur; others may remain invisible and unnoticed. A row during a team meeting is an obvious problem; a furtive conflict between key players might affect team synergy undetected for some time, or may never get uncovered. In the meantime, the project manager keeps wondering why there

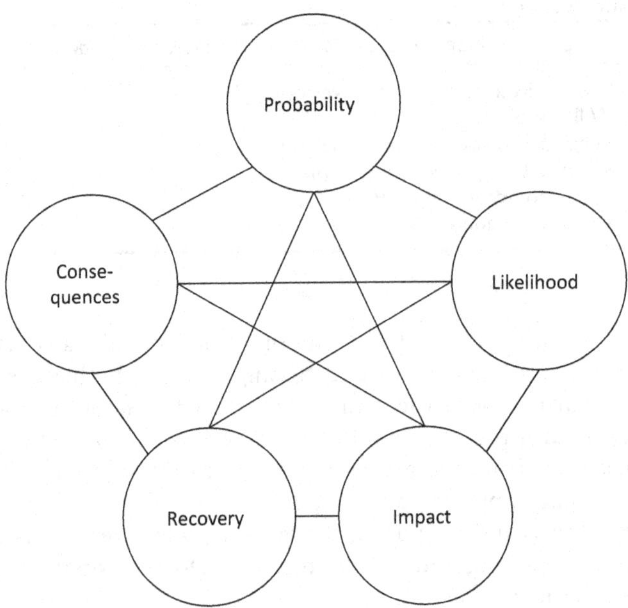

Figure 8.5 The components of risk.

Table 8.2 Aspects of uncertainty related to risk

Risk	*A risk is a possible future event causing a problem.*
Implicit uncertainty	Unidentified risks the project is subject to.
Explicit uncertainty	Will the identified risk strike, where, when, and how?
	What is the appropriate risk response?
	Are the mitigation actions effective?
	What is the degree of residual risk?
	Are the pre-emptive measures cost-effective?

is so little progress. Some problems or issues have a higher *detection threshold* than others, making them more challenging to uncover. Worst-case scenario, the problem is not detected until it reaches the crisis stage.

The first-, second-, and third-order effects to evaluate are the following characteristics: Impact, recovery, and consequences. Imagine falling off your bike on the way to work, the impact being lying on the asphalt with bruises and a bent wheel. The recovery involves walking home and spending $50 on repairs. Consequently, you missed a customer meeting, and a substantial deal for your company was lost. The consequence depends on the problem setting or context it takes place. Had the accident occurred during a Sunday afternoon pleasure ride, there would only be impact and recovery. Assessing the context is essential; the risk of jumping on your bike on a workday versus the weekend varies accordingly.

In the case of a *composite risk,* the impact of one risk triggers a new risk event that sets off another. Due to a punctured car tire, you lose control of the wheel and end up in the left lane, colliding with a meeting vehicle. There is a *cumulative risk* picture to consider in the event of multiple independent risks. The individual risks are not related and might even be low impact, but the sum of the damage can be substantial. Consider a shipping company that operates a fleet of sister ships worldwide. When all ships are at sea simultaneously, the cumulative risk picture is higher than when all ships are safely in port. The fact that the vessels are spread worldwide is essential, so they cannot sink due to a single storm. If the boats are built by the same shipyard and share a similar flaw in the electrical wiring, the fire risk affects all ships independently of their location (Table 8.2).

Problem

A *problem* is a difference between the actual and the desired state or a deviation from a norm, standard, or status quo. The larger the gap, the bigger the problem. Problems can be *multidimensional;* deviations across various aspects exist. A car can have a clutch failure while simultaneously the exhaust gas values are outside the allowed environmental regulations. A *symptom* is how a problem manifests itself. A flat tire will typically cause a car to vibrate, lose balance, and draw to one side. Problems can be *dynamic* or *intermittent* in nature. The latter is harder to fix, as reproducing the problem during fault finding can be challenging. An engine that occasionally does not want to start is hard to troubleshoot for a mechanic if it starts correctly at the repair shop (Figure 8.6).

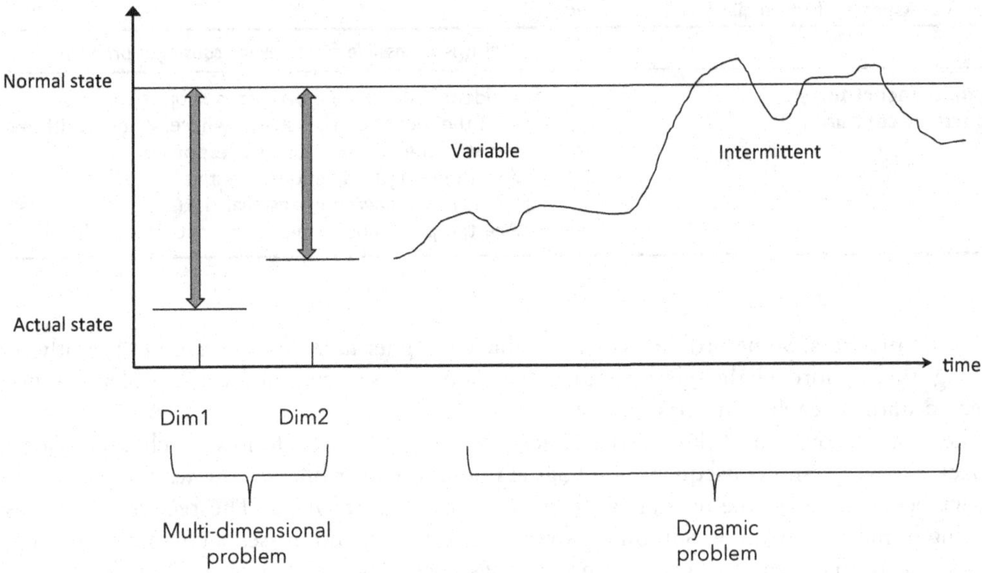

Figure 8.6 Problem dynamics.

Problem awareness involves keeping a watchful eye for symptoms. When analyzing and discussing problems, distinguish between:

- Root cause
- Cause
- Problem
- Symptom.

Addressing problems effectively starts with an accurate definition of the issue. Consider the following problem statement: 'John has a fever.' Fever is a symptom, not the problem. The proper problem description as a deviation from the desired state is: The person in question is in bad shape where he should be healthy. Fever can be caused by various reasons, such as an influenza virus (cause) defeating the immune system. The root cause of infection could be the reduced effectiveness of the immunity system related to malnutrition. If a project is behind a plan due to over-optimistic estimates, lack of reliable estimation capability is the problem, not inefficiency. Cost overruns and missed deadlines are commonly identified as risks or problems but are merely the symptoms of one or several underlying issues.

Projects are resource-constrained organizations and might not be able to handle all problems simultaneously; therefore, a *problem prioritization scheme* is beneficial. Problems can be characterized as:

- *Urgent* or *important* in nature
- Affecting *effectiveness* or *efficiency*.

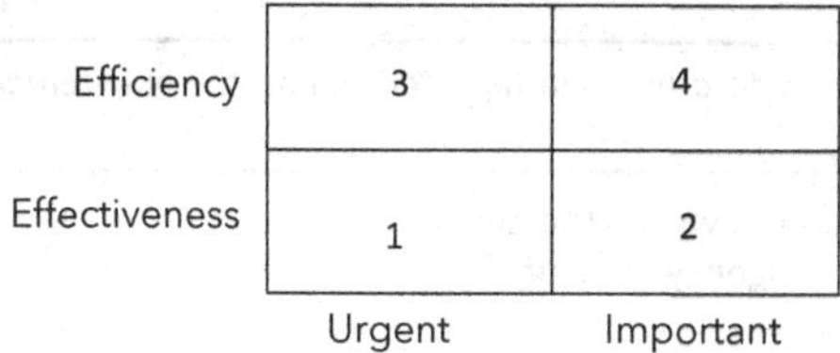

Figure 8.7 Problem prioritization matrix.

Table 8.3 Aspects of uncertainty related to a problem

Problem	A problem *is a difference between the actual and the desired state, a deviation from a norm, standard, or status quo.*
Implicit uncertainty	Undiscovered problems affecting the project outside of the team's awareness.
Explicit uncertainty	Can we detect the symptoms? Do we understand the cause or causes? Are we dealing with a single or composite issue? Have we identified all possible solutions? Are the solutions feasible? What are the time, effort, and resources required for implementation? When and how will we know that it works?

Urgent problems must be resolved immediately to prevent delays, cost increases, or the project from coming to a grinding halt. *Important problems* are issues that do not require immediate attention, and solving them could be postponed. However, all important problems become urgent problems at some point in time. The estimated point where it becomes urgent must be determined and logged for important problems, and an actioned owner must be assigned to address the matter in time. Another distinction is problems that affect *effectiveness* versus problems that affect *efficiency*. A defect preventing a machine from operating is an effectiveness problem; if the device runs but uses more power than usual, it is an efficiency problem (Figure 8.7 and Table 8.3).

Crisis

Just as every risk is a potential problem, every problem can become a crisis. The word *crisis* is usually associated with significant damage or loss of life, where 'significant' is relative and subjective. In the project context, a *crisis* occurs when all thinkable solutions have failed, and the only remaining option is limiting the damage. For example, all attempts to fix a leaking boat have failed, and the ship goes down. Abandoning the ship and going into the life rafts is a crisis decision: The boat cannot be saved, but the crew's lives can. Sometimes when you play the one-breath challenge, a gem appears. When asked to define the difference between a problem and a crisis, a colleague said: 'A problem is something you can work with; a crisis is something you must deal with.'

Example 1. *Imagine lying on the sofa late in the evening and discovering that today is your partner's birthday, and you completely forgot. You rush to the gas station, buy the entire*

Table 8.4 Aspects of uncertainty related to a crisis

Crisis	*A crisis occurs when all solutions to a problem have failed, and the only remaining option is to limit the damage*
Implicit uncertainty **Explicit uncertainty**	What crises are ongoing unbeknown to the team? What is the appropriate contingency measure? What are the possible scenarios? What is the decisive moment to call it a crisis? Who should be informed? What preparations can we make?

bucket of flowers, and say: surprise! Any time before midnight counts as on time. Now imagine finding out the day after. Your only option is to try to reduce the wrath by doing the dishes and house cleaning for the next two months.

Example 2. *A doctor is treating inflammation in a patient's leg. At some point in time, all types of antibiotics and methods have been tried without success. The inflammation spreads through the patient's body and will eventually cause death. The inflammation cannot be stopped; the only remaining option is to amputate and save the patient's life.*

Example 3. *A project goes over time and budget, stretching the available funding of the parent organization to its limits. Actions to bring the project back on track have all failed. Terminating the project to save the company from bankruptcy is a crisis decision.*

Crisis scenarios can be prepared and exercised, but there is always the odd chance of an unforeseen crisis where existing plans are useless. Crisis readiness training focuses on developing effective generic capabilities such as rescue, food, medicine, water supply, medical help, transportation, and evacuation. The real value of a crisis exercise is the ability to improvise, adapt, and reconfigure capabilities to deal with the unexpected situation effectively (Table 8.4).

Measures

Pre-emptive measures

A risk can be accepted if the inconvenience of the problem occurring is deemed minor or a known fix or workaround exists. *Acceptance* implies that no preemptive measures are deployed to affect the nature of the risk, as it is deemed more cost-effective to solve the problem. The time and resources required to solve the problem are considered less than the effort needed for deploying the pre-emptive measures. The risk is entered in the uncertainty log and designated as a *watch-list risk,* meaning watch, warn, and solve any problem on the fly with whatever means available. Keeping track of watch list risks is vital to create awareness and prevent risks from being forgotten and 'rediscovered'. Remember that a single watch-list risk might appear harmless but could play a part in the composite or cumulative risk picture; the total risk picture must be considered when evaluating individual risks (Figure 8.8).

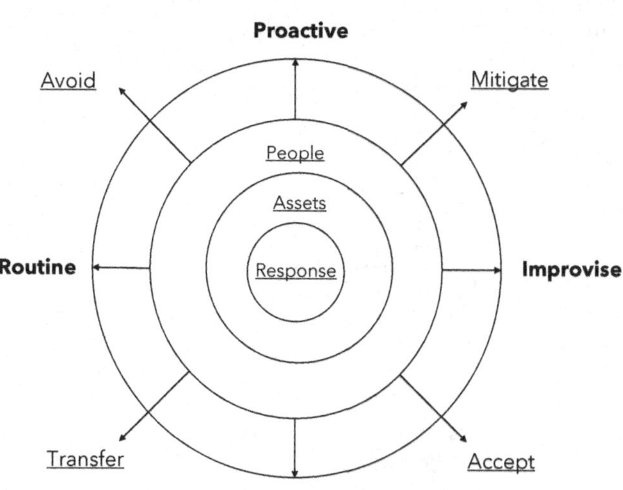

Figure 8.8 Pre-emptive measures in the risk stage.

If the threat posed by risk is unacceptable, a proactive approach is required, and the risk is designated as a *top-list risk* that is addressed through:

1 Avoidance
2 Mitigation
3 Transfer.

Avoidance. If the risk impact and consequences are deemed unreasonable, the proper risk response is to ensure that a problem event never occurs. If the roads are covered with ice, you risk a collision or injury when driving your car to work. To avoid this, you call your boss and ask permission to work from home; eliminating all danger. *Risk mitigation* involves taking actions designed to reduce the chances of the risk from happening, limiting the impact, or a combination of both. Driving slowly in icy conditions would be a combined mitigation action; chances of slipping and sliding are lower, and the dent in your car would be less.

Remember that risk mitigation does not entirely rule out the risk of happening; residual risk remains. *Residual risk* is the remaining degree of risk left after mitigation measure(s) have been deployed. Additional actions, such as risk transfer, can be devised if the residual risk level is deemed unacceptable. *Risk transfer* involves transferring (certain aspects of) the risk to other parties. For example, car insurance shifts the financial risk to the insurance company. The transfer usually has a cost, in this case, an insurance fee.

Countermeasures

Problems can be (Figure 8.9):

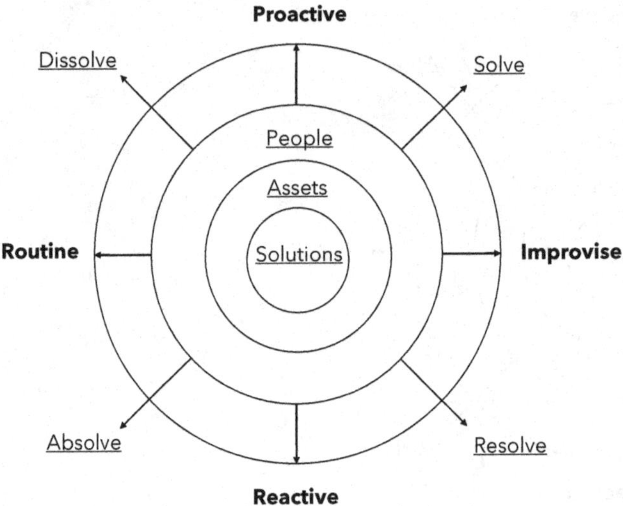

Figure 8.9 Countermeasures in the problem stage.

1 *Absolved*, essentially declaring there is no problem, secretly hoping eventually it will solve itself or go away
2 *Resolved*, implementing a solution or workaround that is good enough for the time being
3 *Solved*, meaning taking measures that yield the best outcome or optimize the situation
4 *Dissolution*, eliminating the problem permanently by redesigning the situation.

Contingency measures

Contingency measures to achieve relief in a crisis are (Figure 8.10):

1 *Endure*, acceptance while making the best out of the situation based on improvisation
2 *Continuity*, ensuring that vital functions remain available
3 *Reduce*, deploy measures to diminish the overall adverse effects wherever possible
4 *Rebuild*, focus on assets and provisions for reconstruction and undoing the damage.

Posture

The fourth component of the measure element is posture. *Posture* is the attitude toward scenario-driven uncertainty; one can choose to be reactive or proactive across the different stages of the continuum. A proactive demeanor involves the definition, preparation, and deployment of (Table 8.5):

1 Pre-emptive measures
2 Countermeasures
3 Contingency measures.

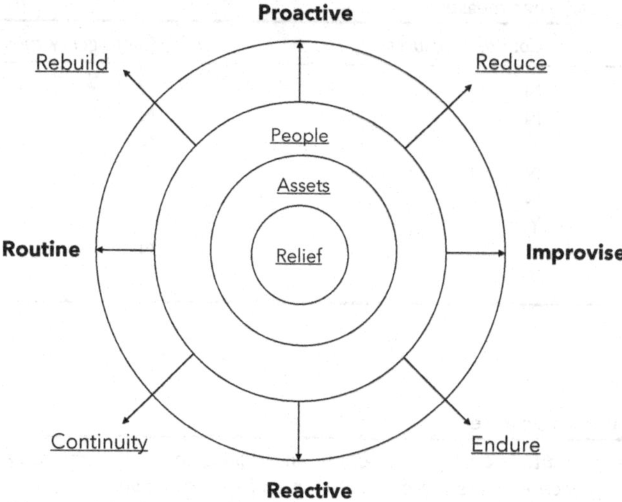

Figure 8.10 Contingency measures in the crisis stage.

Table 8.5 Overview of the available measure per stage

Risk stage	*Problem stage*	*Crisis stage*
Pre-emptive measures: • Accept • Avoid • Mitigate • Transfer	Countermeasures: • Absolve • Resolve • Solve • Dissolve	Contignency measures: • Endure • Reduce • Continuity • Rebuild

Making no preparations (NNN) implies an entirely passive posture, relying on improvisation. A fully active approach supports all measures; for example, in the case of a nuclear power plant, the authorities will demand to prepare plans, standards, and routines for all stages. Each stage has two options, prepare or do nothing, giving 2*2 *2 = 8 possible posture combinations. Note that the problem and crisis stages do not apply if risk avoidance actions are effectively implemented (Tables 8.6 and 8.7).

Techniques

Risk checklist

Risk checklists broaden your horizon, guarding against a narrow risk discovery process and overlooking other areas. The list is based on lessons learned from previous projects and cues to investigate a range of risk types, such as:

Table 8.6 Posture as a combination of different measures

Pre-emptive measures	*Countermeasures*	*Contingency measures*
N	N	N
Y	N	N
Y	Y	N
N	N	Y
Y	N	Y
N	Y	Y
N	Y	N
Y	Y	Y

Table 8.7 Aspects of uncertainty related to posture

Measures	*Posture is the attitude toward event-driven uncertainty; one can choose to be reactive or proactive across the different stages of the continuum.*
Implicit uncertainty	Insensible or ignoring the posture question.
Explicit uncertainty	The most cost-effective combination of options.

- Technology
- Operations
- Finance
- Politics
- Customers
- Business continuity
- Image
- Environment
- Legal.

Risk Response Routine

A fixed procedure when a risk is identified:

- Log an initial description in the uncertainty registry
- Assign a risk owner
- Identify risk triggers that could start a problem
- Assess the risk, probability, likelihood, impact, event recovery, and consequences
- Update the entry
- Decide on a proactive versus reactive approach
- If fully proactive, prepare pre-emptive, counter, and contingency measures
- Add actions to the activity plan or task list
- Identify symptoms indicating that a problem has occurred
- Implement monitoring, if possible
- Create an alert list
- Brief the team.

Ishikawa diagram

An Ishikawa diagram was created by Kaoru Ishikawa, showing the potential causes of a specific event, also called *fishbone diagrams*, due to their shape. They were initially used in product development to ideate the different steps within a given process to determine whether quality control issues can arise related to:

- Workforce
- Machines
- Materials.

Ishikawa diagrams can be used to map risks and risk triggers systematically. For example, stimuli that can cause a flat tire are:

- Riding over a sharp object, like a nail or a piece of glass
- Hitting a curb
- Air valve failure
- A rupture in the rubber walls of the tire
- Overinflation.

Based on the analysis, pre-emptive measures can be designed.

Monte Carlo simulations

A Monte Carlo simulation (MCS) is based on randomly evolving simulations to estimate the values of unknown quantities; for example, the possibility of risks incurring. Decision makers use the technique in a variety of fields to conduct what-if analyses related to:

- Finance and banking
- Portfolio management
- Insurance
- Manufacturing and production
- Engineering
- Logistics and transportation.

A Monte Carlo simulation starts with building a probability distribution model representing all possible results, with a range of values for any factor with inherent uncertainty. Using a random set of input values, the model is run multiple times, using a different set of random values from the input probability distributions. MCS is based on the fact that a random sample exhibits the same properties as the population from which it is drawn. The number of simulations varies from tens to hundreds of thousands depending on the uncertainties related to the value ranges. The result is a range of possible outcomes and their probabilities.

Problem-solving techniques

Various problem-solving techniques exist, some specific to a field or application. The scope of this book is not to provide a comprehensive guide or overview; other more competent authors have done an excellent job already. Most follow a generic approach:

1 Analyze the problem
2 Create a problem statement
3 Devise solution alternatives
4 Select
5 Implement
6 Evaluate.

Principles

Risk is not the sole source of problems

A key thing to realize is that possible adverse events are not the only cause of project problems. Other uncertain factors, such as hidden constraints, dependencies, assumptions, and prerequisites, can result in issues if they are not accounted for in the project plan. Eventually, they will surface during execution and cause trouble. Discovery or becoming aware, however, is not a risk unfolding; the need to incorporate these factors was always there.

Risk awareness starts with defining the secure state

Event-driven uncertainty is a continuum, starting with the secure state where that is inherently safe. Risk awareness begins with knowing your *secure state* as a mental baseline against which risk events can be identified. A boat placed on shore has no danger of sinking. Launching the vessel introduces the risk of going down, while the fire risk existed before. The ship may have problems already past the risk stage, which either become apparent during launch or remain hidden until later during the voyage.

Finding information requires resources

When using a three-point estimate, the *worst-case* number is often associated with things that could go wrong. Remember that finding missing information is another activity that takes up much time—figuring out how to do something and making choices may be more work than the job itself. Typically, in IT, the effort mainly consists of a combination of keystrokes, knowing which ones are the challenge.

Differentiate between issues and problems

Problem and issue are synonymous, but it pays to discriminate between control and creation matters. A *problem* is a creation type of obstacle or shortcoming, like a square peg that needs to fit into a round hole. Other examples are:

- Missing requirements
- Faulty design
- A server unwilling to boot
- Software bugs
- An engine is failing to start.

An *issue* is a control type of complication, dilemma, or dispute. For example:

- Missing resources
- Missing a deadline
- Going over budget.

Provided no penalties are involved, one can solve a missed deadline issue by providing an extension, but a square peg will never fit into a round hole unless something is done about it.

Spotting opportunities is a state of mind

Spotting and capitalizing on opportunities combines attitude and a state of mind. A positive attitude is contagious and transmits from one team member to another. The opposite is also true: When repeatedly confronted with people only discussing risk and problems, it is easy to slide down into a gloomy state of mind and outlook on the world, dominated by trouble and disappointment, inducing a detrimental spiral in a team that can be hard to break out of. Current project problems could result from failure to grab opportunities earlier.

Lack of promptness is the kiss of death to any project

Maintain clear definitions of risks, problems, and crises, their status, and your thresholds. When the situation crosses a predefined limit, act accordingly. Do not mentally stretch these limits by telling yourself 'it isn't that bad.' Addressing a problem while still in infancy can prevent much effort and damage later.

Several triggers do not mean multiple risks

Having several triggers that might cause a problem event to occur does not mean having multiple risks. Overinflation, decaying rubber, hitting a curb, or driving over a sharp object represent the risk of getting a flat tire. Analyzing risk triggers provides a better understanding of the risk probability and helps select preemptive measures.

Problem-solving is not risk mitigation

Risk mitigation reduces the probability and limits the impact before a problem occurs. There should be a logical decision on whether investing time and effort in risk mitigation is the better option to solve the problem. Carrying a spare tire does not diminish the probability of a flat or affect the impact; it is a preparation to fix the problem. Beware of so-called 'risk mitigation measures,' which really are workarounds or fixes for problems.

Risk matrices are mathematical voodoo

One of the tools in traditional project management is called the *risk matrix*. The impact is shown versus the probability using a scale, commonly one through five. An impact with a value of five and a probability of two is multiplied, resulting in a ten. The higher the number, the more substantial the risk. The problem is the scale: Multiplication is only allowed on a ratio scale. A *ratio scale* has a true zero and an equally distanced value between units. The zero is required because zero times some value must be zero. The problem is that our emotions do not follow an equidistant ratio scale.

Try the following experiment, draw a horizontal line with a zero mark on the left. Imagine the following: The lottery calls tell you have won $10 million on your ticket. Make a mark on the line indicating how happy you are. Now imagine the lottery people calling you again. As it happens, you won an additional $10 million on another ticket you bought! Again, set a mark indicating your happiness. Next, determine the interval between zero, your first mark, and the first and second. For most people, the second length is shorter than the first. Although the same event happened twice, the impact is not double, and multiplication has no mathematical meaning.

Imagine lending your pet project, an old-time car you have restored for 20 years, to your beloved daughter. Next, she comes back, crying; the vehicle was involved in an accident and a total loss. You are devastated, ranking the impact five out of five. Then, imagine a police officer coming at the door, sadly informing you that your daughter died in an accident with your classic car. The five-point grief felt now is of another galaxy compared to the previous five points, as you would gladly trash the classic only to get your child back. The previous week's steering committee risk matrix is not comparable to today's, as impact ranges are relative, not absolute.

Avoid the challenge euphemism

Detecting and reporting problems is not a trait of incompetence; hiding or downplaying them is. Some project managers shy the word problem and prefer to use the euphemism 'challenge.' Admitting a problem could easily break the fragile illusion of complete control. Team members avoid the word out of fear of being labeled incompetent. Calling a spade for a spade is vital for a variety of reasons.

For starters, dowsing down a problem can easily result in indifference from the team. Why should the team worry if the leader is relaxed about a problem? Because of indifference, the problem might not get the degree of attention it requires. Most problems tend to grow when left alone, and the cost and time involved in fixing them increases. Therefore, problems must be identified and dealt with as early as possible.

Planning is not hoping for good things to happen

Some might ask: Why only focus on adverse events related to risk, problems, and crisis? What about positive events? First, any known opportunity should automatically be incorporated into the plan; the project should surf on every wave to speed up the course of events. Second, any sound plan is designed to make good things happen.

Artifacts

Uncertainty log

The uncertainty log is a working log continuously maintained with all aspects of uncertainty, such as constraints, working assumptions, issues, risks, problems, open ends, prerequisites, and dependencies. The approved and working version of the project plan is constantly validated, whether it is still realistic to proceed along the chosen path or the need for re-planning exists based on newly acquired information and insights.

Risk response plan

The risk response plan contains detailed steps for implementing pre-emptive, counter, and contingency measures, including required time and cost updates. The extra resources needed may warrant a formal project change request to acquire funding and manning.

Concepts

Risk and problem
Problem and issue
Problem and crisis
Risk and opportunity
Risk event and problem event
Risk telltale and trigger
Risk impact and recovery
Risk impact and consequence
Decision and assessment
Risk mitigation and risk avoidance
Risk probability and risk likelihood
Composite and cumulative risk
Pre-emptive measures and countermeasures
Countermeasure and contingency measure
Favorable conditions and a window of opportunity.

Questions

1 Are risks, problems, and crises being tracked?
2 Does your organization use risk matrices or heat maps? If yes, why?
3 What quantitative risk analysis methods are being used?
4 Is there a risk response routine?
5 Are there cases of false mitigation in the risk register?

Reference

Jozwiak et al. 2015 *Aviation 2015* 19, no. 1:1–6.

Part II: Strategies

Introduction

Know your enemy, and you have half won the battle, stated Sun Tzu. In Part I, project uncertainty was defined by creating a system model and projecting the uncertainty matrix over the elements. Now that we know what we are against, the next question is what to do about it. Imagine being a godlike creature, capable of knowing everything about a project regarding the past, present, and future. For a god, no uncertainty exists; the matrix consists of the known-known field only. Total knowledge is impossible for humans as we cannot foresee the future, but uncertainty reduction is a reasonable, achievable, and economically sensible goal. In Part II, we will focus on the following strategies:

1 Raising information awareness
2 Increasing information availability
3 Improving the effective use of information
4 Maximizing information efficiency.

Theoretical models, practical techniques, and plans are presented to implement these strategies for practitioners in the field.

DOI: 10.4324/9781003431961-11

Chapter 9

Raising information awareness

Introduction

When writing this book, it was announced that two top Spanish transport officials resigned over a failed train project that cost nearly $275 million. The trains were too broad to fit into the tunnels of the northern regions of Asturias and Cantabria, which are not a standard size (Spender, 2023). Another case: In 2022, it became evident that the long-awaited Norwegian search and rescue helicopters were too heavy and could only land on 7 out of 21 emergency hospital landing platforms (Thrane, 2022). Both projects have in common that they are multi-million dollar government projects, with watchdog agencies looking over their shoulder. How is it possible that glaring, obvious information was overlooked? (Figure 9.1)

Temporary or partial blindness was the subject of the book *The Invisible Gorilla* by Christopher Chabris and Daniel Simons (2010). The French psychologists conducted experiments where they showed a short film where two basketball teams make passes to one another, one group dressed in black and the other in white shirts. The viewers are instructed to count the number of passes the team in white makes. A person dressed in a

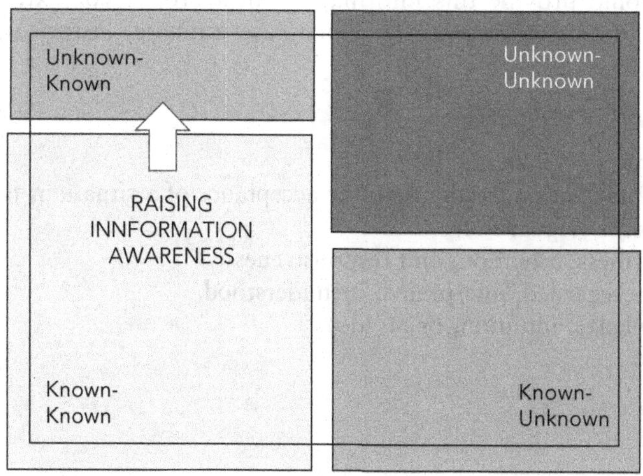

Figure 9.1 The first uncertainty reduction strategy is raising information awareness.

DOI: 10.4324/9781003431961-12

gorilla suit walks through the scene at some stage. Although the gorilla is in plain view, most audience members are so engrossed in their counting activity that they fail to spot it.

Inattentional blindness is a side effect of our ability to focus. Our senses process constant impressions, but you sometimes need to shut things out to get things done. There is a flip side to focusing, project teams can experience reduced awareness or 'information blindness,' sometimes caused by a strong focus on tasks that takes all their attention. The good news is that most people receiving an advanced warning pick the gorilla up immediately and complete their counting task.

An old Dutch saying says: An alerted person counts for two. This research finding is the foundation of the project meta-data technique. By pre-defining critical information, you can dramatically improve the chances of picking up relevant information as the project unfolds. Creating a project meta-data model acts as a pre-warning similar to mentioning a possible gorilla entering the scene. While focusing on the necessary tasks to make the project successful, you keep a keen eye on any essential information passing through the project. This chapter examines raising information awareness by creating a mental model of project meta information.

Definitions

Data is a collection of facts, such as text, numbers, images, or symbols, that do not have significance, meaning, or purpose.

Information is knowledge gained through analysis, research, and interpretation of data within a context.

Meta-data is high-level information about other data, from the Greek μετά, meta, and when used as a prefix, means 'more comprehensive' or 'transcending.' Meta-data is a description of what the data means, but not the content of the message or information itself. When a log states that the car speed is 56, is that 56 miles per hour or kilometers? Are we looking at the speed at a certain point in time, average, or maximum? The meta-data, data about the data, would provide this information. In a project context, 550 work hours could refer to a best-case, most likely, worst-case estimate, historical, or actual number.

Elements

Awareness is the realization, appreciation, recognition, or acceptance of a situation, facts, emotions, experiences, or patterns (Figure 9.2).
Consciousness is a state of alertness, attention, and responsiveness.
Perception is how something is regarded, interpreted, or understood.
Cognition is a sensation, knowledge, intuition, or an idea.

Techniques

Power Kanban

Power Kanban is a combination of project meta data technique and a Kanban board. I created the project meta-data technique (PMDT) for two reasons: One, I have a terrible

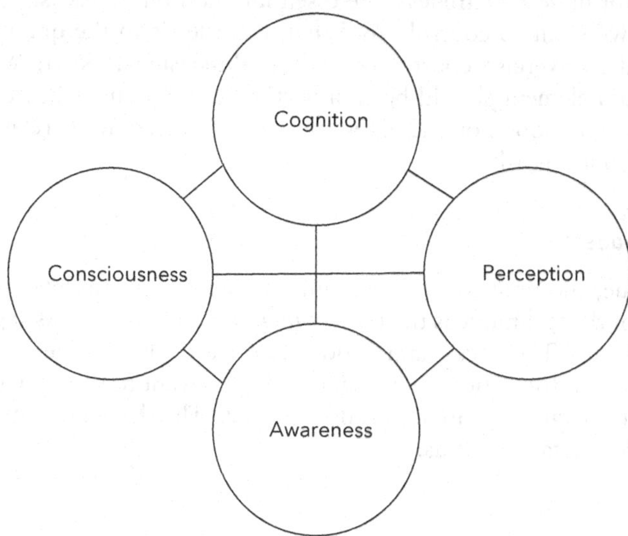

Figure 9.2 The elements of thinking.

memory, and two, I once had a portfolio of 15 small projects and struggled to keep track of things. My role in these projects was merely as an expediter firing tickets into an anonymous IT support system, hoping someone would pick them up. There were many activities to keep track of, and the realization pace was plodding, as the parent organization was a sizeable oil company. Typically, some two months after initiation, a person would inform that a particular task was completed. By then, I had forgotten what the activity was about.

I habitually began to log meta-level information gained in conversations, e-mails, correspondence, and meetings by asking the question: What is the implication of this new information for the project? Is it a task to be done, a constraint affecting the plan, a dependency to factor in, a problem that must be solved, or a decision to be made? The working log approach eventually crystallized into a meta-data model of information types. The log records enabled me to quickly switch contexts and pick up the thread in a project. As a secondary effect, the mental model dramatically increased information awareness, improving the ability to spot essential information moving like monkeys through the scene. At some point, the realization came that the meta-level information structures were generic despite differences in the project assignment.

Creating a mental blueprint of meta-data information will help you to recognize and capture critical information. After a while, picking up cues and recognizing information types becomes an unconscious action like breathing. For example, when a team member raises a question on a topic, and the answer starts with the words 'I think that,' my immediate reaction would be to check whether he is referring to a fact or making an assumption. When someone reports 'having a challenge,' the follow-up question would be whether we are discussing a problem, a constraint, a dependency, or just a job that needs to be done. If someone expresses concern, it could indicate a risk.

When it comes to raising information awareness, the essential question to ask is: What dimensions of the projects do we want to control? And that again leads to the question: What information do we need to exercise control over these dimensions? Next: What relevant attributes of a meta-data element should be captured? The technique is based on the principle that knowing what to look for increases the chances of spotting relevant information, like a heads-up about a gorilla.

Step 1: Create a meta-data model

Although all projects are unique, the premise is that a finite number of meta-data types governs all projects. The heart of the technique is the *project meta-data model*, consisting of meta-data elements and attributes. The meta-data model does not contain the actual information but information about information. For example, do you want to keep track of deliverables? You do. But what information attributes do we need? The deliverable meta-data element could typically have details such as:

- Unique deliverable name
- Team lead responsible
- Approver
- Acceptance criteria
- Work hour estimates (planned, actual)
- Status (not started, in progress, completed, approved).

The meta-data of a decision could look something like this:

- Description
- Owner
- Type (urgent or important)
- Reach (local or global)
- If important, the latest point in time the decision must be made.

Other examples of meta-data structures: A *prerequisite* (PRQ) is a mandatory or essential condition that must be in place before an activity can commence, a problem is solved, or a decision can be made. Typical meta-data attributes are <description>, <latest time in place>, and <owner>. *Constraints* (CON) are either hard or soft in <nature>, <limit> and can be applicable from a certain point in <time>, or <period>. *Interdependencies* (IDP) are reliance on third parties, like other projects, programs, agencies, or suppliers outside the direct control of a project, and can be hard or soft in <nature>. When a company is the sole supplier of a patented product, delivery is a hard interdependency.

Risks (RKS) are given either a top-list <classification>, implying that proactive posture is required, or part of the watch list. A *watch-list* risk means a reactive attitude, but it is not forgotten, and an <owner> is assigned in both cases. *Top-list* risks require a <pre-emptive measure>, a <latest implementation time>, and an <responsible> in charge of the implementation of actions. *Problems* (PRB) can be urgent or important in <nature> and require an <owner>, <counter-measure>, and <latest point in time> to be solved. *Demands* governing activities (DMD) are hard or soft in <nature>, and have an <owner>.

A *crisis* (CRS) requires a <contingency measure>, <owner>. *Open Ends* (OED) are known-unknowns where the exact information is not available right now but can be investigated or researched. For example, an expert must fly in with spare parts to solve an urgent problem. When is the first available flight to the site? What is the arrival time, and what is the cost? Finding out this information is a task with a <question>, <owner>, <status>, <latest point in time>, and an <answer>. Making a *working assumption* (WAS) requires a <description>, an <earliest possible time> for verification, and an <owner>. *Decisions* (DCS) can be of a control or creation <type>, urgent or important in <nature>, have a <status>, an <owner>, and <alternatives> to choose from.

The list may dazzle you at first, but there is a trick to remember. An analogy is that of a compass: The needle consists of epics, decisions, deliverables, activities, and tasks (see Figure 9.3). Realizing epics requires decision making, and decisions determine the deliverables. The epic of a zero-emission house requires a choice (DCS) between wind and solar power; with a turbine or solar panels as main deliverables (DEL). Deliverables are the hub on which the needle rotates, as progress in projects can only be measured in approved deliverables. Creating deliverables requires activities (ACT), that can be split up into one-person tasks (TSK).

The *North group* contains the main elements of the business case, drivers (DRV) stakeholders (STK), and benefits (BEN), and acts as a reference. Without a valid business case, being stakeholders seeing drivers addressed and receiving benefits, there is no project. The *East group* contains prerequisites (PRQ), constraints (CON), and dependencies (DEP). The East is where the sun comes up, and the day starts. Mentally point the needle to the East, and whenever making a decision, define a deliverable or plan an activity; ask yourself: What

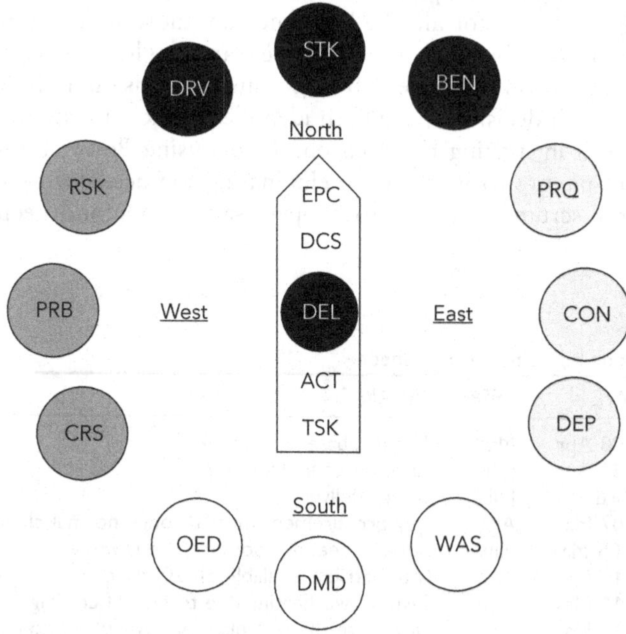

Figure 9.3 The project meta-data technique.

prerequisites, constraints and dependencies are we dealing with? Pointing the needle down is where things go South; it is the tricky domain of working assumptions (WAS) like estimates, demands (DMD), and open ends (OED). The West is where the sun goes down, mentally swing the compass needle and evaluate what risks (RKS), problems (PRB), and crises (CRS) we might have to deal with before the day is over.

Step 2 Create a working log

The second step is to create a working log to capture newly discovered information. In its simplest form, it can be a spreadsheet made available on a share (Table 9.1), or a Kanban board application, for example JIRA. Kanban applications typically have standard ticket types for SCRUM, such as epics, use cases, user stories, tasks, features, issues, and bugs. Create additional ticket types for each meta-data type according to the meta-data model. For example, constraints, dependencies, risks, and issues each have their own card or item type, allowing for filtering. Essentially you are building a product backlog containing different information items relevant to the project, in addition to use cases and user stories.

Next, create dashboards per meta-data type, enabling teams to analyze the project from a specific perspective. For example, a dashboard summarizing all (open) decisions, prerequisites, dependencies, or constraints. Prioritize the backlog items according to urgency and logical sequence. The most urgent problems or decisions go on top, following a logical order going down the list. The advantage of a single working log with dashboards is that all information is available in one place, replacing traditional separate decisions, risks, and issue logs. Also, the different information elements can be linked to epics, releases, or components, providing a complete picture of the status in a single pane.

Create separate boards for each SCRUM or project team, or per project when working in programs. By making boards accessible for all, the left hand can know what the right hand does. For example, a decisions may be local, involving one team, or global, where the outcome affects multiple teams engaged in the project. By accessing the decision dashboard for the project, anyone can see which decisions have been identified, which are still open, who owns it, and who is involved in making the decision. Teams using Power Kanban create a near real time common picture to work from, eliminating the need for tedious status meetings, or waiting for a scrum of scrums to happen, saving time and keeping momentum.

Table 9.1 Example of a project working log using a spreadsheet

ITEM	*DEL*	*STATUS*	*DATE*	*RESP*	*REMARKS*
ISSUE	Design	Open	L 08 Apr	Mark	The database is to small
CON	Software	Action	L 23 Apr	John	Alan, on course week 43
DEP	System	Open	Hard	Julia	Server delivery
DEM	Procure	Action	L 07 May	Alan	Any procurement must through normal channels
TTD	Planning	Action	T 08 May	Paul	Book a meeting room for the review
OE	Planning	Open	L 10 May	Paul	Is the atrium available on 20 May?
RISK	Top List	Action	L 11 May	Paul	System overheating due to lack of cooling
TTD	Planning	Done	L 16 May	Jay	Distribute the test plan for review and comment
PRQ	BC	Resolved	L 10 Feb	SC	Business case approval

Step 3: Follow the SLACK cycle

Power Kanban involves continuous scanning, logging, and information assessment activities, or SLACK cycle: Scan, log, assess, change, keep. *Scanning* involves eliciting information through conversations, discussions, investigations, reviews, meetings, and workshops. Ask follow-up questions regarding the classification and any attributes. Relevant information is categorized and *logged* initially in the working log or directly into the appropriate document. An *assessment* is made regarding the impact or consequences of the uncovered information on the existing approach, plans, situation, and business case. *Change* involves adaptation to plans, and a conscious decision must be made to *keep* existing plans or documents intact in light of emerging information or discard them (Figure 9.4).

The working log provides a litmus test for the current plan's degree of realism, feasibility, and accuracy. Use the working log as a structured means to regularly review and bulletproof your project plans. Select all unaddressed prerequisites, problems, issues, constraints, and dependencies, and assess their impact on the current plans. For example, if a team member is attending a course in week 43, check which assignments are affected by this constraint. Keep an approved and working version of the plans, and update the working version accordingly. A *project change request* is required if the deviations exceed the scope, time, and budget demands. Changes to the contract are achieved through a *variation order*. The working log also functions as a running *history log* of the project and a *handover* or *onboarding checklist*.

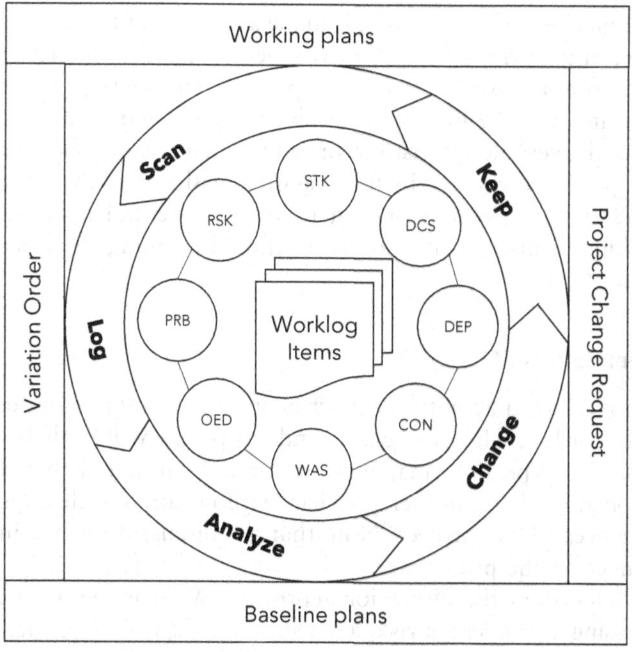

Figure 9.4 Filtering and finding relevant information through linking.

Step 4 Linking and filtering

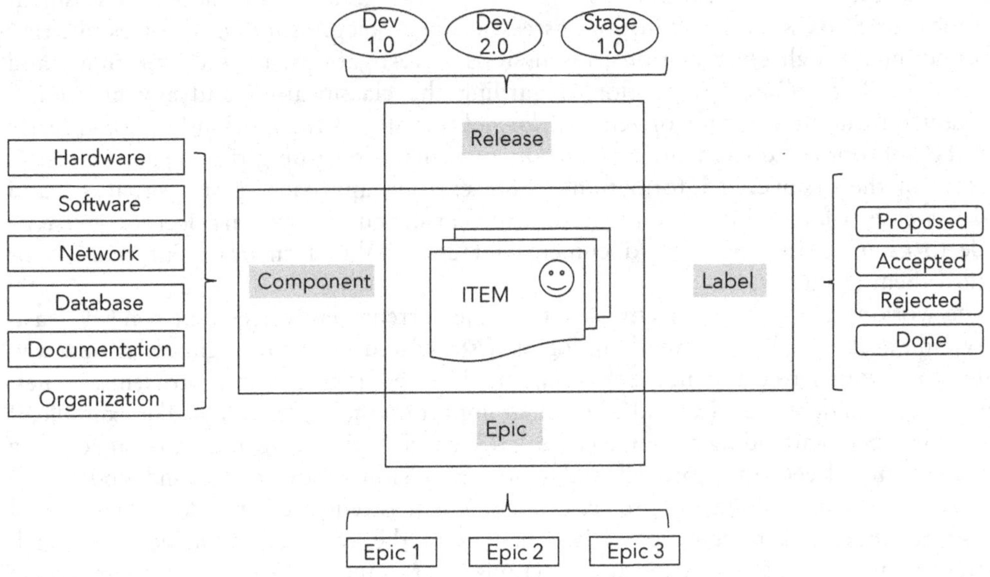

Figure 9.5 Working the Kanban board requires continuous information processing and updates.

Power Kanban works in two ways, first it tricks the mind to help spotting information. Second, using smart linking of board items information is made available. Entering items in a working log is relatively easy, finding the information you need is another matter. As a minimum, link an item to an epic, if possible, to a component representing a project deliverable. In the case of software, add the item to a release. Making smart use of labels enables you to track the status of deliverables, decisions, or requirements across the project. Team members can create their personal worklog by filtering items assigned to them. When conducting sprint planning, select the epic to work on to see all essential information clustered as an input for making realistic plans for realization by taking all essential information into account (Figure 9.5).

Application 1: Minutes of Meeting (MoM)

Making minutes of meetings is a dreaded activity for most people. Two approaches exist: Recording and interpretation. Recording is labor intensive and few people will likely bother to read the extensive minutes. The typical format is as follows: John stated this, Jane disagreed, then the conversation turned to another problem without any conclusions regarding the impact or consequences of the project. Note that the discussion is not interesting, but the outcome and effect on the project are.

The meta-level question is: What does the discussion represent? What is the meta-data element involved? Are we discussing a problem, a risk, a constraint, a dependency, a task to be done, a stakeholder, or a demand? PMDT is an excellent help to create minutes of meetings, translate the discussion to meta-data level, and log in real time using abbreviations and shorthand, enabling you to review and send the MoMs once the meeting has ended.

Taking the meta-data perspective also helps manage conversations, even if the content is highly specialist. I must admit that in-depth technical discussions are often lost on me. Although I may not understand the exact content, I have learned to listen to specific keywords and phrases, like 'I think that... ... .' This makes you wonder, does the person know or merely assume? Look at body language, facial expressions, and listen to the tone of the voice. If a person appears worried or concerned, is there an undiscovered risk or problem that must be articulated?

Regularly summarize your notes during a meeting, and do not be afraid to state that you are lost in a discussion. If confused, ask meta-level questions like: What are we discussing now? Does this represent a risk, a problem, or merely a job that needs to be done? Are we dealing with a constraint or a dependency? Are we assuming, or do we know this for a fact? Let the team dictate what the MoMs say, and facilitate by providing meta-level options. Once the nature of the information is explicit, assess the implications and update the plan.

Analyze the statement, determine what it is, and any follow-up actions, e.g., an ISSUE could be followed up by a TASK to implement a solution or a RISK followed by a TASK to implement mitigations. Note that a single statement can result in multiple working log items.

1 I talked to the PMO. They mentioned that there is a new template for the business case that is mandatory.
2 The I/O for the database is too low; we need to review the design. Upgrading will be a cost, so I guess we need customer approval.
3 By the way, the procurement department mentioned that our hardware supplier warned of extended delivery times due to COVID.
4 We need to review a contract, but we have no one from legal on our team.
5 I heard that John is getting married next month. We should do something together, like drinks and a present.
6 Since no acceptance criteria are mentioned in the contract, we can deliver whatever we want and do not have to do any testing!
7 We think that the design will take, best case, 200 hours, most likely 220, and worst case, 350.
8 Any procurement must follow standard procedures and requires written project owner approval.
9 We need to land a migration strategy soon, the platform is almost ready, and the customer is uneasy.
10 Kim has not responded to the meeting; it seems he never does.
11 Maybe we could use a Kanban board to keep track of our tasks?
12 I was wondering, how can we know whether our solution will do the job?
13 If the supplier delivers the servers too late, our deadline will be impossible.
14 We have no idea when the network department will take our tickets.

Application 2: Analyzing a document

The top-level document for a customer project is the contract, containing essential information as input for the plans. Analyze the agreement by putting the helpful mnemonics in the text.

CONSTRUCTION AGREEMENT

This agreement was made on 23 July 2023 between Mr. P. Johnson (Owner) and Prefab Ltd (Contractor) for the construction project known as Cape Cod House Regent Street 12.

The Contractor shall complete all work stated in the Scope of Work, generally described as a Cape Cod Villa and a garage, reference blueprints provided by the Owner in Annex A. The work shall commence upon receipt of a Notice to Proceed from the Owner, and the lead time is six months to delivery. Because of neighbor considerations, work will be conducted on weekdays between 7 AM and 5 PM, Monday through Friday.

The Owner has secured all documents related to property acquisitions and shall advise the Contractor of the boundaries of the Owner's property. The Owner shall provide connections to establish sewer, water, electric, and telephone lines. Based upon Applications for Payment submitted by the Contractor, the Owner shall make monthly payments. The Owner shall retain fifteen percent (15%) of each amount certified for payment until final payment.

The Contractor shall supervise and direct the Work, using Contractor's best skill and attention. The Contractor shall be solely responsible for all construction methods, techniques, sequences, procedures, and means for coordinating all portions of the work under this contract. Unless otherwise explicitly noted, the Contractor shall provide and pay for all labor, expertise, materials, freight/delivery equipment, tools, construction equipment and machinery, water, heat, utilities, transportation, and other facilities and services necessary for the proper execution and completion of the work.

The Contractor shall enforce strict discipline and order among his employees and shall not employ on the work any unfit or unskilled person in the task assigned to him. The Contractor shall comply with all OSHA and trade-related rules and regulations. The Contractor shall provide the OWNER a list of the names of subcontractors proposed for the central portions of the work. The Contractor shall not employ any Subcontractor to whom the Owner has an objection. The Contractor shall not be required to hire any Subcontractor to whom he has an objection. Contracts between the Contractor and the Subcontractor shall be in line with the terms of this Agreement and shall include the General Conditions of this Agreement insofar as applicable.

After analysis, the contract could look like this:

This agreement was made on 23rd July 2023 between **STK** Mr. P. Johnson (Owner) and **STK** Prefab Ltd (Contractor) for the construction project known as **DEL** Cape Cod House Regent Street 12.

The Contractor shall complete all work stated in the **DEL** Scope of Work, generally described as a **DEL** Cape Cod Villa and a **DEL** garage, reference **DEL** blueprints provided by the Owner in Annex A. The work shall commence upon receipt of a **PRQ** Notice to Proceed from the Owner, and the lead time is **CON** six months to delivery. Because of neighbor considerations, work will be conducted on **CON** weekdays between 7 AM and 5 PM, Monday through Friday.

The Owner has secured all **PRQ** documents related to property acquisitions and shall advise **TSK** the Contractor of the **CON** boundaries of the Owner's property. The Owner shall provide **DEL** connections to establish sewer, water, electric, and telephone lines. Based upon **DEL** Applications for Payment submitted by the Contractor, the Owner shall make **DEL** monthly payments. The Owner shall retain **DED** fifteen percent (15%) of each amount certified for payment until **DEL** final payment.

The Contractor shall **TSK** supervise and direct the Work, using Contractor's best skill **DEM** and attention. The Contractor shall be solely responsible **DCS** for all construction methods, techniques, sequences, procedures, and means for coordinating all portions of the work under this contract. Unless otherwise explicitly noted, the Contractor shall provide and pay for all **DEL** labor, expertise, materials, freight/delivery equipment, tools, construction equipment and machinery, water, heat, utilities, transportation, and other facilities and services necessary for the proper execution and completion of the work.

The Contractor shall enforce **DEM** strict discipline and order among his employees and shall not employ on the work any **PRQ** unfit or unskilled person in the task assigned to him. The Contractor shall comply with **PRQ** all OSHA and trade-related rules and regulations. The Contractor shall provide to the OWNER a **DEL** list of the names of subcontractors proposed for the main portions of the work. The Contractor shall not employ **CON** any Subcontractor to whom the Owner has an objection. The Contractor shall not be required to **CON** employ any Subcontractor to whom he has an objection. Contracts between the Contractor and the Subcontractor shall be in line **REQ** with the terms of this Agreement and shall include the General Conditions of this Agreement insofar as applicable.

Legend:

STK	Stakeholder
DEL	Deliverable
TSK	Task
PRQ	Prerequisite
DEM	Demand
CON	Constraint
REQ	Requirement
DCS	Decision

Extract the items from the contract into the working list and group per category to provide an overview. The discovered items are input into the various plans.

Principles

It is easy to miss something you are not looking for

You might have seen landscape pictures with the statement: Find the sniper. A camouflaged sniper hides in the bushes, trees, plants, sticks, and stones. However, expert camouflage makes them impossible to detect without special training; another sniper would see the telltales of a hidden opponent based on knowing what to look for, combined with experience based on years of training. As the aphorism goes: It takes one to know one. Constructing a mental metadata model is the first step in understanding what to look for; practice is the other. Eventually, picking up essential information will become an unconscious habit like breathing.

Beware of the activity trap

Another detrimental effect, besides temporary blindness, is the 'activity trap.' Peter F. Drucker first described this phenomenon in his book *The Practice of Management* (Drucker 1993). The team gets so engrossed in their current activities that they lose sight of their original objectives regarding project results, benefits, and contribution to the vision. Whatever the activity, ask yourself: What is the deliverable here? Second, how does the deliverable address drivers, and provide benefits for stakeholders, or the North reference.

Project work is messy by nature.

Although project meta-data technique sounds like a nice and clean process, in practice, it is erratic, like a pinball bumping into and bouncing off things all the time in any direction:

- While looking for a resource to do a task, you discover a new stakeholder, the boss (stakeholder register update)
- The boss points out some requirements that are missing in the opinion in the project (result breakdown structure update)
- Provides guidelines on how the person prefers to work (demands, working log update)
- While informing you that the person in question plans to get married in two weeks, and a three-week holiday has been granted (constraint, uncertainty log update)
- The planned absence initiates the need for a stand-in to cover the honeymoon period (stakeholder update), and a handover (task plan update)
- Upon request, the boss provides the hourly rate (budget update).

Prepare for information overflow.

Especially at the beginning of a project, you will get a large amount of seemingly random information thrown at you. The key to handling this continuous flow of information is to establish a working version of a plan for each area, e.g., a stakeholder register, result breakdown structure, PERT plan, budget, and uncertainty log at the very start of the project. Subsequently, every bit of information you have or uncover can be categorized into an information model element, resulting in an update or a change in an accompanying sub-plan.

Minimize the meta-data elements.

Avoid creating extensive meta-data models; large models make the cure worse than the pain. As a guideline, more than 20 meta-data elements are too much. If the granularity is too high, searching for an appropriate meta-data type becomes a chore defying the purpose. Restrict yourself to essential elements like constraints, dependencies, risks, and problems. When you are faced with creating a new element or an attribute, start with the attribute option and see if this works out. For example, a resource is an attribute to a task or activity rather than an element.

Working assumptions are a necessary evil.

Although often frowned upon, making assumptions cannot always be avoided. When writing a business case or a project plan, the steering committee expects you to present projections about the cost and expected benefits in hard numbers, estimates that are working assumptions until confirmed to be true. All plans are elaborate working assumptions about how you believe things could evolve, and time will show whether you were right. The rules for working assumptions are as follows:

- Only assume if you must
- Be conscious about assuming
- Log the assumption
- Assign an owner
- Determine the earliest point in time when the assumption can be verified.

Working assumptions are one of the most critical meta-data objects, spot, and log, as making them comes naturally, and the fact that they were made is quickly forgotten. Note that assumptions can be complex structures. When you wrote down that the work hours estimate for a task was 60, remember that you had John's experience in mind, with him having a good day, being able to work undisturbed, and with all tools and materials in place. Write it down, and make a calendar note or task on the earliest verification date.

Uncovering a known-unknown is uncertainty reduction.

Discovering yet another known-unknown and adding it to a growing list may not seem like much progress, but it is progress as it provides improved visibility on what to work with.

Master the one-breath challenge.

If you cannot articulate the difference between a constraint and a dependency on a conceptual level, it is unlikely that you can recognize the meta-data type in daily hectic project life. Practice the one-breath challenge as the skill of defining accurate and granular concepts support the project meta-data technique.

Artifacts

Project meta-data model
Abbreviation list
Project working log
Minutes of meeting.

Concepts

Cognition and perception
Awareness and consciousness
Data and meta-data
Data and information
Prerequisite and precondition
Assumption and working assumption
Demand and constraint.

Questions

1 Create a meta-data model that captures the information needs of your current project.
2 Set up a document structure to support the SLACK cycle.

References

Chabris, C.F., and D.J. Simons. 2010. *The Invisible Gorilla: How Our Intuitions Deceive Us*, New York: Random House

Drucker, P.F. 1993. *The Practice of Management*, New York: HarperCollins

Spender, T. 2023. *Spain officials quit over trains that were too wide for tunnels*, *BBC News*. [online] BBC. Available at: https://www.bbc.com/news/world-europe-64717605

Thrane, K.T. 2022. *Norges Nye Redningshelikopter Kan Fortsatt Ikke Lande i Oslo*, *NRK*. fra-sea-king-fra-12.-desember-_-men-kan-ikke-lande-over-alt-1.16215536 64717605 [Accessed: April 15, 2023].

Chapter 10

Maximizing information availability

Introduction

The second strategy to maximize the known-known area is to increase information availability by moving the availability line in the uncertainty matrix to the right. A known-unknown is information you want to know but do not have. The premise is that any known-unknown information not confirmed positively as a fact is an assumption, and the rules for working assumptions apply: Log, assign an owner, and determine the first opportunity for validation. In this chapter, we will structure the known-unknown information into distinct categories and use calculations, simulations, and models to create forecasts or hypothesis that can be tested to reduce uncertainty (Figure 10.1).

The first category is open ends, referring to information that might not be available in the spur of the moment but can be obtained through investigation. The next differentiator is information about future events, which may be deterministic or stochastic. The outcome of phenomena that follow natural laws can be calculated. For example, the time of sunrise in your present position twenty years from now is deterministic. Although the movement of the planets can be accurately predicted for years, the ten-day weather is a combination of forecasting based on observations collected from satellites and ground stations across the globe and fed into stochastic models. Stochastic events or systems require computer models

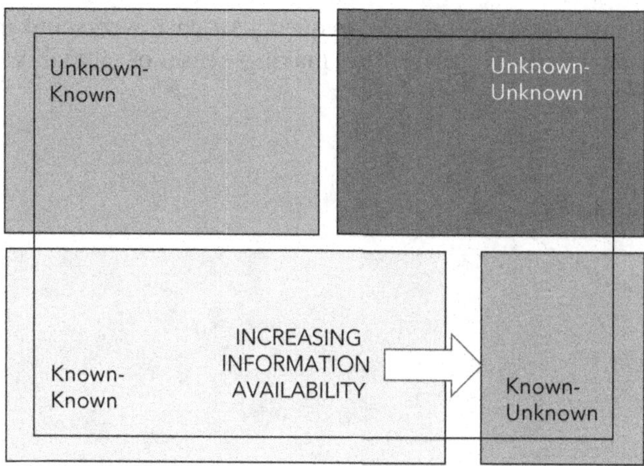

Figure 10.1 Uncertainty reduction strategy number two is to increase information availability.

DOI: 10.4324/9781003431961-13

to consider families of random variables to provide insight into the likelihood of scenarios occurring.

Beyond calculations, forecasts, and simulations, the last resort is to hypothesize. Any project is unique and uncertain, but we can ask generic questions and use models to rationalize about the answer. For example, the strategic contribution of a project can be visualized using the four-phase model, which presents archetypes of strategies. This chapter will give a set of universal questions regarding any project and introduce models to make hypotheses providing preliminary answers to be confirmed during project execution.

Definitions

A *prediction* is a statement about what you think will happen based on subjective considerations. Anyone can predict anything, and it does not require knowledge or skills, or information. For example, a 5-year-old might predict that aliens will land in New York Times Square on May 25, 2032.

A *forecast* is an estimation of a future event incorporating and projecting forward data related to the past in a pre-determined and systematic manner.

Interpolation is finding intermediate data points based on a discrete set of known data points (Figure 10.2).

Extrapolation in mathematics is estimating values of a variable beyond the original observation range or applying human experience to project, extend, or expand the known expertise into an area not known or previously experienced.

Regression is finding the best fit between data points to determine the mathematical function that best describes the observations.

A *deterministic* model produces the same results for a set of inputs based on a formula, logic, or algorithm. For example, converting degrees Fahrenheit to Celsius and back.

A *probabilistic model* is the opposite, predicting the likelihood of future events in a random process or experiment, like rolling a die.

Probability and statistics are similar when analyzing the *relative frequency of events;* however, *probability* deals with predicting the likelihood of future events based on a theoretical and ideal world.

On the other hand, *statistics* involves analyzing the frequency of past events and measuring the extent to which our world is perfect by making sense of actual world

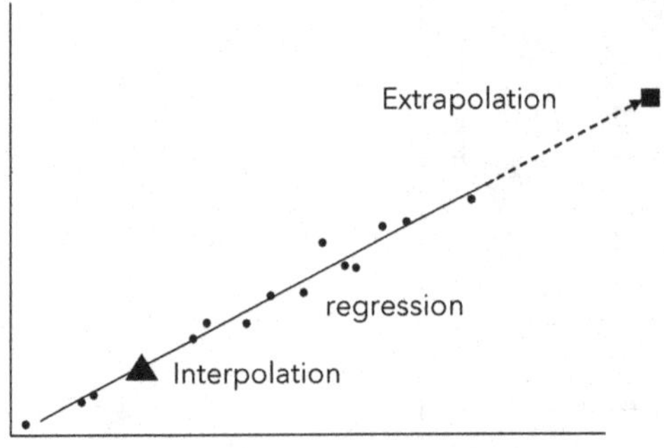

Figure 10.2 Interpolation, extrapolation, and regression.

observations. For example, in probability theory, the chances of a die are 1/6; the statistical perspective is to roll the dice multiple times and see whether the dice is accurate or loaded. In summary, probability theory enables us to find the consequences of a given ideal world, while the statistical approach allows us to measure the extent to which our world is perfect.

Stochastic models present data that predicts outcomes while accounting for certain levels of randomness in the phenomenon. A stochastic process is a collection of random variables, often used to represent the evolution of some random property or system over time.

Stochasticity and randomness differ in that the former refers to the modeling approach, and *randomness* relates to phenomena themselves, although in practice, these two terms are often used synonymously.

Elements

Investigation

The *investigation* systematically collects objective facts while discarding false information, eliminating uncertainty. The starting point for analysis is the project drivers, ensuring that projects are initiated for the right reasons. It is not uncommon that the problem definition changes as the project evolves. Another variant is that the initial assignment covers but a small part of a more significant problem. Alternatively, other matters must be fixed before the initial issue can be addressed (Figure 10.3).

The next logical step is investigating whether the project has been done before, within or outside your organization. A common bias is to believe that the parent company is unique and implicitly its projects. See what can be learned from others regarding solutions, estimates, things to do, and things not. Also, check all information sources. Is the current knowledge based on facts, assumptions, or presumptions? Information from top management can come with authority, but that does not automatically make it true or accurate.

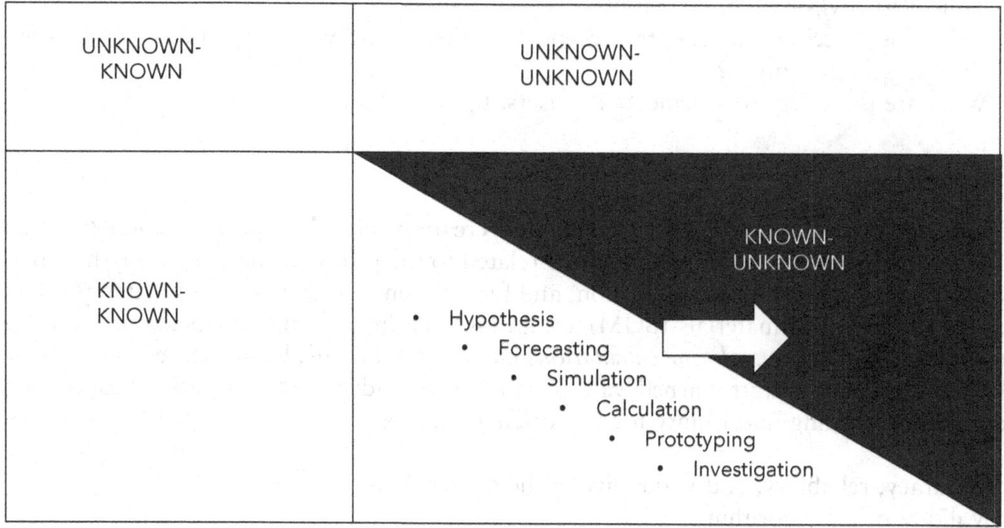

Figure 10.3 Approaches to rationalize about known-unknowns.

Prototyping

When a solution's technical workings, feasibility, or safety are in doubt, a prototype is created to prove the idea can work. The prototyping process develops an idea for a new product or service into a functional production item. A prototype can either focus on the workings or functionality, alternatively, on the production process. A prototype demonstrating feasibility has limited features; only the questioned functionality is implemented and often made to scale to reduce building time and cost. A *mock-up* is a scale or full-size product or system model used for demonstration, design evaluation, or promotion but contains no functional parts. Typical prototyping methods are:

1 *Physical modeling* to make a realistic representation using materials like wood, clay, cardboard, craft paper, or 3D printing, either to scale or full size
2 *Wireframe* is a standard prototype for websites, software user interfaces, or digital tools, showing the navigation structure and content and providing a first impression of how users interact
3 *Virtual or augmented reality* enables users to walk through a construction or production site using virtual reality goggles to assess the design from different angles at full scale
4 *Video animation* visualizes the product as an animated video or explains its use
5 As the investment and threshold for coding are low, a *software demonstrator* containing the key features of the final product.

Questions to consider regarding prototyping are:

- What is the purpose of the prototype? Feasibility, demonstrator, promotion, or training
- Who is the audience? Users, designers, managers, executives, or investors, and what is their primary interest
- What are the testing conditions to demonstrate use, design flaws, and wear? Laboratory, controlled environment, or real-life
- What does success look like, the acceptance criteria, and what constitutes a reason for changing the prototype?
- What are the safety requirements for users, bystanders, and the environment?

Calculations

Calculations come in two types: Control and creation related. Typical *creation types of calculations* are engineering computations related to the project's domain: Strength, force, elasticity, torque, heat loss, combustion, and fuel efficiency. Calculations of material needs related to the bill of materials (BOM) are an essential input into cost calculations on the control side. Other *control-type calculations* include work hours, lead time, resource needs, slack earliest, latest start, earned value, actual cost, and benefits. Generic questions or comments regarding uncertainty for any calculation are:

- Accuracy, reliability, and variability of the source data
- Validity of the algorithm
- Is the calculation done correctly?

- Are there alternative ways or different algorithms available to calculate the property?
- What if the answers from different algorithms deviate?
- Does the answer make sense, and is it helpful?

Simulation

The difference between simulation and forecast is that *simulation* is about mathematical models that epitomize natural world conditions, operations, events, or the actual behavior of a system, while a *forecast* is an estimation of a future state. Is the phenomenon governed by laws or random? A subtype is a chaotic system; although following rules, a slight difference in initial conditions can yield significant diverging outcomes making long-term behavior prediction of the system impossible in general.

Lorenz (1963) defined *chaos* as when the present determines the future, but the approximate present does not approximately determine the future. For example, a different release position of a pendulum will convey a different evolution of motion, even though the natural law governing the movement is constant and no random elements are involved. The initial condition may also change due to measurement errors or rounding errors in the model, resulting in diverging outcomes that can make deterministic systems unpredictable (Figure 10.4).

A *static model* provides a snapshot of the process at a specific moment, while dynamic models represent a changing phenomenon developing over time. The outputs of static models solely depend on the inputs and model variables. On the other hand, *dynamic models* consider inputs from the current time and previous points in time, implying that the variables in dynamic models are functions of time. Static models do not factor in process evolution, so they are unsuitable for dynamic processes. For example, the learning process of a project team will not be fixed; with sufficient focus, the group will learn how to learn together. Finally, natural phenomena, systems, or processes can be *discrete* or *continuous* in nature; discrete modeling is used when the exact point in time of an event can be pinpointed, and there are no changes in the state between events (Figure 10.5).

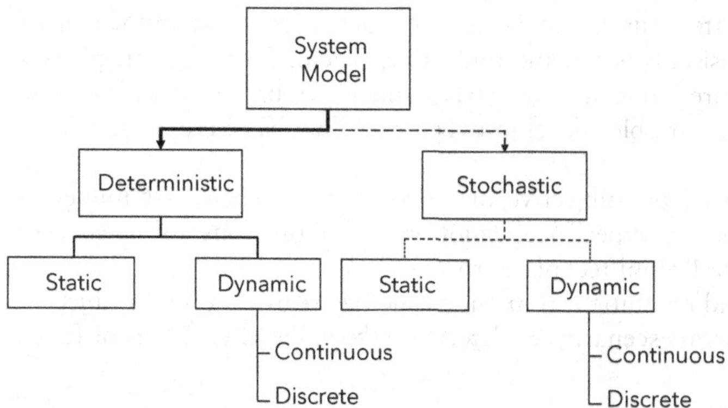

Figure 10.4 Type of simulation models (Shishvan and Benndorf 2017)

Source: Reproduced under Creative Common License: Attribution 4.0 International CC BY 4.0, https://creativecommons.org/licenses/by/4.0/, with minor changes).

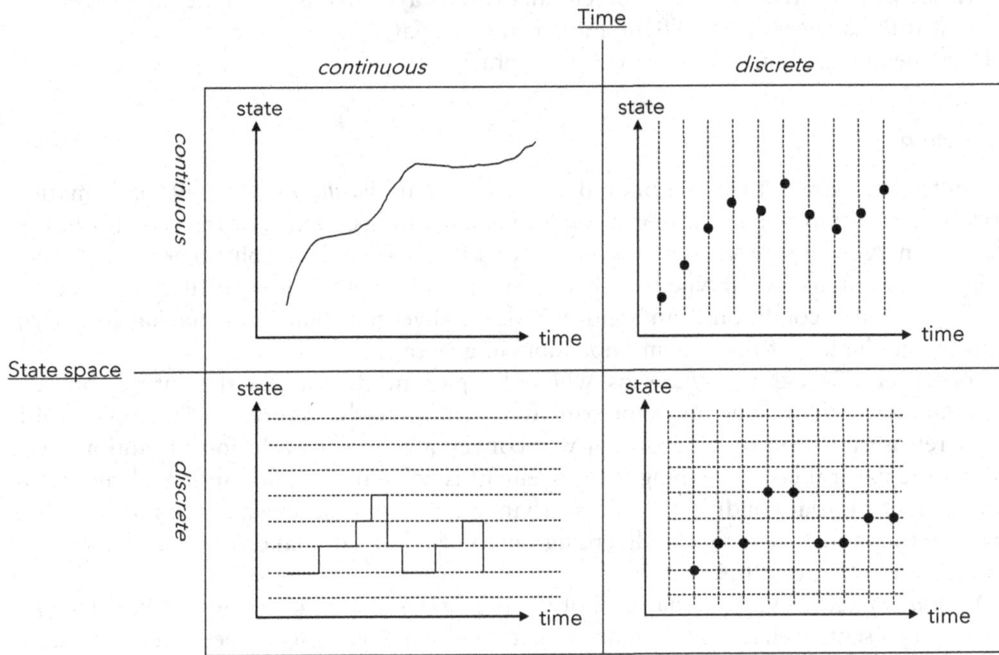

Figure 10.5 Continuous versus discrete simulations (Holzer, Wuchner, and de Mee 2010).

Source: Copyright notice: The author grants EASST e.V. non-exclusive rights of publication free of charge. Exclusive publication rights have not been and will not be given to any other publisher. The readers will be granted the right to read this article and distribute it without changes).

Forecasting

Forecasting plays a significant role in our daily life, such as the weather, stock markets, prices of food and gasoline, the closing price of stock each day, units sold, inflation, or unemployment. Forecasts estimate future events' characteristics, properties, and values for scenario analysis, planning, decision making, and budgeting. The underlying principle is to determine an observation's future values or state based on previous observations, often visualized as projections of how variables develop over time. Two basic types exist:

1 *Qualitative forecasts* are based on subjective human judgment when past numerical data is not available, gathering experience, emotions, and opinions using surveys, questionnaires, panels, or the Delphi technique to gain insight
2 *Quantitative forecasts* depend on statistical methods such as regression using objective data or causal models to generate scenarios to determine the value of variables or future behavior of systems.

Forecasting efforts must be:

- Related to relevant properties or variables of the projects
- Unambiguous and understandable

- Traceable, regarding the logic and data used
- Timely to allow for proactivity
- Value for money.

Hypothesis

When investigation, prototyping, simulation, and forecasting fail to produce sensible answers, the final resort is to establish a *working hypothesis*: An asserted notion as a provisional conjecture regarded as highly probable in the light of facts to guide project execution. The starting hypothesis is the definition of success. Launching projects without the notion of what success is like traveling without a destination; no matter where you end up, the purpose of the trip is achieved. Although projects are unique, there are universal questions to ask in any project:

1 How is organizational *coherence* affected?
2 What are the *relations* to other change initiatives?
3 What is the *strategic direction?*
4 What is the *nature* of the project?
5 Which types of *deliverables* are involved?
6 What is the *technological* challenge?
7 What is the degree of innovation *novelty?*
8 What is the *nature* of the project domain?
9 What is the degree of *change?*
10 What are the stakeholder *attitudes?*
11 What is the *financial* perspective?
12 What are the *prerequisites?*
13 What are the *governance* limits?

We can develop relevant working hypotheses regarding the answers to these questions using various models, which will be presented in the next paragraph.

Techniques

Ikigai—coherence

Well-functioning organizations are like fine-tuned machines; the effects of the change induced by the project can potentially affect all other elements of the parent organization. The Ikigai model is a Venn diagram depicting the raison d'être of the organization from different perspectives (Figure 10.6):

1 The mission of the organization is to provide value to *customers* using capabilities and preferably by following a strategy
2 *Regulators* govern the capabilities and assets necessary for the mission, like governmental agencies, standardization, and industry branches
3 *Suppliers* provide assets and the qualified personnel necessary to achieve the vision
4 Organizations serve a purpose for *fifth parties;* for example, by providing a dividend to the shareholders.

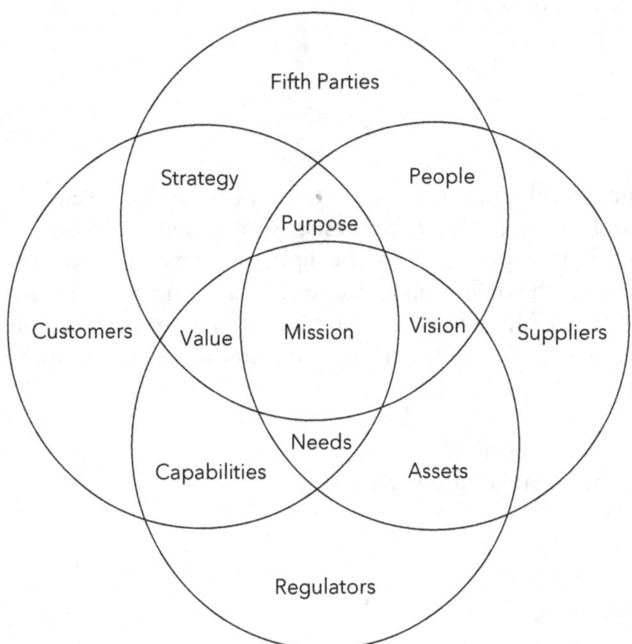

Figure 10.6 The Ikigai Venn diagram depicts different views on the raison d'être of the organization.

The effects of the project assignment on the coherence between all elements of the parent organization must be evaluated and to ensure that the overall performance is improved. For example, a project designed to create new capabilities may require different types of assets delivered by new suppliers, including additional personnel, overseen by regulators requiring proper licenses.

The four-phase model—strategic direction

Projects are defined proactively as part of strategy implementation or may be initiated as a reaction to sudden threats, opportunities, problems, or perceived risks. An important question is the strategic direction of the change induced by the project assignment. The four-phase model (Hardjono, 1995) identifies four primary strategies that an organization can pursue. The model identifies two basic orientations for organizational improvement, which are dichotomies (Figure 10.7):

- Focus on *control* versus *change*
- *Internal* versus *external* focus.

The combination creates four ideal types of *strategic orientations for change*:

a *Effectiveness,* a market-driven orientation toward delivering demanded value

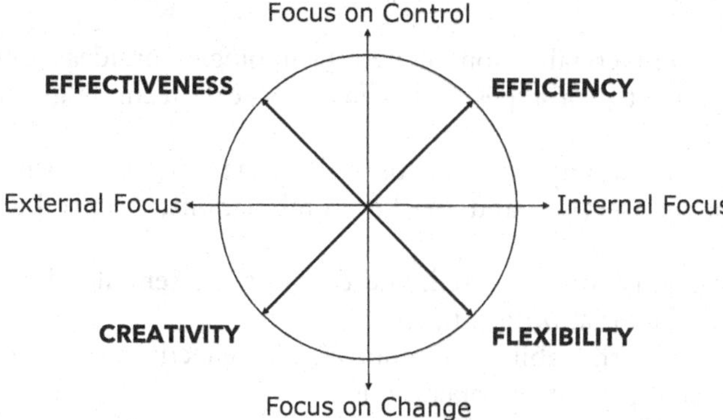

Figure 10.7 Strategic alignment: The simplified four-phase model (Hardjono 1995, reproduced with permission).

b *Efficiency* is a productivity-driven direction toward reducing the time, materials, and cost required to create value
c *Flexibility* is a people-driven orientation designed to increase agility
d *Creativity* is an innovation and adaptation-driven adjustment to develop new value types or cheaper, better, or cleaner production technologies.

Analyze the assignment to determine its strategic direction and assess the alignment between the project and the organizational strategy. Note that not every project has a strategic component, nor does it have to. Doing a large-scale maintenance overhaul of the production systems organized as a project is an immediate need requiring no strategic guidance. Projects addressing emerging urgent problems or changing conditions like new laws affecting the business must be prioritized, strategic alignment or not.

Core capabilities—project nature

The core capabilities that deliver value to the customer are (Figure 10.8):

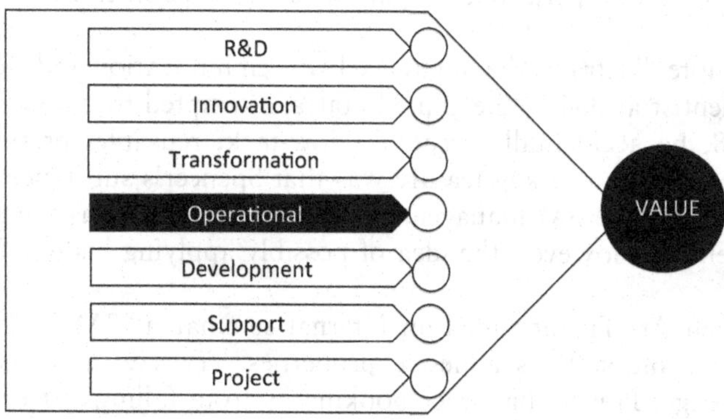

Figure 10.8 The core capabilities of the organization.

1 *R&D capability* is the ability to invent new products, services, production, or manufacturing techniques
2 *Innovation capability* is the commercialization of new technologies or ideas, transforming research and development prototypes and laboratory-scale technologies into full-scale operational capability
3 *Transformation capability* is the ability to transform the organization to shift to fundamentally different product, service, and market combinations, or production technologies
4 *Operational capability* is the ability to create, sell, and deliver the essential value that represents the raison d'être of the organization to its customers
5 *Development capability* refers to the ability to improve the effectiveness and the efficiency of the business as usual part of the operations
6 *Support capability* sustains the other core capabilities of the organization by providing what is indirectly needed regarding people and assets
7 *Project capability* refers to the ability to select and run the right projects for the organization effectively and efficiently.

A key strength of organizations that organize around capabilities, is the potential to quickly shift mission by rearranging base capabilities into new constellations. The U.S. Coastguard operates a large fleet of ships, helicopters, and fixed-wing aircraft and can quickly redirect their mission depending on the situation's needs or emerging threats ranging from fishery patrol, counter-drug surveillance to anti-pollution and vessel inspection.

Organizational development, change, and transformation are often used interchangeably in management; in this book, I will use development and transformation for consistency; in the case of *development,* the mission, products, and services remain the same, and the focus is streamlining operations to improve efficiency. *Transformation* capability implies shifting to other products, services, and markets. For example, Toyota started in the mechanical loom business and switched to manufacturing cars. In the Toyota Production system context, development means continuous improvement, or kaizen (Ohno, 1988).

Note the difference between business support and support of the product or service. A taxi service requires regular car cleaning and maintenance. Companies need everything from cleaning services, catering, training, and security. Invoicing and sales are not part of the support capability but the operational capability's sub-capabilities to drive revenue.

The story behind the post-it note illustrates the difference between innovation and R&D capability. Spencer Silver, a scientist at 3M in the United States, attempted to develop an extra-strong adhesive. In 1968, he accidentally created a low-tack, reusable, pressure-sensitive bond. Such glue did exist; the new key feature was that Spencer's substance did not smudge. But what to use it for? The 3M management showed no interest as the glue was deemed too weak to be helpful. However, the idea of possibly applying his development stuck in Spencer's head.

The breakthrough came when Art Fry attended an internal seminar at 3M in 1974 hosted by Spencer Silver, who promoted his adhesive properties. Fry saw a potential application to a practical challenge: Preventing paper bookmarks from falling out of his hymnal when he sang in church. Fry developed bookmarks using Silver's adhesive, preventing them from leaving residue and sought to interest others within the 3M company. That concluded the R&D stage of the Post-It note.

The innovation stage took several years to perfect the design and production. Significant challenges involved creating equipment and processes to manufacture the notes, keeping the adhesive in place, and maintaining a consistent range of adhesion. The Post-It Note was put on sale in 1977. Today, the Agile community is jokingly regarded as the biggest sponsor of the Post-It Note. Transformation capability, the ability to adapt and renew the organization and move to new markets and products, is based on products and technologies resulting from innovations done by others (Flavell-While, 2012).

The critical question is to define the nature of the project; the core capability model provides a classification scheme. Initially, the Post-It note is an example of an R&D project that delivered a prototype, evolving into an innovation project to set up the sticker's marketing, sales, and production lines. Projects can be designed to improve the effectiveness or efficiency of existing capabilities or add new capabilities to an organization. For example, a consumer electronics company making TVs and radios using existing bought patents may choose to add R&D capability to do fundamental research themselves.

Project master planning—relations

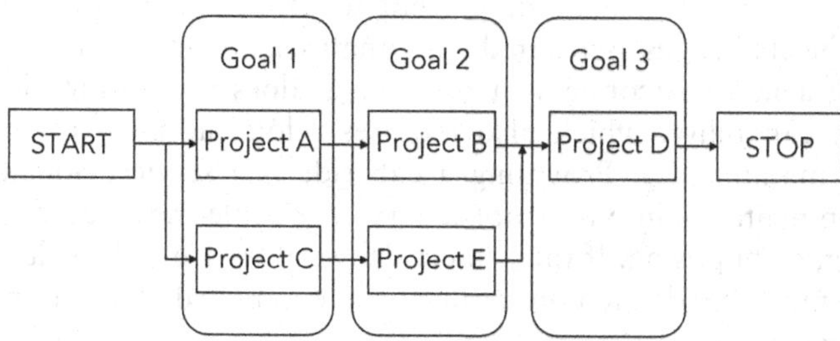

Figure 10.9 Inter-dependencies at the project level.

Aggregated network planning at the project level illustrates the projects' interdependencies, including the critical path. At the project level, projects in a program might appear independent, i.e., could be run in parallel; however, it is prudent to create a network plan at the top-level deliverable level, to check for hidden dependencies that may require coordination (Figure 10.9).

Elemental value grid—value

What domain deliverables must the project produce besides the control type of deliverables, like plans and reports? Fundamental domain types are (Figure 10.10):

1 Products
2 Services
3 Opinions, and
4 Capabilities.

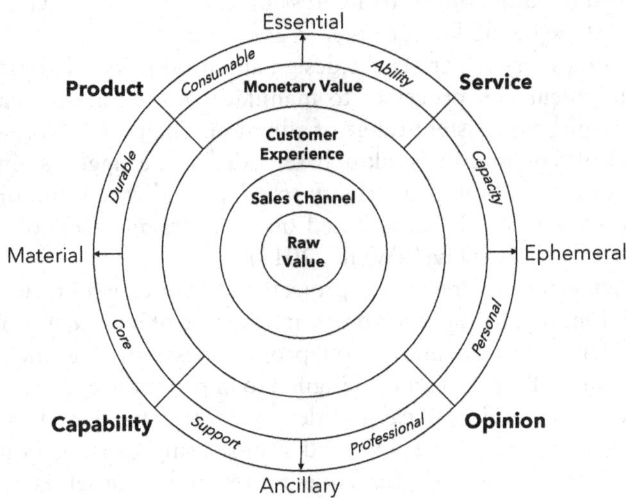

Figure 10.10 The types of project deliverables, markets, and sales channels.

The difference is subtle but essential. Understanding what to deliver in the domain is crucial to project success, as the challenges associated with analysis, design, creation, and acceptance differ. Developing a new helicopter is a product; it does not automatically provide aerial transportation capability, which also requires pilots, licenses, training, storage, a landing spot, and maintenance. Providing a cab ride is a service. Soliciting political, religious, or environmental opinions is not a service; people may be open to suggestions, rejecting, arguing, or opposing. If the project deliverables are to be sold, the customer value proposition must be defined in terms of the targeted market, sales channel, and customer experience.

Technology-capability matrix—technological challenge

A universal question is the size of the technological leap the project makes. Does the project create existing value using new capabilities or a new deal using existing capabilities? Toshiba is a known manufacturer of air-conditioning systems. Developing a more recent model based on a liquid refrigerant evaporating would be an example of existing value using existing technology. Tesla's flagship, the Model S, debuted in 2012 and represented new value based on existing technological elements such as batteries, electrical motors, and computers rearranged creatively. Before the Tesla Model S, electric cars were compact short-range city vehicles; the Model S was a full-size sedan with a range matching that of cars powered by combustible engines. A sleek design combined with perks like free charging announced a new era in automobiles (Figure 10.11).

What the business concepts of Uber and Airbnb have in common is that they provide existing value through new capabilities: Using the app, any car or home owner can offer its services to customers, accept reservations, and accept payments without first having to

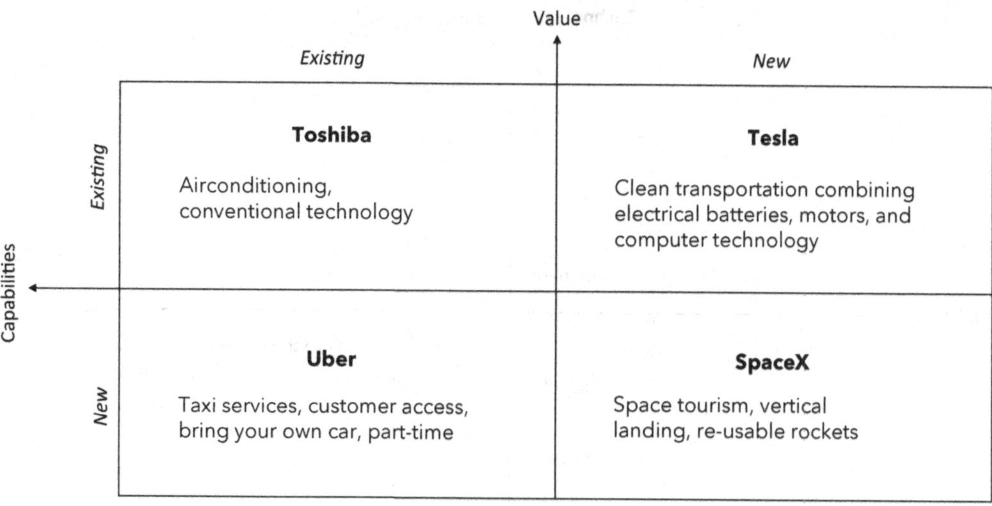

Figure 10.11 The technological challenges.

invest in the underlying IT infrastructure and applications. Uber and Airbnb create virtual marketplaces where supply and demand meet, based on free software as a service (SaaS), creating income by taking a cut from the revenue generated by the traders. Finally, SpaceX introduced a new value: Space tours using new capabilities like reusable rockets with vertical landing capability.

The diamond of innovation—novelty

A project must create a unique result that provides benefits to the organization. Some results are more novel, complex, or technologically advanced than others. Creation uncertainty can be assessed using the diamond analysis tool (Shenhar and Dvir 2007). The diamond tool is a grid using four axes that describe the nature of the project from the following points of view (Figure 10.12):

a Novelty
b Technology
c Complexity
d Pace.

The *novelty* describes the level of innovation of the project result on the following scale:

- Derivative, an extension of an existing product
- A platform is a new generation of a current product, like a new car
- New to the market, taking an existing product into a new market, for example, commercial GPS, which was initially a military system
- New to the world; no one has seen it before, for example, the Segway.

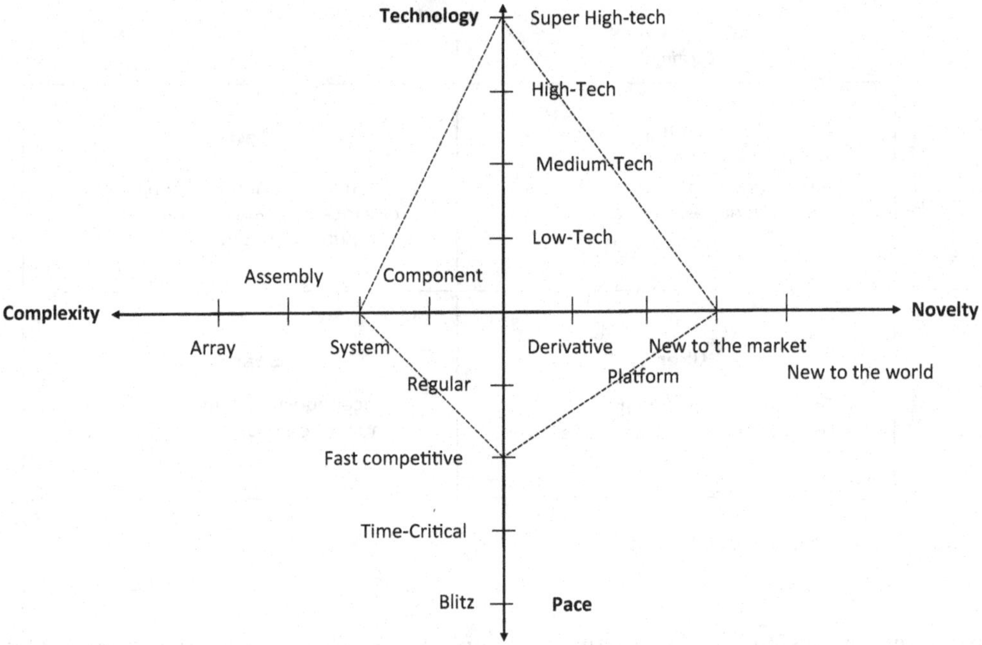

Figure 10.12 The diamond of innovation (Shenhar/Dvir 2007, reproduced with permission).

The amount of *technology focus* on a project, ranging from:

- Low tech, no new technology is used
- Medium tech, mostly existing technology with some new features
- High tech, using recent, but existing technology for the first time
- Super high tech, non-existing technology must be developed by the project.

The *complexity* of the product's functionality and the complexity of the organization that is undertaking the project:

- Component, no function on its own, a simple element in a product
- Assembly, an actual product capable of doing one function or part of an extensive system (video projector
- A system, a multifunctional product containing subsystems (ship)
- Array; multiple systems working together to achieve a common purpose (city subway system).

The *pace* is the urgency of the project:

- No time pressure
- Fast/competitive, being ahead of the competition
- Time-critical, missing a definitive deadline implies complete failure
- Blitz is an urgent situation where an immediate response is needed.

The results of the diamond tool assessment can help the team to adapt the project organization, staffing, procedures, documentation, checks, and balances to tackle the uncertainties. A diamond analysis will be unique to each project. The further you end up on a scale, the higher the level of creation uncertainty. Be aware that large projects can consist of deliverables with different characteristics. Some parts of the result might be straightforward, such as a building, while others might be more complex or uncertain, requiring a different approach.

CYNEFIN framework—domain nature

A project may involve changing the workings of the parent organization, the environment, or society. How well do we foresee the effects of our interventions? Do we understand the causality between our actions and the positive or negative consequences that may result from the change? The Cynefin framework is a system-thinking approach to assess the situation regarding predictability and complexity and select a suitable method to make changes developed by Kurtz and Snowden (2003). The Cynefin framework recognizes the following domains (Figure 10.13):

a *Obvious*, where causality or the relationship between cause and effect is evident, the approach is to Sense - Categorize - Respond, and it is likely to exist a best practice that can be learned or copied from others or precedence
b *Complicated,* in which the relationship between cause and effect requires analysis or some other form of investigation by experts, the recommended approach is to Sense - Analyze - Respond, and good practice applies
c *Complex,* in which the relationship between cause and effect often only becomes apparent in retrospect, but not in advance, the approach is to Probe - Sense - Respond, and one can develop an emergent practice
d *Chaotic,* in which there is no relationship between cause and effect at the systems level, the suitable approach is to Act - Sense - Respond and needs to discover a novel practice

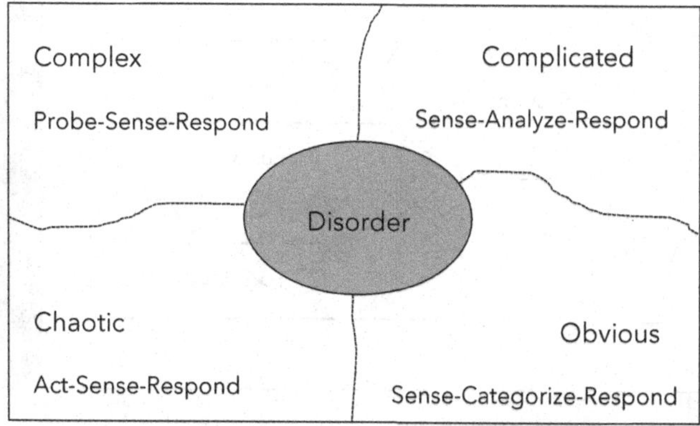

Figure 10.13 The CYNEFIN framework (Kurtz, Snowden, 2003). Reprint Courtesy of IBM Corporation © 2003.

e *Disorder,* which is the state of not knowing whether causality exists, to begin with, and decision-making is purely by luck or intuition.

The boundary between obvious and chaotic can be regarded as catastrophic: complacency leads to failure. It is not unlikely that a differentiated approach might be required, where different parts or deliverables of the project fit into various domains.

Caution: The boundaries between the realms are not hard defined, and as a result, the risk exists that the project is the disorder area without the team being aware of it.

The project footprint—degree of change

Another question is the degree of change a project makes to the parent organization (Figure 10.14).

The project footprint technique defines the relative project size by providing a map of the project's footprint on the organization. The project footprint model consists of the following:

- Organization
- Value chain
- Production systems
- Processes
- Information and communications technology (ICT)

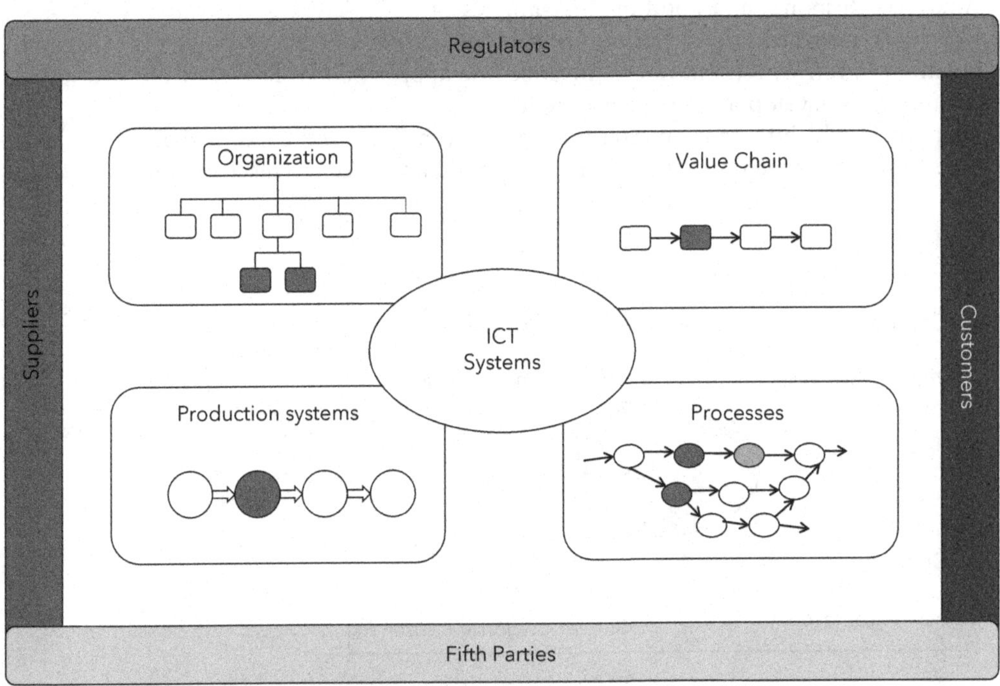

Figure 10.14 The project footprint model for assessment the degree of change.

- Regulatory bodies
- Suppliers
- Customers
- Fifth parties.

The areas that the project will change create the 'footprint' of the change. For example, a production machine is at the technical end of its life, and a project team replaces it with a new one from the same manufacturer with roughly the exact specifications. Replacing the machine involves shutting down the production line, removing the old device, installing the new one, conducting an acceptance test, and handling production start-up. Although replacing the machine is a 'big' project in absolute size, the project affects only a single dimension in relative terms: The production system.

As the new device is like the old one, no changes to other elements must be directed and coordinated. Suppose the company decides to add a new part to the value chain. In that case, you can expect that this requires additional production means, added processes, and new organization units and that the project will involve changes for both customers and suppliers, changing five out of nine dimensions. A project could be 'small' in absolute size, but if it scores on all aspects in the footprint analysis must be threatened with extra caution.

VUCA grid—stakeholder attitude

What is the expected position of the stakeholders toward the project? VUCA is an acronym that describes the volatility, uncertainty, complexity, and ambiguity of general conditions and situations to enhance insight and foresight in the behavior of trends, forces, groups, and organizations. The VUCA model describes the following domains (Figure 10.15):

- *Volatility,* nature, and dynamics of forces and catalysts that affect or create change
- *Uncertainty* refers to a lack of relevant information, the absence of predictability, the prospects for a surprise, a low sense of awareness, and understanding of causality in issues and events
- *Complexity,* intricate patterns of forces, the confounding of issues, turmoil, and disorientation surrounding organizations

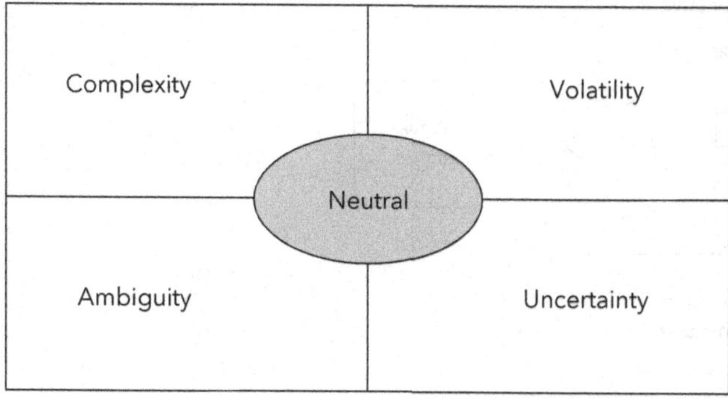

Figure 10.15 The VUCA grid.

- *Ambiguity,* the haziness of reality, the potential for misreads, and the mixed meanings of conditions; vagueness about cause-and-effect.

The project must continuously identify and track relevant trends and forces exerted by various stakeholders, analyze their meaning and behavior, and place them in their applicable quadrants.

Budgeting—financial perspectives

Using various financial techniques, such as earned schedule (Lipke, 2012) and earned value (PMBOK version 6, 2017), the economic uncertainties of the project can be analyzed from different points of view (Figure 10.16):

1 The Business Perspective
    - Project Cost
    - Revenue
    - Return on Investment
    - Net Present Value
2 The Planning Perspective
    - Periodical Cost
    - Cumulative Cost, or Planned Value (PV)
    - Budget at Completion (BAC)
    - Management Reserve
    - Contingency Reserve
3 Cash Flow Perspective
    - Expenses
    - Invoicing

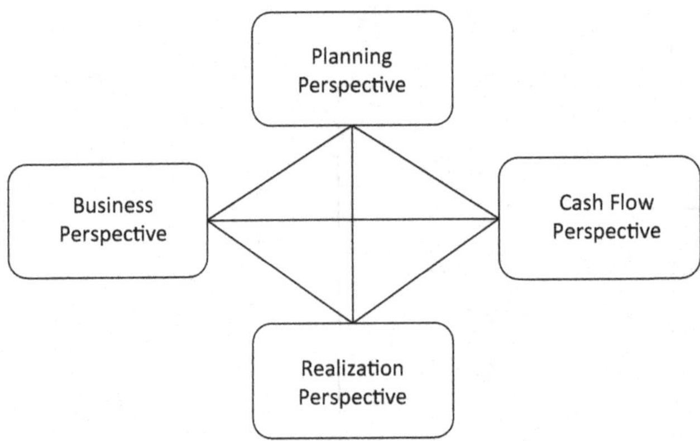

Figure 10.16 The financial perspectives on the project.

4 Realization Perspective

- Actual Cost
- Earned Value
- Estimate at Completion
- Earned Schedule (Lipke, 2009).

For a complete overview of earned value–related concepts, see PMBOK version Six.

Stage gate transition—conditions

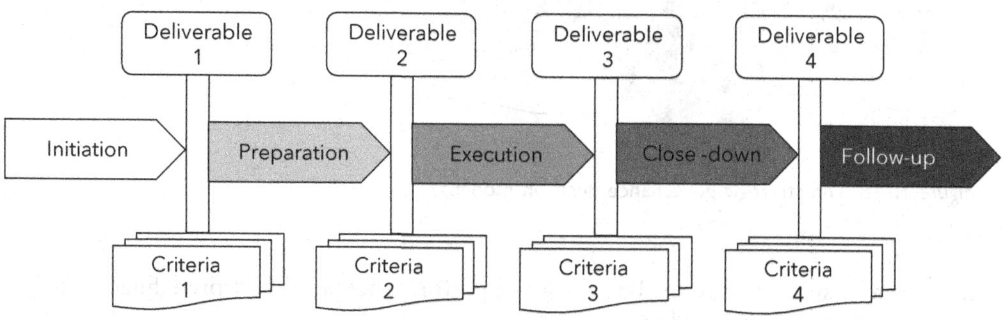

Figure 10.17 Decision gateways between stages with predefined criteria to proceed.

A classic approach to control is to divide a significant assignment into more miniature, more manageable project life-cycle stages separated by decision gates. A *decision gate* is a conscious decision to move from one stage to the next by asking: Are the prerequisites in place to move on? Successful application of the stage gate transition technique depends on predefining the criteria for passing each stage. Do the results of the previous stage warrant going forward? If the results are deemed insufficient or defective, the stage is redone or put on hold. Other typical prerequisites are sufficient funding, resource availability, and project priority (Figure 10.17).

Strategic governance decisions—operating limits

Strategic project governance is an agreement on performance and evaluation criteria between the project manager and the organization. The actual performance of the project is reviewed against these predefined criteria. By defining rules and standards beforehand, one can prevent the organization from getting sucked into successive costs or time increases without a conscious decision at the strategic level on whether to proceed with the project (Figure 10.18).

Projects require regular follow-up at both strategic and tactical levels to succeed. It is not uncommon for management to treat many projects as 'fire and forget missiles.' The project is defined and handed over to the project manager and team to complete the job. In most surveys investigating why projects fail, lack of management support is a prominent reason. An essential part of the follow-up is establishing performance

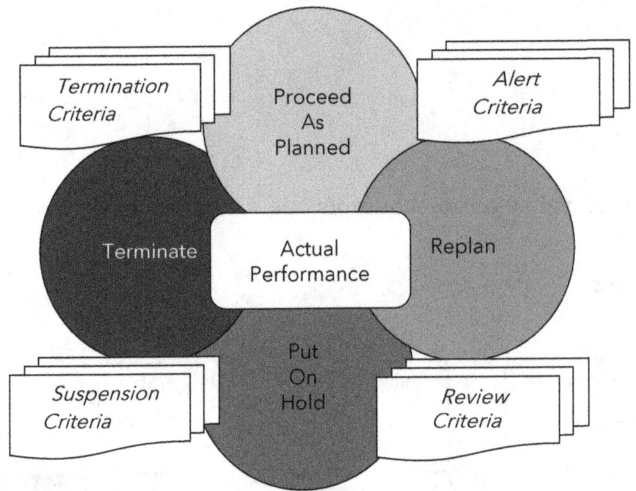

Figure 10.18 The strategic governance decision model.

monitoring and success criteria. Based on the performance level and predefined criteria, strategic decisions can be made to:

- Continue as planned
- Re-plan
- Put on hold
- Terminate.

Alert criteria are a set of predefined boundaries for the work. If any of these boundaries are exceeded, the owner must be informed. Consider a car repair scenario where the brakes are making noises. An example of an alert criterion could be that the owner must be notified if the predicted repair price reaches 25% above the original price quote. Apart from time and cost deviations, alert criteria could be newly identified problems, risks, or critical planning assumptions that prove wrong.

Review criteria are used to assess whether the assumptions made when planning the repair are still valid; for example, the cause of the problem or the price estimate for the job. In this case, the price was based on the reason for the noise being normal wear and tear. The additional steering system failure was not foreseen. A suitable review criterion would be the discovery of any extra problems.

Suspension criteria are used to determine whether the project should be put on hold, in this case, to investigate other options, like buying another car or waiting until the next payday. *Termination criteria* determine when to abort the project, for example, by defining the maximum cost and time limit. Because the car is old, a termination criterion of, let us say, $600 could be established. You want the brakes to be repaired, but not at all cost. Considering technical life expectancy and sales value, spending more than $600 on the car is not economically viable.

Principles

Known-unknows are a fact of life

The most likely thing you will see when you finally reach the top of the mountain is another mountain. After figuring out a known-unknown, one or more new ones will emerge. Do not go into the pitfall of figuring out every missing bit of information before moving on; known-unknows will always be there.

Do not guess

A common reaction when a piece of missing information is identified is to start guessing. Instead, identify the suitable approach, investigation, simulation, and forecasting, and assign an action item to a team member in the working log.

Any estimate is known-unknown

Any estimate is a particular case of a working assumption, and any project plan qualifies as such. Until confirmed information exists, all estimates must be validated continuously to establish a confidence level.

Beware of the comma

Do not get deceived by statistically calculated numbers, convincingly presented in a spreadsheet with three digits behind the comma, providing an impression of accuracy. If the difference between the best-case and worst-case estimate is 500 hours, displaying the PERT average as 150,796 can lull you into a false sense of security.

Allow for estimation iterations

When an artillery gun makes a long-range shot, several variables like distance, wind, temperature, humidity, and the effects of Earth's rotation go into the calculation. Despite sophisticated models, the shot is expected to miss. After the first hit, fire corrections are applied, and eventually, the accuracy is improved. Getting the first numbers out is essential when assessing and estimating known unknowns, even though the ballpark may be high. Allow for emerging information to narrow the gap in iterations.

Simulation models are not built equal

No universal model can accurately simulate any project problem, decision, or risk. To build a reliable simulation model, you must analyze and understand the nature problem and the tools available for its resolution, then select a proper model.

Simulation is both science and art

Making mathematical simulation models may appear to be hard science; however, intuition and creativity play a significant role in their creation. If no reliable data is available, the model's probabilities are expert opinions, a euphemism for someone's best guess based on experience or analogy. The only way to improve is to evaluate the accuracy of the models with the actual data obtained afterward, analyze, adjust, and learn.

Working assumptions are a necessary evil

Making assumptions is generally considered a bad practice but is inevitable in project work. During the inception stage, assumptions must be made regarding the potential benefits. In the preparation stage, plans are made, and essential known-unknows are assumed based on forecasts, calculations, or an educated guess effort. Any estimate is a special case of an assumption. When you have no choice but to add value to a missing piece of information, make a *working assumption.* The following rules apply:

1 Only make working assumptions when there is no other option
2 Make conscious assumptions
3 Write the assumption down and assign an owner
4 Determine the earliest possible point in time when the assumption can be verified.

Examples:

1 A house painting project is estimated to take 32 hours, with four equal sides at 8 hours per side. Once the first side is painted, the working assumption can be verified.
2 The burndown rate for a SCRUM team is estimated at 20 points; on completing the sprint, the actual speed can be compared with the planned rate.

Make clean budgets

Keep your financial models clear, and avoid combining elements of different perspectives into a single spreadsheet.

Artifacts

Working log entries and updates
Models and output
Planning updates
Estimates.

Concepts

Prototype and mock-up
Deterministic and stochastic
Stochastic and random
Forecast and prediction
Simulation and forecast
Hypothesis and assumption
Strategic direction and strategic alignment
Complex and complicated

Chaotic and obvious
Product and service
Purpose and value
Process and value chain
Assembly and component
Innovation and transformation.

Questions

1 Using the Ikigai model, assess what elements of the organization will be affected by the changes induced by your project.
2 What is the strategic direction of your project in terms of the four-phase model?
3 Using the core capability model, describe what capabilities(s) your project creates or improves.
4 Draw a network project master plan showing the interdependencies between projects in the parent organization.
5 Using the elemental value grid, what is the type of deliverable of the project?
6 What is the technological challenge based on the capability matrix?
7 What is the focus and level using the diamond of innovation?
8 What is the nature of the project domain in the CYNEFIN model?
9 How big is the degree of change based on the project footprint?
10 Using the VUCA grid, what are the expected attitudes of the stakeholders toward your project?
11 Describe the financial perspectives on the project based on the business, planning, cash flow, and realization budget.
12 Using the stage gate transition model, describe the conditions that must be met to warrant going to the next stage.
13 Describe the criteria for the strategic governance decisions.

References

Flavell-While, C. August 15, 2012. *Spencer Silver and Arthur Fry: The chemist and the tinkerer who created the Post-it Note.* [online] The Chemical Engineer. Institution of Chemical Engineers. [Accessed April 14 2023].

Hardjono, T. 1995. Ritmiek en organisatiedynamiek: vierfasenmodel: met aangrijpingspunten voor organisatorische interventies ter vergroting van de effectiviteit, efficiency, flexibiliteit en creativiteit. Phd. Technische Universiteit Eindhoven. DOI: 10.6100/IR449363

Holzer, R., P. Wuchner, and H. de Mee. 2010. "Modeling of Self-Organizing Systems: An Overview." *Electronic Communications of the EASST* Volume 27. DOI: 10.14279/tuj.eceasst.27.385

Kurtz, C.F., and D.J. Snowden. 2003. "The New Dynamics of Strategy: Sense-Making in a Complex and Complicated World" (PDF). *IBM Systems Journal* 42, no. 3: 462–483.

Lipke, W. 2012. "Earned Schedule, Contribution to Project Management." *PM World Journal* I, Issue II – September 2012

Lorenz, E. 1963. "Deterministic Non-periodic Flow." *Journal of the Atmospheric Sciences* 20, no. 2: 130–141.

Ohno, T. 1988. *Toyota Production System: Beyond Large-Scale Production*, Cambridge MA: Productivity Press.

Project Management Institute. 2017. *A Guide to the Project Management Body of Knowledge*, 6th edt. Pennsylvania: PMI

Shenhar, A., and D. Dvir. 2007. *Reinventing Project Management: The Diamond Approach to Successful Growth & Innovation*, Boston: Harvard Business School Press.

Shishvan, M., and J. Benndorf 2017. "Operational Decision Support for Material Management in Continuous Mining Systems: From Simulation Concept to Practical Full-Scale Implementations." *Minerals* 2017, 7, no. 7:116. 10.3390/min7070116

Chapter 11

Improving information effectiveness

Introduction

In the previous chapters, we focused on maximizing the known-known area by raising information awareness and increasing information availability. This chapter will focus on the effective use of this information. *Information effectiveness* is the ability to make the right decisions, take adequate actions, and develop sound solutions given the available information (Figure 11.1). *Information efficiency* is the time, effort, and resources required to locate, process, and interpret information. There can be no efficiency without effectiveness; information efficiency will be covered in the next chapter.

Any decision, assessment, or solution is as good as the information it is based on, and known-known information seldom comes without problems. Although known to be relevant and available, the information can be incomplete, inaccurate, stale, noisy, or ambiguous. But effective use of information not only relies on information quality. Making sensible decisions requires knowledge, guidance, and insight. Although we like to see ourselves as rational beings, psychological research shows that even basic algorithms outperform human experts as they are consistently given similar input, unaffected by human whims and impulses

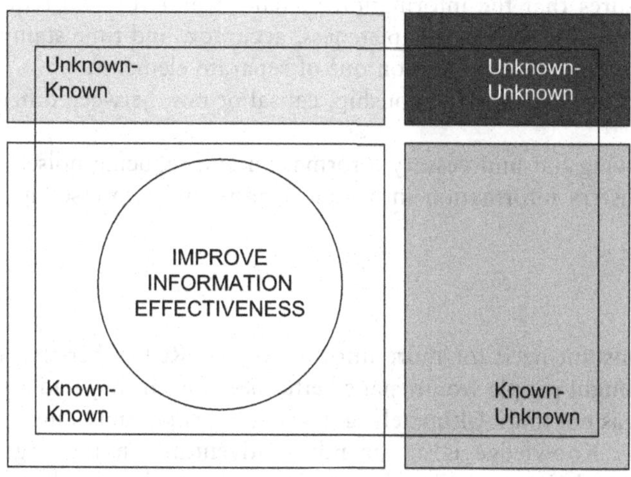

Figure 11.1 Making maximum effective use of know-known information.

DOI: 10.4324/9781003431961-14

(Kahneman 2011). Even with pertinent information, we may err due to time pressure, multitasking, biases, emotions, a lapse in attention, lack of expertise, or judgment. Acquiring more known-known information must lead to systematic knowledge development, guiding actions, and developing the wisdom to make the right decisions.

This chapter presents the OODA loop model for knowledge development created by J. Boyd, a fighter pilot, instructor, and the father of modern U.S. aircraft development. The essence of the OODA loop is that success in war, conflict, or competition depends on the quality and tempo of the cognitive processes of the leaders and their organizations. The popular but narrow interpretation is that victory depends on going through the OODA cycle faster than the opponent (Osinga 2005). In the project context, opponents can be negative stakeholders or competitors engaged in a race to the market. The more common enemy, however, is time, cost, and resource constraints. With each misguided decision, incorrect action, erroneous solution, or failing hypothesis, the remaining reserves are depleted while deadlines approach without deliverables to show.

Although presented as a technique, the OODA loop is merely a mental model to make decisions and take action followed by continuous adaptation based on multiple feedback loops. Given the uncertainty inherent to project assignments, there will rarely be sufficient known-known information; one can only make best-effort flexible plans and use emerging information as the situation develops to its advantage. Most people will worry about making the right decision. The OODA loop forces you to focus on how to determine whether the chosen decision was correct. Although Boyd's ideas started in the cockpit, the universal message is about adopting a vigilant mindset to constantly seek confirmation or contradiction on the correctness of decisions and the effects of actions.

Definitions

Information validation identifies relevant information pertinent to a problem, challenge, decision, action, or task.

Information verification ensures that the information matches standards and requirements, such as coming from a reliable source, completeness, accuracy, and time stamp.

Information combination creates new information out of separate elements.

Information correlation is to establish the relationship, causal or not, between different information elements.

Information reduction is leaving out unnecessary information and reducing noise.

Information aggregation clusters information into logical units and expresses it in a summary form.

Elements

The running gag about the constant need for more information is: 'Remember the time before the internet when we thought people would make better decisions if they had access to more information? Well, it was not that.' Ultimately, gathering information is a means to an end: To amass knowledge. Knowledge is an unending adventure on the edge of uncertainty (Bronowski, Bragg, and Gower, 1974). Acquiring more knowledge will reduce decision tension to an extent. *Knowledge* is facts and truths on a particular subject within a specified context, acquired through training and learning applied to achieve a specific

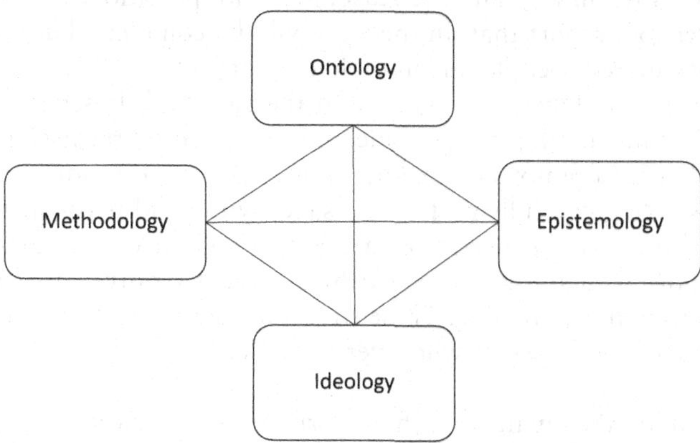

Figure 11.2 A systems perspective on knowledge.

purpose. *Wisdom* is the ability to make correct judgments and decisions gained through experiences in life and conscious evaluation of chosen paths. More knowledge enables the team to make the right decisions, assess, evaluate, solve, or act. Knowledge can be broken down into (Figure 11.2):

1 *Ontology* is a coherent set of concepts and categories in an area or domain that shows properties and the relations
2 *Epistemology* represents the theory of knowledge, concerning its methods, validity, and extent, including the distinction between justified belief and opinion
3 *Methodology* is the systematic study of methods and their application
4 *Ideology* is a set of ideas and ideals shaping theory and policy in an area or topic.

Techniques

OODA loop

Known information, defined as available information where its relevance is understood, may suffer from several issues:

1 *Information completeness* refers to missing pertinent information; only parts of the puzzle are available
2 *Unreliable information* cannot be trusted for reasons such as a disputable source or lateness
3 *Conflicting information* is inconsistent or contradicting with other trusted information on the same topic
4 *Noisy information* contains some relevant but primarily irrelevant information—*noise*—and making it is hard to discriminate the essential parts
5 *Confusing information* has a complex structure or is hard to interpret and build a coherent story for the purpose

6 *Ambiguous* information allows for more than one reasonable interpretation
7 *Dispersed information* relates to a report that, in theory, could be complete, but exists in parts within the minds of different people, or multiple documents
8 *Disinformation* and *misinformation* have in common that they are both false; the first one is intentionally wrong. Disinformation has become an industry; opportunists use it to expand their power by shaping opinions or making money. Disinformation targets the weakest link—people—sending carefully crafted messages with solid psychological triggers like fear, hate, or disgust. *False narratives* are the next-level disinformation where actual events are reported in twisted ways to fit a main narrative, however, always with a grain of truth to make it credible. These stories are sent coordinated over multiple channels, and messages are repeated whenever possible.

In addition to problems related to the quality of the information foundation, human decision-making has several structural flaws, like biases, group thinking, or simple mistakes. We need to accept that our plans are most likely flawed to some degree and that we neither can foresee all the consequences of all our actions and decisions. As an implication, we must build adaptive project organizations capable of rethinking plans, activities, or the entire project method and approach if necessary. As the project evolves, we must seek feedback, evaluate, learn, and adjust. Boyd's OODA loop model effectively illustrates a mindset of overcoming and winning.

John Boyd retired from the U.S. Air Force was a lieutenant colonel, having flown the F86 Sabre during the Korean War. Later, he became a fighter pilot instructor at the Nellis Airforce Base in Nevada. He earned the nickname '40 second Boyd' as he bet any pilot he could get in a firing position within 40 seconds in air-to-air combat, a venture he tended to win. Later, he became the father of modern American air tactics and was involved in developing the F15 and F16 fighter aircraft.

Boyd's philosophy was that uncertainty pervades everything, representing fundamental and irresolvable characteristics of our lives, no matter how good our observations and theoretical models are. Boyd created a comprehensive strategy theory in *A Discourse of Winning and Losing* (Boyd, 2017), stating that the only way to deal with uncertainty is to recognize the extent to which one's mental model is correct and the ability to use different models simultaneously (Osinga 2005).

From a methodology perspective, the OODA loop is a sequential process model with inputs, outputs, controls, and feedback loops (Figure 11.3). Although the initial ideas were born in a cockpit, after his fighter pilot and instructor career, Boyd immersed himself in studies of ancient battles, combining strategy with knowledge from various scientific fields. Over the years, he made several presentations that slowly evolved into concrete ideas through discussions with the public. Eventually, he went beyond the military application, and the OODA loop became a process for organizations to deal with unforeseen circumstances through adaptation and learning from unfolding events. The more significant theme of the model is organizational agility to prosper and survive, rather than plain winning over an opponent (Osinga 2005).

Strictly speaking, the OODA loop is not a technique but a mental model where organizations are seen as systems that evolve and adapt. In the project context, the *observation process* gathers information about the project context, unfolding situations, events, and actions. Observation is guided by the project meta-data model, combined with experience and intuition. The next step is *orientation*, analyzing the meaning of new information, in combination with existing information, within a context of cultural norms and personal

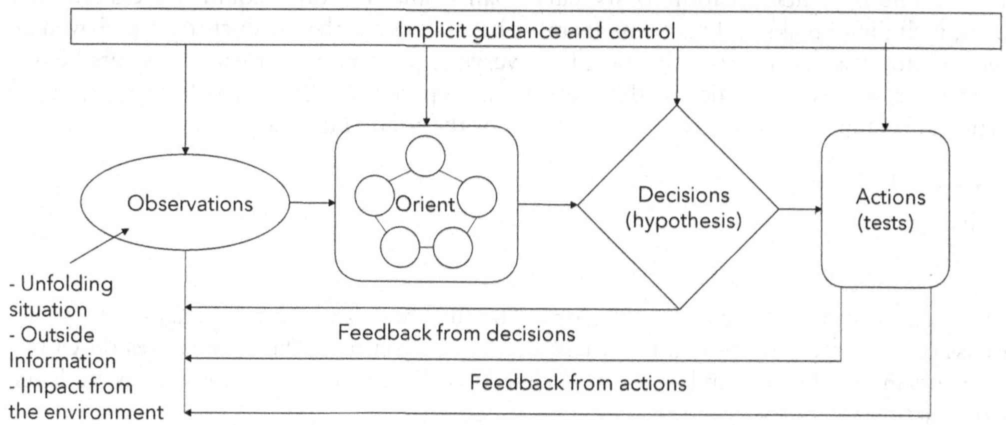

Figure 11.3 The OODA loop.

experience. Orientation involves various sub-processes such as correlation, combination, analysis, and synthesis.

The third process is the *decision;* alternatively, forming mental models or developing a *hypothesis* about the state of the world. The decision process is guided by the parent organization's mission, vision, strategy, project business case, plans, policies, laws, and ethical guidelines. The final process is *actions* or *testing the hypothesis.* Although the model structure is sequential, all operations are continuous and unceasingly reinforced by multiple feedback loops. Known-known information will rarely be complete and is often tainted. We must assume that the outcomes of our actions and decisions will differ from our expectations or hypothesis and determine if our efforts were correct based on feedback. Emerging information from observations must be evaluated on how they impact the project's scope, business case, mandate, overall approach, and plans.

Reviews

Peer review is the most common form of reviewing information; a representative group of stakeholders inspects the documents. A facilitated meeting is held where people can provide input, ask questions, and discuss the content in free-form discussions. A peer review aims to detect errors and defects as early as possible. The document is sent out before the meeting, and the session is facilitated with a focus on walking through the entire content while ensuring that all reviewers' voices are heard.

A *structured review* aims to ensure that the product is complete and accurate and that there are no misunderstandings while safeguarding that applicable standards have been followed. The roles in a structured review are:

- Review manager (responsible for planning and implementing the review)
- Scribe (writes down the comments; this can be the product's manufacturer)
- Participants (selected people who comment on the product).

The maximum number is four to six participants, and sessions should not exceed two hours, including breaks. All participants must have access to the product to be reviewed at least two to three days before the meeting. Everyone must prepare their comments before the meeting. If anyone comes to the meeting unprepared, the session will be postponed. Participants submit in advance a list with any of the following actions:

- Delete
- Change
- Add

to correct any faults, defects, or omissions. The function of standard changes is to avoid discussions and focus on pointing out flaws and imperfections. The scribe notes down the comments in the observation list during the meeting. On completion, a decision is made on further action:

1 Approved
2 Conditionally approved (provided the agreed changes are made)
3 Improve the document
4 Rejected.

On completion, the scribe distributes the notes, including the attendance list, comments, and decisions, for signature to all participants.

Principles

Effectiveness before efficiency

Effectiveness is about making the right decisions, solutions, and actions. Efficiency is a secondary requirement, as one cannot be efficient without effectiveness. Making a wrong decision but claiming that few resources were used in the process of making mistakes is senseless. When a patient dies during surgery, claiming that the team wasted limited time and resources is not acceptable. The misunderstanding about effectiveness and efficiency runs deep; project success and project management, in general, are primarily associated with the efficient use of money and resources, rather than achieving the aim.

Define confirmation

Effective decision making is not solely concerned with choosing a suitable alternative. It is equally important to define how and when you can know whether you are right or wrong based on feedback—defining confirmation implies knowing what to look for and ensuring that effective feedback loops are in place to check.

Sequential is not step by step

The OODA loop is a sequential process, but sequential does not mean step by step. All functions are continuously running, including the feedback loops, examining the world in multiple information channels, perspectives, mental pictures, and impressions. Boyd's thesis is that the larger the variety in media, dimensions, and models, the better we can adapt to an uncertain reality.

A higher speed is not necessarily better

A popular interpretation of the OODA loop is that victory comes from going faster through the loop than the opponent. In the project context, a misunderstanding is that fast decisions will save time and money. In practice, careful decision making is critical, while delaying a decision to the last possible moment can be advantageous to keep options open and allow for emerging information to improve insight. But there is a caveat, postponing a decision is only valid if new information is likely to emerge. Ask yourself: What more will we have learned by then that we do not know now?

The D and A processes entail more than decision and action

Decision making is about selecting alternatives generated by the orientation process; however, the orientation process also generates mental images about the state of the world. In Boyd's view, these models or schemas represent hypotheses that can be validated. Hypothesizing in projects is not limited to technical aspects but applies to a wide range of control dimensions. Any plan, related to deliverables, activities, benefits, or cost, is a hypothesis.

Success translates into approved deliverables and measurable benefits

Although military in origin, the OODA loop evolved from aerial combat to Boyd's view on individual and organizational development, adaptation, and learning. Unless the project is dealing with active negative stakeholders or is engaged in a race with a business competitor to capture a market share, there is no opponent. Like in golf, the opponent is yourself; your skill and decisions determine how many strokes it will take to complete a course. Success in project terms can be seen as approved deliverables; victory means actual benefits worth the effort and money.

Artifacts

Working log updates
Project plan updates
Project change request
Variation Orders.

Concepts

Using one breath, explain out loud the fundamental difference between:

- Information effectiveness and information efficiency
- Disinformation and misinformation
- Decision and hypothesis
- Correlation versus combination

- Analysis versus synthesis
- Aggregation versus reduction
- Ontology and methodology
- Epistemology and ideology
- Wisdom and knowledge.

Questions

1 Can you provide recent examples of disinformation and misinformation?
2 What documents, models, or policies provide implicit guidance and control to your project?
3 Provide an example where your project made observations, orientation, decisions, and actions following the OODA loop.

References

Bronowski, J. 1974. *The Ascent of Man*, Boston MA: Little Brown & Co.
Kahneman D. 2011. *Thinking Fast and Slow*, New York: Farrar, Straus, and Giroux.
Osinga, F. 2005. *Science, Strategy and War, The Strategic Theory of John Boyd*. Phd. Universiteit Leiden.
Boyd, J. 2017. *A Discourse on Winning and Losing, Maxwell Air Force Base*, Alabama: Air University Press

Chapter 12

Maximizing information efficiency

Introduction

Once effective information use is within reach, the next priority is improving efficiency: Minimizing the time and resources required to access and process information. Once you have identified the need for a specific known-known information item, how long does it take until it is at your disposal? What effort is required to get the information in the proper format and distributed to the right team members? Information tends to be dispersed like islands of knowledge. The vision is to create waterways of information, like small brooks connecting, and growing into a river (Figure 12.1).

Typically, in IT-related tasks, doing the job is merely making some clicks on the screen, while finding the correct information to do the task takes the bulk of the time. Another challenge is finding the right person and getting the authorization to do so. The next inefficiency comes from gaining access to information systems, requesting roles and credentials, and waiting on approvals from people outside the project. If you do not have the information, the next logical question is: Who knows anyone that might have it? Finding the right person to talk to may take time.

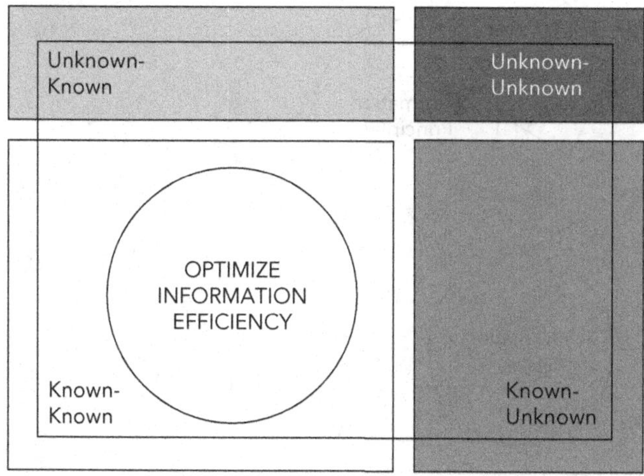

Figure 12.1 Optimizing the efficiency of processing and distributing known-known information.

DOI: 10.4324/9781003431961-15

Data processing takes time, raw data needs to be reduced, filtered, aggregated, and maybe visualized in graphs and tables; processing can be done manually or automatically. A source of inefficiency is offline interfaces; typically, the information comes from different systems and applications, with a spreadsheet as an offline interface. Although a project is a unique assignment, many process steps or processes are repetitive, like logging hours and reporting to the steering committee.

Since all projects are on the clock and resource constrained, looking at the information organization from an efficiency angle is worthwhile. Careful analysis of information needs, system design, implementing information roles and responsibilities, and optimizing and automating information tasks can be an investment that soon pays off. This chapter will make a blueprint for information efficiency by closely examining the project information needs, organization, principles, structure, and systems.

Definitions

Routine information refers to a habitual, regular, or repetitive procedure, such as writing hours in a project, that is predictable and a possible candidate for automation.

Unique information is related to a single event, unique problem, decision, or action, requiring a custom search to identify relevant information, gathering, transformation, and visualization.

A *document* is any carrier of data containing text, pictures, drawings, or tables on any physical, electronic, or digital media.

Elements

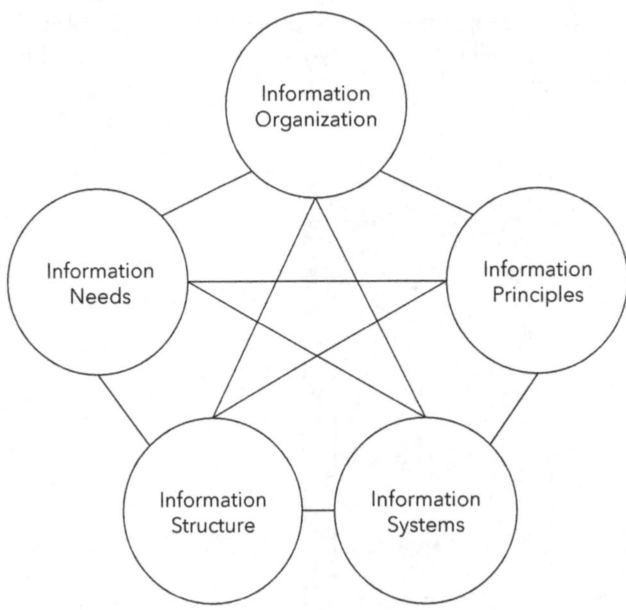

Figure 12.2 The elements of the information design.

Information systems break down into (Figure 12.2):

- Logical design
- Physical design
- Interfaces
- Communication
- Storage
- Backup.

Defining the *information structure* involves the design of the project meta-data model, and *document structure*, stating a document's purpose, hierarchy, and template development.

Information principles govern the design and use of information, for example:

- Information shall have a single source of truth
- Access to sensitive information is based on the need to know
- Delivery must be on time
- Information accuracy, meaning that the information is correct and without mistake
- Information integrity is the trustworthiness of information and ensuring that it cannot be tampered with
- Information security relates to protection against unauthorized use of information.

The *information organization* defines the roles and responsibilities for generating, handling, reviewing, and auditing information. Typical roles are:

- *Author*; the person writing or creating the document
- *Reviewer*; checks the documents for accuracy, completeness, layout, spelling, versioning, requirements, standards, or legal aspects.
- *Approver*; validates the appropriateness of the document from a business or organizational perspective, the timing for implementation, and authorizes the paper from an effective date
- *Owner*; responsible for the operational use of the document, distribution, and maintenance.

The *AORA matrix* provides an overview of the information organization's document types, functionaries, and duties.

The *information needs* depend on the roles and responsibilities for different deliverables, as expressed in the RACI matrix (responsible, accountable, consulted, informed). To take responsibility, information is required to support cognitive processes. The primary cognitive processes are (Figure 12.3):

a Situation awareness
b Threat and opportunity assessment
c Decision making
d Direction and tracking.

Situation awareness is continuously gathering information about essential elements of your environment, organization, and project. Based on this information, threats and opportunities are assessed. If needed, decisions are made and implemented using direction and tracking. Following the outer loop is not mandatory; in case of short reaction times or everyday

Figure 12.3 Mapping the basic types of information needs.

situations, actions are implemented directly using the short circuit. The arrow between the situation awareness and the direction and tracking process illustrates this option.

Car example: A driver needs situational awareness regarding the vehicle and its environment, such as direction, speed, location, other traffic. The dashboard provides the status of the car's systems; windows and mirrors present a picture of what is happening outside. Based on the situation awareness picture, the driver evaluates the situation and identifies possible threats and opportunities. A threat might be an animal suddenly crossing the road; an opportunity could be a much-needed gas station. When facing complex threats and opportunities, decision making is necessary. *Direction and tracking* involve executing the appropriate response using the car's controls, like the wheel and brakes. A *reflex* or *standard response* could be hitting the brakes when you spot a person in front of the vehicle.

Information systems provide the following functions:

- Logging
- Filtering
- Reduction
- Aggregation
- Transformation
- Visualization
- Distribution
- Updating
- Backup
- Storage
- Recovery.

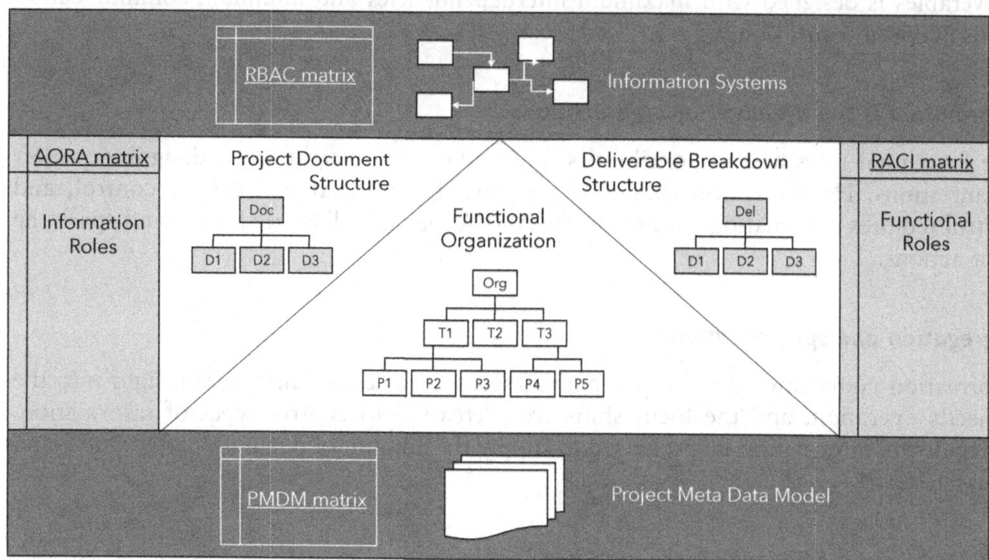

Figure 12.4 Designing for information efficiency.

Techniques

Optimizing for information efficiency pulls several techniques together (Figure 12.4):

a Functional organization design, the organization chart (organigram) shows steering committees, teams, and positions in the project organization
b The RACI matrix connects people and their functional roles (responsible, accountable, inform, consult) with the elements of the deliverable breakdown structure
c A project document structure is created defining the hierarchy and purpose of the different project documents
d The AORA matrix displays the information roles per document related to the author, owner, reviewer, and approver
e The information system design provides an overview of the project's internal data systems, interfaces, and data flows
f A role-based access control (RBAC) matrix provides an overview over the different functional roles and information system access
g The project meta-data document matrix (PMDM) connects information types with documents.

Principles

The deliverables determine the organization

The deliverables determine the type of people and resources needed, defining the organizational structure. The choice of the organizational units responsible for creating deliverables is designed with maximum interdependencies and minimum communication needs between teams in mind.

Information is the lifeblood of organizations

The functional roles and responsibilities often take the limelight when designing project organizations. However, you cannot be responsible for what you cannot control, and control requires information. Designing the AORA matrix will create insight and spark the right actions.

Aggregation and specialization

Information going toward the top is aggregated to provide a conceptual insight into the project's operation, and the focus shifts from creation to control types of information. Going down, information is specialized to supply the amount of detail needed to direct and complete tasks.

Onboarding and offboarding are vital moments

Creating an onboarding checklist, RACI, AORA, RBAC, PMDM, and matrices speed up the integration of the new people in the organization, increasing the efficiency of the on-boarding process. Remember to revoke access right when offboarding and request leavers do a file cleanup to save others from rooting through outdated information.

Preplanned responses save time and energy

When identifying information needs, create as many standard responses as possible between the situation awareness process and direction and tracking process to speed up reaction time and prevent creating bottlenecks higher up in the organization.

Who is who in the zoo?

Knowing someone who might know is also information; this could be people inside or outside the project and is a part of situation awareness. Creating social arenas for the project helps informal networks to grow.

Organizational design is an unceasing process

Adjusting and optimizing the organization is a continuous process, and the structure may change during the different stages of the project life cycle.

Artifacts

Information systems logical design
Information systems physical design
RACI matrix
AORA matrix

RBAC matrix
PMDM matrix
Project metadata model
Project document structure.

CONCEPTS

Aggregation and specialization
Routine and unique information
Information needs and information structure
Situational awareness and situation assessment
Information organization and functional organization
Information integrity and information accuracy
Document author and approver
RACI and AORA matrix.

Questions

1. Does your project have a Deliverable Breakdown Structure?
2. Create a RACI matrix
3. Does your project have a document structure?
4. Create an AORA matrix.

Postface

Have you ever been on an inspiring course, coming back to your job equipped with fresh knowledge, ideas, and insights? Only to discover that nothing has changed a week later? To avoid this from happening after reading this book, you need to ask yourself: Where to go from here? Based on the insights gained, what will you do differently in your next project to increase your chances of success? Here is some advice. Mastering uncertainty is the starting point to achieving project success systematically. The first step to mastering uncertainty is to develop a granular terminology, as you cannot control what you cannot define. Continue with the one-breath challenge, shorten and sharpen your formulation, and look for new challenging word pairs. Extend the game to your team, or colleagues.

The second step is to start modeling. The systems model presented in this book is not the ultimate answer; it is my perception of a project and probably not yours. The way from here is to start thinking for yourself; creating your model is the most effective way to increase knowledge and gaining insight. The good thing about models is that they can be compared and their relative merits and flaws debated, a significant improvement over discussions that tend to boil down to a mere exchange of opinions.

As for model building there are two approaches: Build your model from scratch or adapt the presented version from this book to suit the specifics of your assignment, domain, or parent organization. System thinking modeling implies making decisions about extending the model in width by adding a new element at the top level or in depth by creating components in an underlying sub-system. Where to place the system boundary is essential; too wide a border creates complexity, while too constrictive may lead to overlooking critical elements.

Looking back, my hardest decision was to add 'threat' and 'opportunity' as components to the context element, a choice which can be contested. Why not add threat and opportunity as top-level elements? As stated, the presented model is not perfect, but perfection is not the goal. Models are a means to an end; actionable insight will come when you start modeling yourself. Anyone can question the presented model; learning comes from making your own, and more insight can be gained by comparing models.

Modeling is only helpful if it explains what we see in practice. Theoretical models complement empirical observations and vice versa. If the model does not confirm what reality shows, adapt or reject the model, and start anew. Another option is to select another modeling approach, like process thinking, to get a fresh perspective when stuck. Ultimate wisdom is when we can explain the concept of uncertainty using any modeling discipline, be it systems thinking, capability thinking, process, or functional analysis.

Starting with a systems thinking approach has significant advantages, as it provides an overview of the subject and can visualize complex behaviors resulting from the underlying

DOI: 10.4324/9781003431961-16

structure of interacting elements. Another advantage is that it prevents circular definitions, where the meaning of one element is based on the description of another. For example, if your model contains a risk and a threat element, the risk definition cannot state that a risk is a threat, implying that the elements are identical.

Finally: The applied method is universal with regards to scientific areas; creating a systems model of projects and analyzing uncertainty by projecting the uncertainty matrix over the elements can be applied to any other domain outside project management. Projects are a crossroads of disciplines, and our best hope for improving the theoretical foundation and practical capabilities is to achieve cross-pollination with other sciences.

Index

Note: Locators in *italics* represent figures and **bold** indicate tables in the text.

Printed in the United States
by Baker & Taylor Publisher Services

Printed in the United States
by Baker & Taylor Publisher Services